THE BLACK AMERICAN IN BOOKS FOR CHILDREN:

Readings in Racism

second edition

Edited with an Introduction
by
Donnarae MacCann
and
Gloria Woodard

THE SCARECROW PRESS, INC.
Metuchen, N.J., & London • 1985

List of permissions begins on page vii

Library of Congress Cataloging in Publication Data
Main entry under title:

The Black American in books for children.

Includes bibliographies and index.
1. Children's literature, American—History and
criticism—Addresses, essays, lectures.   2. Afro-
Americans in literature—Addresses, essays, lectures.
3. Racism in literature—Addresses, essays, lectures.
4. Race relations in literature—Addresses, essays,
lectures.   5. Children—United States—Books and
reading—Addresses, essays, lectures.   I. MacCann,
Donnarae.   II. Woodard, Gloria.
PS173.N4B57 1985   810'.9'9282   85-10893
ISBN 0-8108-1826-4

CONTENTS

Part III: Racism in 20th-Century Fiction and Biography

Part IV: Racism in Contemporary Picture Books

Part V: Racism and Publishing

Part VI: International and Legal Perspectives

v

ACKNOWLEDGMENTS

Rae Alexander: "What Is a Racist Book?" Reprinted from *Interracial Books for Children Bulletin* (Vol. III, #1, 1970) by permission of the Council on Interracial Books for Children, 1841 Broadway, New York, N.Y. 10023.

Nancy L. Arnez: "Jake and Honeybunch Go to Heaven" (A Review). Reprinted from *The Crisis* (March, 1983) by permission of the Crisis Publishing Co., 186 Remsen Street, Brooklyn, N.Y. 11201.

Beryle Banfield and Geraldine L. Wilson: "The Black Experience Through White Eyes—The Same Old Story Once Again." Reprinted from *Interracial Books for Children Bulletin* (Vol. 14, #5, 1983) by permission of the Council on Interracial Books for Children, 1841 Broadway, New York, N.Y. 10023.

Beryle Banfield: "Racism in Children's Books: An Afro-American Perspective." Reprinted from *The Slant of the Pen* edited by Roy Preiswerk (World Council of Churches, 1980) by permission of the author.

Jessie M. Birtha: "Portrayal of the Black in Children's Literature." Reprinted with permission of the Pennsylvania Library Association.

Jeanne Chall, Eugene Radwin, Valarie W. French, Cynthia R. Hall: "Blacks in the World of Children's Books." Reprinted with permission of the authors and the International Reading Association, 800 Barksdale Road, P.O. Box 8139, Newark, Delaware 19714.

Paul C. Deane: "The Persistence of Uncle Tom: An Examination of the Image of the Negro in Children's Fiction Series." Reprinted from the *Journal of Negro Education* (Spring. 1968) by permission of the author.

Donald B. Gibson: "Mark Twain's Jim in the Classroom." Reprinted from the *English Journal* (February, 1968). Copyright © 1968 by the

permission of the Council on Interracial Books for Children, 1841 Broadway, New York, N.Y. 10023.

Albert V. Schwartz: "*The Cay*: Racism Still Rewarded." Reprinted from *Interracial Books for Children Bulletin* (Vol. III, #4, 1971) by permission of the Council on Interracial Books for Children, 1841 Broadway, New York, N.Y. 10023.

Rudine Sims: "*Words By Heart*—A Black Perspective." Reprinted from *Interracial Books for Children Bulletin*, (Vol. 11, #7, 1980) by permission of the Council on Interracial Books for Children, 1841 Broadway, New York, N.Y. 10023.

Dorothy Sterling: "The Soul of Learning." Reprinted from the *English Journal* (February, 1968). Copyright © 1968 by the National Council of Teachers of English. Reprinted with the permission of the National Council of Teachers of English.

Isabelle Suhl: "The "Real" Doctor Dolittle." Reprinted from *Interracial Books for Children Bulletin* (Vol. II, #1 and 2, 1969) by permission of the Council on Interracial Books for Children, 1841 Broadway, New York, N.Y. 10023.

Judith Thompson and Gloria Woodard: "Black Perspective in Books for Children." Reprinted by permission from the December 1969 issue of the *Wilson Library Bulletin*. Copyright © 1969 by The H. W. Wilson Company.

We extend our special thanks to the Council on Interracial Books for Children for its generous contribution of articles.

Illustrations

David McKay, illustrator. *The Adventures of Huckleberry Finn* by Mark Twain. Grosset and Dunlap, 1948.

Eric Palmquist, illustrator. *The Adventures of Huckleberry Finn* by Mark Twain. Tidens Förlag, 1957.

INTRODUCTION

WHEN THE FIRST EDITION of this book was published in 1972, we began with a reference to urban uprisings and organized boycotts against the schools. It was a period of social upheaval, but also an era of hope and increasing social awareness. Advances in equity and justice (so it was thought) could be anticipated provided important areas of Black history could become better known throughout the culture at large. Books in schools and libraries were understandably viewed by some as the primary instrument for conveying that knowledge.

At the present time, this hope for social progress has been substantially undermined by retrogressive actions. We see affirmative action programs under a continuous barrage—under the kind of attack represented in the Bakke case on school admissions. We read reports of the need for continuing litigation to equalize voting rights—to overcome the gerrymandering and at-large voting devices that have been employed to make Black American candidates unelectable. Such problems point to glaring ironies in our political life, and they suggest to educators an urgent question: Are such maneuvers engendered by anxiety in the dominant cultural group, by fears that have their roots in the early years of socialization? When children's books, for example, offer negative, unexplained images of the Black family, economy, and personality, then segregation and various forms of domination are not unlikely outcomes. And another predictable consequence is the lessening of opportunities for the Black child.

The number of racist children's books about Blacks did not show a great increase over the last dozen years, but some racially biased publications were inexplicably singled out for high honors and laudatory reviews. These titles can therefore be expected to enjoy a continuing and wide circulation, and to have a greater cultural penetration than the typical work of fiction will have. It is in this professional response to biased images that the least progress has been made.

If the United Nations Declaration on the Rights of the Child were accepted in spirit, such approval for white supremacist messages would perhaps be less frequent. Principle 10 of that declaration reads:

The child shall be protected from any practice which may foster racial, religious, or any other forms of discrimination.

A few practical implementations of this principle did begin to take shape in the early 1970s, but as civil rights organizations became less vociferous, the trend slowed down. Progressive changes in the policies of the American Library Association, for example, were rescinded by the mid-1970s, as will be described later in this Introduction. Interracial children's literature is still, therefore, the arena of conflict between two social theories: 1) the idea that public institutions in the United States, such as schools and libraries, are democratically based and offer each child an equal opportunity; and 2) the idea that such institutions represent, in many instances, cultural and political monopolies, and that the minority child needs specific, legalistic forms of protection.

To take the second position (a position this book supports in some detail) is not to limit the development of children in the majority culture. A white supremacist orientation cannot help but be destructive to white children in the long run, since it undermines the health of the whole society. Intergroup education is a deep, enriching way to protect children in each cultural subgroup. It involves a socialization process that does not condone feelings of ethnic superiority. And concurrently, it does not allow feelings of intense futility and self-worthlessness to accumulate year after year because of a youngster's group identification. Literature for children that supports a consciousness of self-worth and interracial harmony is a vital part of the socialization of children as it takes place within public institutions.

In the pages of this second edition, children's literature specialists, educators, creative artists, sociologists, and cultural historians discuss cultural issues and evaluate books about Blacks—books that are, for the most part, lacking in cultural authenticity. Articles from the first edition have been retained if their timeliness has not greatly diminished, and some of the theoretical issues that we explored in the first edition (e.g., intellectual freedom) are reexamined in this new Introduction. We are still in basic agreement with Barry N. Schwartz and Robert Disch when they stress the seriousness of negative stereotypes, myths, and images:

Of the various ways in which white racist fantasies and attitudes have found release—from lynching to "goodwill" tokenism—perhaps none has had a more

destructive effect and proved to be more intractable than the web of stereotypes, myth, and image spun around the lives of nonwhite Americans. . . .
The nonwhite in America has been consistently degraded and dehumanized,
through ignorance, malice, or both, by publishers, writers, film makers, artists, scientists and scholars. . . [1]

Child Development Issues

Children develop over time as readers of literature, as people with a
well-defined sense of self, as abstract as well as concrete thinkers.
People who work and live with children need to be aware of age
trends. They need to observe the changes that occur as children deal
with such concepts as identity, vicarious experience, authority, and
historical time. Books on children's literature often refer to the general
conceptual stages studied by Jean Piaget (the sensorimotor stage ending at about age two; the preoperational stage ending at about age
seven; the concrete operational stage ending at about age eleven; and
the formal operational stage ending at fourteen and later). But the
early development of racial awareness and how it can evolve along
positive or negative lines—these are subjects with much less coverage
in the professional literature of education, librarianship, and the arts.

 The appearance of racism in early childhood is well documented.
Martha W. Carithers, in a review of the literature on racial cleavage,
writes:

No matter at what point in [the child's] school life desegregation takes place—
kindergarten through high school—the child does not approach integration *in
vacuo*. This early awareness of racial difference, along with the values attached to such differences, play a part in the formulation of the stereotypes
which the child carries with him [or her] through [the] school years. [2]

 Phyllis A. Katz, sociologist at City University of New York, noted
that "the relative imperviousness of adult prejudice . . . strongly suggests that predispositions acquired at early developmental levels may
form the irrational but potent foundation for racism." [3]

 With respect to outside influences upon the child's self-esteem,
psychologist Kenneth B. Clark, writes: "Children who are consistently rejected understandably begin to question and doubt whether
they, their family, and their group really deserve no more respect from

the larger society than they recieve."[4] And in the Harvard University Press publication, *Black Child, White Child; The Development of Racial Attitudes* (1971), Judith D. R. Porter notes that it is exposure to the stereotypic reading materials out there in that larger society that is an important factor in the creation of prejudice. There is considerable agreement about the conclusion that a person's self-concept is shaped by social interactions of one sort or another, since every one of the contributors to an anthology on Black self-concept held this view.[5] How well the child copes with these social interactions depends to some degree upon the child's age.

As readers of fiction, children also change as they become older. They relate to vicarious experience with varying intensity. Richard Beach has reviewed a number of studies that indicate age trends in this aspect of child behavior. Readers, he writes, showed "a progressive development from predominantly an emotional/engagement type of response in the elementary grades to increased description/retelling in the junior high grades to a decline in engagement and description and an increase in interpretation in the senior high school grades."[6]

Learning to separate fiction from non-fiction is a skill that develops gradually, as Arthur Applebee discovered in his research for the book, *The Child's Concept of Story.* He writes:

It is a long time before [children begin] to question the truth of stories. . . . And though they will eventually learn that some of this world is only fiction, it is specific characters and specific events which will be rejected; the recurrent patterns of values, the stable expectations about the roles and relationships which are part of their culture, will remain. It is these underlying patterns . . . which make stories an important agent of socialization. . . ."[7]

In the end, it isn't the fictional or nonfictional features of a work that have the greater significance; it is the cultural patterns conveyed in both modes.

Research on authority figures also takes note of age trends. And given the authoritative status of books and their authors, it is important for book selectors to be acquainted with data about the child's sense of authority. For example, Dolores Durkin found that the oldest children as well as the youngest tend to seek justice in the authority person.[8] Robert Loughran found that adolescents still make their judgments under the moral constraint of authority figures.[9] The important point, therefore, is that children are probably disinclined to doubt what they read. Critical reading requires growth in years, as well as some specific help in learning to examine the world skeptically.

The child's slowly emerging conception of historical time should be considered in relation to book selection, especially since some prominent authors are reintroducing demeaning epithets in children's books on the ground that the epithet (for example, "nigger") is historically accurate. But a child's understanding of comparative measurements is not achieved at an early age. Children sometimes know a verbal symbol (e.g., the terms "more," "less," "long ago"), but various tests have shown that the concepts themselves are understood vaguely, partially, and even incorrectly.[10] With regard to the child's comprehension of historical dates and their implications, an age trend has been traced that shows eleven years of age as the point when more than three-quarters of the children tested understood the meaning of historical dates. Another group of researchers place a full understanding of chronology at an even later age: sixteen years.[11] As to the broader historical perspective that takes account of fairness to a foreign group, children at age thirteen or fourteen have been found to demonstrate some sensitivity.[12]

In the works of historical fiction about most American ethnic groups, insulting epithets are not generally employed. For one reason or another, the child's late-developing capacity to understand what chronology implies is respected. Consequently, there is reason to doubt the legitimacy of pleas for an historical use of the term "nigger." And writers who have recently used the term are suspect in another sense: they indicate neither the ironic implications of "nigger" when it was used historically by Blacks, nor its use as part of a protective "mask." (Opal Moore's essay in this anthology—"False Flattery and Thin History"—examines this problem in detail.)

In other words, child development concerns are very unequally attended to in children's book circles. Whether the narrative introduces issues related to self-esteem, to the fine line between fantasy and reality, to authority figures, or to historical time, it seems clear to us that ethnicity should not be presented as a stigma and a burden. Yet some books about Black Americans continue to be irresponsible in this respect.

Child development studies and their insights are suggestive, not absolute. When they indicate a general age trend, they are helping us define the realm of childhood, not limit its constituents. If we ignore the most well-grounded definitions that specialists have been able to achieve, then we may find ourselves neglecting both the child's rights and the child's rich potential for enjoyment of the arts.

Concerns of Artists and Critics

Critics of the arts are sometimes concerned that excessive weight may be given to social themes. The British critic of children's books, Margery Fisher, writes:

Children's fiction is more often than not reviewed and analysed for its content and not for the sum of its parts, so that a book of limited literary value, perhaps weak in character-drawing or insipid in vocabulary, can be recommended because it delivers a strong message on an important question. This approach to books for the young must eventually dilute their quality as mainstream literature. As a creative artist the writer is more susceptible to pressure of this kind from his public than musicians or artists are. We have yet to find a way of manipulating a chord so that it directly teaches, we accept that music must make its point more subtly. [13]

Although this statement does not mention the reader explicitly, Ms. Fisher seems interested in the reader as well as the writer and the finished work. She implies that the reason critics reject the "weak" and "insipid" has something to do with a work's failure to engage the reader. A three-way process in literature has been recognized for decades as a vital part of literary theory. In 1942 Thomas Pollock noted three phases in any complete linguistic process: the psycho-physiological activity of the writer which results in signs, the signs per se, and the "psycho-physiological activity of the hearer or reader in response to the signs." [14] In short, communication implies the presence of an audience.

In a heterogeneous society, the audience's ethnicity is not automatically pertinent to a literary experience, but it becomes significant if the writer introduces the subject. In such cases, the writer's respect for the subgroup hinges upon unstereotyped depictions, and upon how well the author is acquainted with the particular culture. In *Shadow and Substance: Afro-American Experience in Contemporary Children's Fiction*, Rudine Sims notes the inadequacy of fiction about Afro-Americans in which the "Afro" dimension is excluded. The details of Black home, family, and community life are unknown and unexpressed, and consequently the Black reader cannot be engaged in such a work to the same extent as the white reader, and the white reader is apt to be misled and confused by an indistinct portrait. "Universality," writes Sims, is "achieved in a rather facile manner, by viewing Afro-Americans with a tunnel vision that permits only one part of the duality of growing up Afro-American to be seen at a time."[15]

The "strong message" that Fisher sees as pressuring writers and encouraging inferior literature is therefore a much more subtle problem than she indicates. Much depends upon who is sending the "message" and who is receiving. For years writers have been putting strong messages in books that are widely referred to as "outstanding," but the racist messages in these same books have apparently been imperceptible to most of the white book critics. The treatment of the "message" has seemed "artistic"—understated—only to the white readers. In some children's literature journals (e.g., *The Horn Book Magazine*) this cultural blindness or naïveté is so extensive that racism is singled out as an "issue" or "message," while other culture-related thematic materials are viewed as the proper sphere of literary criticism. Thus in a 1977 *Horn Book* editorial, critics who take note of racial bias are labeled "vigilantes":

. . . an "issues approach" to children's books is not literary criticism at all. . . . Using the methods of vigilantes to track down messages in children's books is an exercise in profound futility and a cruel misuse of literature.[16]

Another problem with Margery Fisher's warning to critics is in her comparison of music, painting, and literature. The abstractions of music, in particular, are different in kind, not just degree, from the abstractions of literature. Malcolm Cowley has explained this difference:

Literature is not a pure art like music, or a relatively pure art like painting and sculpture. Its medium is not abstract like tones and colors, nor inorganic like metal and stone. Instead it uses language, which is a social creation, changing with the society that created it. The study of any author's language carries us straight into history, institutions, moral questions, personal strategems, and all the other aesthetic impurities or fallacies that many new critics are trying to expunge.[17]

Because language is so indissolubly connected with "history, institutions, moral questions, and personal stratagems," meaning and style can never be neatly separated in works of realistic fiction. A theme discussed throughout this book is the need for Black perspective as well as artistry in children's books, a concept referred to as "thinking Black," or writing from "inside rather than outside." When a book is created from this vantage point, it is likely to be aesthetically effective, as well as socially and psychologically authentic. Whether authors are Black or white, if they do not have the perspective that places value on Black identity, they cannot create a truly individualized characterization of a Black person and the whole work suffers. As noted in "Black Perspective in Books for Children" in this collection, stereotypes are by nature dull; they reduce personality to a formula; they are based on assumptions about *all* members of a community or ethnic group. The simplistic notions conveyed by stereotypes make inferior art, for they lack both depth and vitality.

Fantasies represent a marginal case for book critics because in that one genre an author can ignore characterization to some extent and yet produce a consistent, "humorous," fantasy world. Writers can use real world settings as they fit into the fanciful scheme, but also get by without writing "from the inside" about human personality. In a book such as *The Story of Dr. Dolittle,* the fantasy world is, in a technical sense, well-conceived, but the portrayal of Blacks is pernicious. Therefore the critic is forced to choose between two groups of values. On the one hand, he or she must consider the racism and its psychological damage to the child, and on the other hand, consider certain kinds of narrative competence. But even aesthetically we can question whether "Dr. Dolittle" is a great character, knowing now more about what he represents. The ethnocentricity he expresses has become an acknowledged anachronism in a world that lends support to the UN's "Declaration on the Rights of the Child."[18]

When Rae Alexander says in her essay in this book that "I was on the child's side, all the way," she is not advocating "message" books in the propagandistic sense of that term. Rather she is in accord with the UN Declaration and also with Thomas Pollock's description of the dynamics of literature. Pollock writes:

The existence of the actual work of literature itself is of primary importance. Its importance depends, however, not on its character as a static object, but on its potentialities as a medium capable of communicating a controlled experience to readers. The study of the work of literature in its character as a potential stimulus for the response of readers is therefore . . . the most important branch of literary investigation from the points of view both of the individual reader and of society.[19]

Equal Rights and Intellectual Freedom

Human rights and freedoms gained new clarification in the 1960s and 1970s as many people began to look more closely at the concept of accountability. For example, it is noted in *Equal Education* by John E. Hughes and Mary O. Hughes that while the state has the right to demand of children their presence for instruction in a school, the child has the concurrent right to demand an "appropriate and reasonable [educational] program for his [and her] needs."[20] If this were not the case, the child would face a no-win situation, because "the effects which an inappropriate or unreasonable program may have on our young citizens are often beyond the capability of their parents to counterbalance or the school to correct."[21] Since an instructional program includes use of library materials, library policy needs to reflect an accommodation between the concepts of freedom and accountability.

Defining "appropriate" and "inappropriate" is not easy, but the *Brown vs. Board of Education* case is some help because it focuses attention on "the stigma arising from the assumption of white supremacy," according to Kevin Fong, a staff member of the *Harvard Civil Rights-Civil Liberties Law Review*.[22] Fong states that it is not an adequate response to dismiss cultural pluralism as an issue of sociology. Rather it is a question of law because forced assimilation, like forced segregation, presumes that "white is right"—that Euro-American groups are innately superior. Minority group students have, therefore, legitimate grounds for protest when white supremacist materials are imposed on them, and the exercise of these rights does not do damage to the exercise of intellectual freedom. A law professor at Yale, Thoman I. Emerson, has written:

Where the government expression operates as a monopoly or near monopoly, some principles of limitation to absolute freedom of expression may be necessary. Such a situation arises, for example, in the field of education, which is a nearly closed system under the control of the government.[23]

One response to this "monopoly" problem—to an educational milieu containing largely monocultural materials and personnel—is the placement of racist materials in restricted collections. One of the writers represented in this collection, Jessie M. Birtha, recommends that racist classics be placed in historical research collections rather than in children's libraries. The debate revolving around this kind of recommendation is illustrated by a case in 1971 in San Jose, California. The head librarian of the San Jose Public Library stated the position of the American Library Association's (ALA) Intellectual Freedom Committee: "to remove the book [*Epaminondas and His Auntie* by Sara Cone Byrant] would be outright censorship and to place it in the Research collection would be a subtle form of the same thing."[24] He criticized the National Association for the Advancement of Colored People (NAACP) as follows:

It is ironic . . . that the NAACP, which has fought so valiantly against the suppression of ideas regarding the contributions of black citizens to American History is now cast in the role of suppressor of ideas with which [that] organization disagrees.[25]

This comparison involves things so vastly disproportionate that the whole fallacious character of the librarian's argument should have become apparent. The exclusions and distortions in the teaching of American history about Blacks have been well documented and are now widely admitted. Yet this fact is, in the view of the San Jose librarian, equivalent to what would be taking place if a racist children's book were transferred to a research collection. Such superficial comparisons have often been used as a means of evading social change. But beyond the invalid comparison, there is a noticeable deficiency in perspective when someone refers to racism as merely an idea "with which [that] organization disagrees." This view is out of line with the findings of psychologists, who maintain that racism is something destructive to the human personality—destructive to both the perpetrator and the target.

The position of ALA's Intellectual Freedom Committee is that the age of the borrower must never be allowed to interfere with the circulation of books—that parents, not librarians, are the sole legitimate arbiters. But this presumes that parents are acquainted with the books—that they could, if they wished, function like children's librarians and use their bibliographic knowledge in serving their own children. There is no system within the fields of publishing, librarianship, or education that gives parents the information they would need to serve as such advisers, much less "arbiters" as some ALA sections envision.

It is not surprising, therefore, that this position was modified by the Children's Service Division (now called the Association for Library

Service to Children) in 1973. A more equitable and defensible social policy is suggested in "The Statement on Reevaluation of Library Materials for Children's Collections" adopted by the Children's Services Division Board of Directors. The statement reads in part:

Librarians must espouse critical standards in selection and reevaluation of library materials. It is incumbent on the librarian working with children to be aware that the child lacks the breadth of experience of the adult and that librarians have a two-fold obligation in service to the child:

1. To build and maintain collections of materials which provide information on the entire spectrum of human knowledge, experience and opinion.

2. To introduce to the child those titles which will enable him [sic] to develop with a free spirit, an inquiring mind, and an ever-widening knowledge of the world in which he [sic] lives.

And the "Statement" concluded:

The Board of Directors of the Children's Services Division, American Library Association, supports the Library Bill of Rights and Free Access to Libraries for Minors. Reevaluation is a positive approach to sound collection building and should not be equated with censorship.[26]

Unfortunately, in 1976 the Division rescinded its "Reevaluation" statement at the behest of ALA's Intellectual Freedom Committee (IFC). But its central points remain valid: that children are not adults, and that taking account of child development (especially problems of self-image) is not censorship.

As the IFC was working to rescind the more pluralistic guidelines, it was also rewording the Library Bill of Rights and its "Interpretations" so that all criteria dealing with racial stereotyping would be disallowed. Thus in an issue of the *Newsletter on Intellectual Freedom* in 1983, ALA's official position was summarized in these terms:

Whether or not [a book] is guilty of racial stereotyping, according to ALA policy as enunciated in the Library Bill of Rights and elaborated in the policy on Diversity in Collection Development, this is not for librarians to judge. Libraries should strive to include in their collections the broadest diversity of materials, representing all points of view and tastes, including ones which may be personally offensive to the librarians.[27]

But in contradistinction to this policy and its assumptions that stereotyping is just a matter of "taste" or "viewpoint," there is a more pluralistic policy implied in another ALA publication, *Cultural Pluralism and Children's Media* (a work prepared under the auspices of the American Association of School Librarians). Avoidance of stereotyped materials is a strain that runs through nearly all the essays in this publication. In writing about Afro-Americans in children's fiction, Catherine Annelli writes: "It is expected that fiction selected for black children will be free from stereotyping and unflattering racial characterization."[28] In discussing literature and American Indian people, Cheryl Metoyer writes: "Critical to the improvement of children's materials about American Indians is the concern that librarians avoid materials that perpetuate stereotypes and misinformation."[29] Guidelines suggested by Asian Americans Florence Yoshiwara and Vivian Kobayashi include the criterion that a work transcend stereotypes.[30]

It appears then that since the first edition of this book in 1972, the American Library Association has been defining itself more and more as a battleground for conflicting perspectives on equal rights and intellectual freedom. Much of the conflict revolves around the legal definition of children as a specific and special class. But leading First Amendment theorists do not see this definition as problematic. As Thomas I. Emerson notes,

The world of children is not strictly part of the adult realm of free expression. The factor of immaturity, and perhaps other considerations, impose different rules. . . . Regulations of communication addressed to children need not conform to the requirements of the First Amendment in the same way as those applicable to adults.[31]

If children are to be given an equal chance to learn, they cannot be thrust into an alien, hostile educational environment, however "freely expressed" someone considers it to be.

The philosopher Mortimer Adler creates a simple line of division between creative liberty and social repsonsibility. He writes: "It is proper for the prudent man [sic] to supervise the ways in which works of art reach their audience, to say, not what shall be made, but what shall be received and by whom and under what conditions."[32] Writers write what they must out of their own experience; society accepts or rejects what it must to guarantee equal opportunities for the young.

Professional Tools for the 1980s

Despite the continuing production of racially biased books, and their continuing support by critics and institutions, some advances have been made in supplying the field with professional tools. First, the Coretta Scott King Award (a prize given under the auspices of ALA's Social Responsibilities Round Table) has been gaining in influence since its inception in 1970. Consequently, books by Black American authors comprise a growing collection that is gaining in prominence and accessibility. This award honors the Black author who has created the year's most distinguished children's book or young adult book. A similar award honors a Black illustrator.

An important publication of the last decade has already been mentioned: Esther R. Dyer's *Cultural Pluralism and Children's Media.* It is a series of position papers that explain the cultural and literary approaches advocated by Afro-American, Asian American, Native American, and Hispanic American educators. We also referred to Rudine Sims' *Shadow and Substance; Afro-American Experience in Contemporary Children's Fiction*—an extremely valuable overview of the Black aesthetic as it relates to children's literature. It offers a well-organized grouping of critiques that highlight both the problems and the advances made over the past dozen years.

John R. Cooley's *Savages and Naturals: Black Portraits by White Writers in Modern American Literature* contains detailed essays about cultural distortions in works by Stephen Crane, Vachel Lindsay, Eugene O'Neill, William Faulkner, Eudora Welty, and others. Cooley analyzes two forms of primitivism in characterization. The first equates Blackness with terror or destructiveness; the second depicts the "natural" Black American as childishly naïve and pastoral. These are the facile stereotypes that "yawn invitingly and deceptively before the white writer" who is "attempting to describe black lives."[33] The book should be of great interest to children's librarians, as well as adult librarians, book critics, and scholars.

The Council on Interracial Books for Children (CIBC), established in 1965, has produced a wide variety of curriculum guides, filmstrips, and pamphlets designed to combat racism (as well as sexism, handicapism, etc.) in education. Eight times a year it publishes *Interracial Books for Children Bulletin,* and its first book-length publication, *Human (and Anti-Human) Values in Children's Books; New Guidelines for Parents, Educators and Librarians,* was issued in 1976. This book begins with an eloquent essay on social values in their relation to literary values, and contains a sampling of reviews that demonstrate the application of the recommended guidelines. In conjunction with the National Education Association and the Connecticut Education Association, the Council prepared a landmark instructional kit entitled "Violence, the Ku Klux Klan and the Struggle for Equality." Another breakthrough is CIBC's multicultural textbook and teacher's guide, *Embers: Stories for A Changing World,* for grades four to six. It was published in 1983.

In 1977 we compiled for Scarecrow Press a multicultural anthology of articles entitled *Cultural Conformity in Books for Children.* A number of books are discussed in the section on literature about Blacks—publications we have not tried to cover in this book. In addition to these critiques, *Cultural Conformity* gives the reader an efficient means of comparing the forms of stereotyping that five different cultural groups have been subjected to.

In this second edition of *The Black American in Books for Children* we have centered our attention on some of the newer, widely publicized novels and picture books, and books from the past that continue to have a strong cultural influence. We have included an additional essay on a book that some consider to be the most widely taught novel in the United States, *The Adventures of Huckleberry Finn,* and we have added some assessments of publishing trends, and an interview with the head of Third World Press, a small press concentrating on Black culture. The concluding section offers the perspectives of a Swiss sociologist and an American lawyer. The section on "Black Perspective" has been expanded with essays by the president of the Council on Interracial Books for Children, Beryle Banfield, and the distinguished author Eloise Greenfield. A selected number of pieces in this section have been carried over from the first edition, and have not been changed. Their purpose is to trace the broad issues related to children's books vis-a-vis the Black aesthetic, not to focus attention on particular titles.

"Perspective," said the novelist Richard Wright "is that part of a poem, novel or play which a writer never puts directly upon paper. It is that fixed point in intellectual space where a writer stands to view the struggles, hopes, and sufferings of his [sic] people."[34] The writers about Black perspective in this anthology are aware of that "intellectual space" and concerned that images faithfully represent it. In *The Black Aesthetic,* Carolyn F. Gerald expresses the same concern and points to the vast responsibility of the image-maker:

Why is image so central to a man's [sic] self-definition? Because all images, and especially created images, represent a certain way of focusing on the world outside. . . .

We cannot judge ourselves unless we see a continuity of ourselves in other people and in things and concepts. . . . The black child growing into adulthood . . . seeing white protagonists constantly . . . experiences [life] in someone else's image . . . sees, in other words, a zero image of [him/herself].

Our work at this stage is clearly to destroy the zero and the negative image-myths of ourselves by turning them inside out. . . .

No one can hand us a peoplehood, complete with prefabricated images.

The artist then, is the guardian of image. . . .[35]

Notes

1. Barry N. Schwartz and Robert Disch. *White Racism: Its History, Pathology, and Practice.* (Dell Publishing Co., 1970) p. 383.
2. "School Desegregation and Racial Cleavage, 1954–1970: A Review of the Literature" in *Journal of Social Issues,* 26 (Autumn 1970) 26.
3. Phyllis A. Katz. "The Acquisition of Racial Attitudes in Children" in *Towards the Elimination of Racism,* ed. by Phyllis A. Katz. (Pergamon Press, 1976) p. 125.
4. Kenneth B. Clark. *Dark Ghetto: Dilemmas of Social Power.* (Harper, 1965) p. 64.
5. James A. Banks and Jean D. Grambs. *Black Self-Concept: Implications for Education and Social Science.* (McGraw-Hill, 1972) pp. xiv, xv.
6. Richard Beach. "Issues of Censorship and Research on Effects of and Response to Reading" in *Dealling with Censorship,* ed. by James E. Davis (National Council of Teachers of English, 1979) p. 140.
7. Arthur Applebee. *The Child's Concept of Story.* (University of Chicago Press, 1978) pp. 38, 52–53.
8. Dolores Durkin. "Children's Concept of Justice: A Further Comparison with the Piaget Data" in *Journal of Educational Research* 52 (March 1959) 256.
9. Robert Loughran. "A Pattern of Development in Moral Judgments Made by Adolescents, Derived from Piaget's Schema of Development in Childhood" in *Educational Review* 19 (1967) 79–98.
10. Gustav Jahoda. "Children's Concepts of Time and History" in *Educational Review* 15 (1962) 88.
11. *Ibid.,* pp. 96–97.

12. *Ibid.*, p. 99.
13. Margery Fisher. "Rights and Wrongs" in *Top of the News* 26 (June 1970) 376–377.
14. Thomas Clark Pollock. *The Nature of Literature*. (Princeton University Press, 1942) pp. 203–205.
15. Rudine Sims. *Shadow and Substance: Afro-American Experience In Contemporary Children's Fiction*. (National Council of Teachers of English, 1982) pp. 37, 41.
16. "Da Capo" in *Horn Book Magazine* 50 (October 1977) 502.
17. Malcolm Cowley. "Criticism: A Many-Windowed House" in *The Saturday Review* 44 (August 2, 1961) 11.
18. Over the past dozen years, two preeminent authors have revised their novels to eliminate the racism: Roald Dahl (*Charlie and the Chocolate Factory*) and P. L. Travers (*Mary Poppins*). But *The Story of Dr. Dolittle* still receives strong support. For example, in *20th Century Children's Writers* (2nd ed., 1983) the critic, Caroline Moorehead, trivializes the problem of racial slurs in Lofting's books by calling them "thoughtless lapses" and saying "they should not be allowed to spoil [the books'] real worth."
19. Pollock, pp. 203–204.
20. John E. Hughes and Mary O. Hughes. *Equal Education*. (Indiana University Press, 1972) p. 152.
21. *Ibid.*
22. Kevin M. Fong. "Cultural Pluralism" in *Harvard Civil Rights-Civil Liberties Law Review* 13 (1978) 169.
23. Thomas I. Emerson. *Toward a General Theory of the First Amendment*. (Random House, 1963) p. 113.
24. "NAACP vs. Epaminondas" in *Wilson Library Bulletin* 45 (April 1971) 718.
25. *Ibid.*
26. "CSD Board Action: Statement on Reevaluation of Children's Materials" in *Top of the News* (November 1972) 15–18.
27. "The Enemy Is Us?" in *Newsletter on Intellectual Freedom* (March 1983) 31, 36. It is worth noting that the larger context in which these policies have emerged includes ALA's own sponsorship of a racist film entitled "The Speaker" (an educational film that attempts to clarify intellectual freedom issues and the First Amendment). The film's grossly stereotyped characterizations of Blacks include the violent, brutish "militant," the lazy, let's-get-it-over-with committee member, the teacher who is guided in both cultural and political affairs by her paternalistic white colleague, and so on. As long as ALA functions as sponsor for a production so uniquely hostile to Blacks, the charge that culturally pluralistic librarians are "enemies" can be expected.
28. Esther R. Dyer, comp. *Cultural Pluralism and Children's Media*. (American Library Association, 1978) 34.
29. *Ibid.*, p. 22.
30. *Ibid.*, p. 49.
31. Emerson, p. 91.
32. Mortimer Adler. *Art and Prudence*. (Longmans, Green, 1937) pp. 449–450.
33. John R. Cooley. *Savages and Naturals: Black Portraits by White Writers in Modern American Literature* (University of Delaware Press, 1982) p. 185.
34. Richard Wright. "Blueprint for Negro Writing," in *The Black Aesthetic* ed. by Addison Gayle, Jr. (Anchor Books, 1972) p 323.
35. Carolyn F. Gerald. "The Black Writer and His Role" in *The Black Aesthetic* ed. by Addison Gayle, Jr. (Anchor Books, 1972) pp. 349, 351, 353, 354.

Part I

BLACK PERSPECTIVE: THE BASIC CRITERIA

1. WRITING FOR CHILDREN—A JOY AND A RESPONSIBILITY

Eloise Greenfield

IT IS A JOY to write for children. In addition to the satisfactions that derive from creative activity, there is a sense of sharing the world with someone who hasn't been in it very long. It's a joy.

And yet, there are times when I wonder why anyone would want to write, to suffer the pain and frustration of trying to trigger a flow of words that won't come, and be racked by the fear that a door has slammed and locked the words inside forever. At those times I have to say to myself, "This has happened before, I've had this terror before, the words will come, they'll come." I try to remember that although words do sometimes flow unbidden from their source, it is often just this suffering, this tension, that awakens my African muse.

Almost every writer has experienced this terror and the rush of relief and gratitude that accompanies, finally, the rush of words. It is not easy, therefore, to admit that the Muse is not infallible, that she must be continually challenged as to the validity of her offerings, but we must have the courage to face that fact. Our audience is too vulnerable, too impressionable, for us to entrust our art entirely to this force that lies somewhere in the subconscious mind, that repository of accumulated knowledge, attitudes and emotions. Both the rational and the irrational, the healthful and the harmful reside there as the result of a lifetime of conditioning.

In this society, our conditioning has been, to a great extent, irrational and harmful. This country was built on a foundation of racism, a foundation which is only slightly less firm after centuries of Black struggle. Attitudes toward women, toward men, attitudes regarding age, height, beauty, mental and physical disabilities have been largely of the kind that constrain rather than encourage human development. To perpetuate these attitudes through the use of the written word constitutes a gross and arrogant misuse of talent and skill.

Librarians, no less than writers, have a responsibility to challenge their own conscious and subconscious beliefs, as well as the validity of the books they select. Standing as they do between authors and children, they are the conduit through which book messages flow. The importance of their role as selector cannot be overemphasized. Nor can the importance of the question they must ask: What is the author saying?

There is a viewpoint which denies the relevance of this question, that holds art to be sacrosanct, subject to scrutiny only as to its esthetic value. This viewpoint is in keeping with the popular myth that genuine art is not political. It is true that politics is not art, but art is political. Whether in its interpretation of the political realities, or in its attempts to ignore these realities, or in its distortions, or in its advocacy of a different reality, or in its support of the status quo, all art is political and every book carries its author's message.

In the area of Black-oriented literature, much of what is communicated is venomous. Considerable attention has been devoted by sociologists to the study of the targets of racial abuse and oppression. The trauma, the damage to the spirit, the stifling of creativity, the threat to mere physical survival, have been well documented. Not enough attention, however, has been given to the study of those who, because of their conditioning, manifest delusions of grandeur, delusions that the whiteness of their skin makes them somehow special. The necessity to keep these delusions well nourished, to fortify them against any invasion of reality, makes these people menaces to society. Some of them are writers. They wield word-weapons, sometimes overtly, sometimes insidiously, yet they disclaim all responsibility for what they say, being merely objective observers of the human scene, or secretaries transcribing the dialogue of characters over whom they have no control. Is it the writer's fault that the characters just happen to be racist?

Children need protection from these word-weapons. They need protection in the form of organizations such as the Council on Interracial Books for Children and Black literature journals such as *Black Books Bulletin,* and they need librarians who care. The library can and should become the center for regular and systematic education of children in the dynamics of racism as it occurs in literature. Even the youngest school-age child can be told: "There are some people in the world who are very sick. Some of them are so sick that they don't want you to know what a wonderful being you are."

Until children are knowledgeable enough to defend themselves, racist books must be kept out of their reach, as any other deadly weapon would be. To say this is not to demean the intelligence of children, but to recognize the power of communication to influence the thought, emotions and behavior not only of children, but also of adults. The tens of billions of advertising dollars effectively spent each year attest to this fact. And consider this—there must have been a time in our recent history when there was only one Farrah Fawcett-Majors, and now there are at least three in every square mile of the North American continent.

The books that reach children should: authentically depict and interpret their lives and their history; build self-respect and encourage the development of positive values; make children aware of their strength and leave them with a sense of hope and direction; teach them the skills necessary for the maintenance of health and for economic survival; broaden their knowledge of the world, past and present, and offer some insight into the future. These books will not be pap—the total range of human problems, struggles and accomplishments can be told in this context with no sacrifice of literary merit. We are all disappointed when we read a book that has no power, a story that arouses no emotion, passages that lack the excitement that language can inspire, But the skills that are used to produce a well-written racist book can be used as well for one that is antiracist. The crucial factor is that literary merit cannot be the sole criterion. A book that has been chosen as worthy of a child's emotional investment must have been judged on the basis of what it is—not a collection of words arranged in some unintelligible but artistic design, but a statement powerfully made and communicated through the artistic and skillful use of language.

We are living now in a period of rapid growth comparable to that one year in the life of adolescents when they have trouble keeping up with the changes occurring in their bodies. We are struggling to keep up with our new understanding as we unlearn myths that have existed for hundreds—in some cases thousands—of years, and as we challenge the concepts that have defined us and our goals.

Webster's New World Dictionary, for example, defines the word success as: "the gaining of wealth, fame, rank, etc." I am incensed each time I read it. To take beings who have the potential for infinite growing, infinite giving of their ideas and talents, of their caring, and to commend for their greatest efforts aspirations that glorify two of the basest of human attributes—greed and egotism—and not be ashamed to set it down in print, is a harsh self-indictment by the society in which we live. And this from a society that boasts of being civilized.

But we are learning. Though few of us here today will live to see it, there will come a time when positive attitudes will be so ingrained in the fabric of our society, so pervasive, that constant examination of our artistic expressions will no longer be necessary. Our art will reflect us, and we will be in a state of health. For now, though, we have work to do. We will make mistakes sometimes. We will have periods of conflict and confusion. But we owe it to children, we owe it to posterity, and we owe it to ourselves to persevere. Our place in history demands it.

2. RACISM IN CHILDREN'S BOOKS: AN AFRO-AMERICAN PERSPECTIVE

Beryle Banfield

ANY WELL-ROUNDED CONSIDERATION of racism in children's literature and textbooks must proceed on the following premises:

1. Literature and textbooks reflect the values of a society and serve to perpetuate and reinforce these values.

2. Every intellectual discipline, i.e. the social sciences, philosophy, is pressed into service to provide the theoretical and "scientific" support for these values.

3. Educational institutions play a critical role in the reinforcement and perpetuation of these values, first, by the socialization of teachers and students so that they internalize and accept these values and, second, by the cultivation and development of scholars who will continue to present theoretical arguments in support of these values in increasingly sophisticated ways.

4. Every form of communications media is utilized to guarantee the widest possible dissemination of those ideas considered valid and desirable by a society.

Given the above stated conditions, in a racist society children's tradebooks and textbooks must be viewed as one of the most effective tools of oppression employed by a dominant majority against powerless minorities. The effectiveness of the educational institutions in socializing students to accept racist values guarantees that there will be an ever renewing supply of persons from which the creators, editors, and publishers of materials which espouse these ideas will be drawn. This has important implications, both for the methodology and criteria employed in analysing such materials and for the development of any programme to eliminate racism in children's materials and to counteract their damaging effects on *all* children.

The United States: Model for Analysis

Any analysis of racism in children's materials in a society must take into account the values of that society and the ways in which those values are projected and supported by intellectual disciplines and societal institutions. Only within such a framework can the function and effect of racism in children's materials be fully understood and the correct responses made to their devastating impact upon the minds and psyches of young people.

An excellent model for this type of examination is the United States, a racist society ever since its inception when the first boatloads of English people landed upon its shores with firmly internalized convictions of their superiority over the "heathen Indian" and the "barbaric African". An analysis of the development of racism in its literature and textbooks done in an historical context reveals that not only do these materials reflect the racist values of the United States society throughout its two hundred year history, but also they appear to express these values almost as if by demand at critical periods in the history of the Afro-American. They thus serve to reinforce racist ideas and constructs projected by "scientific theories" which are based on racist assumptions and which perpetuate historical distortions and degrading stereotypes. It becomes readily apparent that evidence of racism in literature and textbooks, far from being eliminated as time passes and the society presumably becomes more enlighted, consistently reappears in successive historical periods in increasingly subtle and sophisticated forms—making it ever more difficult to detect, and therefore all the more insidious and dangerous.

Well-developed racist stereotypes of the Afro-American began to emerge in the early 1800's in the pre-Civil War period. The ideology that was developed to justify the plantation system of slavery was already well entrenched in the southern states. It was based on three racist myths: (1) the black was by intellect and temperament naturally suitable to be the slave of the white; (2) slavery was the natural lot of the African and so ordained by the Creator; (3) rigid discipline and severe controls were necessary and beneficial to the African barbarian. Southern statesmen such as John C. Calhoun lauded the plantation system as a "near perfect society", and as a "little community with the master at its head, who concentrates in himself the united interests of capital and labour of which he is the common representative". Political writers argued the benefits of the system to the slaves in sentiments similar to those expressed by George Fitzhugh in *Cannibals All or Slaves without Masters* (1853):

> Our slaves till the land, do the
> coarse and hard labour on our

roads and canals, sweep our
streets, cook our food, brush
our boots, wait on our tables,
hold our horses and fill all
menial offices. Your freemen
at the North do the same work
and fill the same offices. The
only difference is, we love our
slaves and are ready to defend,
assist, and protect them.

Three Stereotypes

Here we see the emergence of the ever-recurring theme of the plantation tradition of literature. Slavery was idyllic, pastoral, and beneficial
to the inferior black. It was during this period that three of the stereotypes identified by the eminent Afro-American critic, Sterling A.
Brown, began to evolve. The Contented Slave, the Wretched Freeman, and the Comic Negro: the buffoon, the ridiculous, the postur-
ing—the hopelessly inept.

One of the earliest writers in this tradition was John P. Kennedy
whose *Swallow Barn* (1832) is unequalled in its idyllic portrayal of
slavery and picturesque slaves. He describes the "little negroes" who
showed their slim shanks and long heels "in all varieties of their
grotesque nature". Slavery is beneficial to the black, rhapsodizes Kennedy, since "in spite of the inconveniences of shelter, there was no
want of what in all countries would be considered a reasonable supply
of luxuries". Furthermore, Kennedy reasons:

(The Negro) is in his moral condition a dependant upon the white race. . .
Apart from this he has the helplessness of a child. . . This helplessness may
be the due and natural impression which two centuries of servitude have
stamped upon the tribe.

Not all writers shared Kennedy's rose-coloured perceptions of
the pastoral quality of plantation life. The ex-slave Frederick Douglass
had this terse and cogent comment:

It is the boast of slave-holders that their slaves enjoy more of the pastoral
comforts of life than the peasantry of any country in the world. My experience
contradicts this (1855).

Of these early writers it is Edgar Allan Poe who has had the most enduring fame and most devastating impact upon the minds and souls of white and black students. Generations of adolescent students have been helpless against the pernicious effects of his *Gold Bug*, as they were assigned this "classic" to read by teachers who were either oblivious to its racism or who had already internalized the racist values of the society. Poe made no secret of his own racism. He emphatically "denied that Negroes are like ourselves the sons of Adam and must therefore have like passions and wants and feelings". It was only natural that this racism should be apparent in *The Gold Bug*, considered by Poe to be his finest literary effort. Indeed, it was awarded a major literary prize in 1843.

In the book, Poe carries the stereotypes of the Contented Slave—the faithful, stupid black servant—and the Comic Negro to the ultimate in racism. The servant, Jupiter, although manumitted, refuses to leave "Massa Will", a formerly wealthy southern gentleman who is now somewhat "unsettled in mind". In this passage, Jupiter, after having caused "Massa Will" to make an error in calculations while trying to locate buried treasure, is asked to identify his left eye:

"Oh my golly, Massa Will! Ain't dis here my lef' eye for sartain?" roared the terrified Jupiter, placing his hand upon his *right* organ of vision.

A. F. Watts, an Afro-American university professor, graphically recorded his response to *The Gold Bug* in the short story *Integration: Northern Style:*

We are reading Poe's *Gold Bug*. . . Now this is what kills me. Jupiter is afraid of the dead bug! . . . Here's Jupiter acting like a jackass. None of the white fellows are afraid. Nobody's scared but Jupiter. He's rolling his eye-balls which are, of course, very white and talking like an ignoramus and murdering the king's English. Then there's this word "nigger" that's going to be read out loud by somebody in just a few minutes. And there's me, the only one of me in the whole class. . . There must be at least two whole pages sprinkled with "massa" and "nigger". When it comes my turn to stand up and read . . . if I don't draw that same stinking part! Jupiter's part. The "nigger" part! Me!

Watts' white classmates did not share his distress at having to read Jupiter's lines. One of them was "reading and grinning and glancing around the room all at the same time. . . . 'Ain't this a hell of a joke!' he seems to be saying."

"Ill-equipped to Survive in Freedom"

The trickle of literature in the plantation tradition became a veritable flood in the Post-Reconstruction period. This was the period of greatest racist attack against Afro-Americans—a period aptly described as *The Nadir (1877–1901)* by the Afro-American historian, Rayford Logan. The Hayes-Tilden Compromise, giving the presidency to Rutherford B. Hayes in return for the withdrawal of federal troops from the South, put an end to the promise of Reconstruction and abandoned the ex-slaves to the violent racism of their one-time masters. Many former slave-holders had always perceived the newly freed blacks as a threat to their economic and political power. They moved quickly to reimpose what was, in effect, a new form of slavery and to reaffirm the political and economic dominance of whites. Lynching, forced labour of blacks, and the passage of Jim Crow laws became the order of the day.

In almost obscene counterpoint to the escalation of violence against the blacks, there was an intensification of the pastoral plantation myths as justification for the virtual re-enslavement of the Afro-American. Afro-Americans were projected as being ill-equiped to survive in freedom and as longing for the "good old days before the war" when they were secure in the idyllic and protected atmosphere of the plantation. Two decades later, these myths would be given support by the newly emerging social sciences. More degrading stereotypes also made their appearance at this time. To quote Rayford Logan:

He (the Negro) was a thief and a drunkard.
He used big words which he did not understand.
He liked fine clothes and trinkets.
The inevitable razor-toting Negro made his appearance. Stealing was the main characteristic.

Joel Chandler Harris and Thomas Nelson Page were the foremost purveyors of these intensified racial myths. Page contributed *Two Little Confederates* (1888) to the store of racist juvenile literature. The standard stereotype of the contented, dependent, freedom-fearing slaves is well illustrated by the following excerpt. The mistress of the plantation has just called the slaves together to advise them that the Yankees are approaching and they are free to leave.

"Balla, I want you to know that if you wish to go, you can do so".
"Hi, Mistis———" began Balla, with an air of reproach; but she cut him short and kept on.
"I want you all to know it". She was speaking now so as to be heard by the cook and the maids who were standing about the yard listening to her. "I want you all to know it—everyone on the place! You can go if you wish; but, if you go, you can never come back!"
"Hi, Mistis", broke in Uncle Balla, "whar is I got to go? I wuz born on dis place an' I 'spec' to die here, an' be buried right younder". And he turned and pointed up to the dark clumps of trees that marked the graveyard on the hill, a half mile away, where the coloured people were buried.
"Dat I does", he affirmed positively. "Y' all sticks by us, and we'll stick by you".
"I know I ain't gwine nowhar wid no Yankees or nothin'," said Lucy Ann, in an undertone.
"Dee tell me dee got hoofs and horns", laughed one of the women in the yard.

Page would have his young readers believe that freedom was so distasteful to the blacks that they eagerly cooperated in hiding their Confederate masters from the Union Army. Lucy Ann, the slave, has just volunteered to aid the Union officers in the search for her two young masters on the pretext that she wants to be free.

She came straight down the passage towards the recess where the fugitives were huddled, the men after her, their heavy steps echoing through the house. The boys were trembling violently. The light, as the searchers came nearer, fell on the wall, crept along it, until it lighted up the whole alcove, except where they lay. The boys held their breath. They could hear their hearts thumping. Lucy Ann stepped into the recess with her candle, and looked straight at them. "They ain't in here", she exclaimed.

It is interesting to note that *The Two Little Confederates* was reissued in 1976 in a specially bound edition together with *The Little Colonel* by Anne F. Johnston (1896).[1] This is the same "Little Colonel" whose recreation in the dimpled image of Shirley Temple with Bill Robinson as her smiling, genial, dancing, faithful family retainer has been stamped on the minds of generations of American children for at least four decades through the media of movies and television.

From Moral Instruction to Political Retaliation

Joel Chandler Harris is generally credited with the collection and preservation of African folk-tales known to thousands of Americans as *The Tales of Uncle Remus*. Hailed as the one who best "knew and understood the Negro", Harris exerted great influence on this type of literature. His Uncle Remus was the epitome of the "plantation Negro": in the words of his creator, "an old Negro who had nothing but pleasant memories of the discipline of slavery". Harris' racism blinded him to the true nature of the slave's use of the folk-tale. In the African homeland, the folk-tale was a vehicle of moral instruction and the trickster-hero was often punished. Under slavery, it became an instrument of political retaliation and a technique of survival under an oppressive system. For the slaves, these stories exemplified the truth of a proverb common in many West African countries: "Even the poor and weak can outwit the rich and strong".

Harris therefore, in his ignorance, wrote condescendingly:

He (the slave) selects as his hero the weakest and most harmless of all animals and brings him out victorious. . .
It is not virtue that triumphs but helplessness. It is not malice but mischievousness.

Harris made his own contribution to the myths of the Contented Slave and the Wretched Freeman in his *Free Joe and the Rest of the World* (1887):

The slaves laughed loudly day by day, but Free Joe rarely laughed. The slaves sang at their work and laughed at their frolics but no one ever heard Free Joe sing or saw him dance. There was something painfully plaintive and appealing in his attitude, something touching in his anxiety to please.

The Bobbsey Twins series, one of the most popular and enduring ever devised for children, made its appearance in 1904. The cook, Dinah, is the ultimate stereotype of the Contented Slave, the Buxom Mammy, and the superstitious, watermelon-eating, eye-rolling, thieving black.

An examination of an original passage of *The Bobbsey Twins in the Country* and a revised version issued forty years later is instructive in terms of the perpetuation of racism on different levels, From *The Bobbsey Twins in the Country* of 1907:

Just then Dinah, the maid, brought in the chocolate, and the children tried to tell her about going to the country, but so many were talking at once that the good-natured coloured girl interrupted the confusion with a hearty laugh.
"Ha!Ha!Ha! And all you-uns be goin' to de country!"
"Yes, Dinah", Mrs Bobbsey told her, "and just listen to what Aunt Sarah says about you", and once more the blue letter came out, while Mrs. Bobbsey read: "And be sure to bring dear Old Dinah! We have plenty of room, and she will so enjoy seeing the farming".
"Farming! Ha! ha! ha! Dat I do like. Used to farm all time home in Virginie!" the maid declared. "And I like it fust-rate! Yes, Dinah'll go and hoe de corn and" (aside to Bert) "steal de watermelons!"

In the 1950 edition Dinah, now a "plump, good-natured Negro woman", responds in this manner to the invitation:
"Farm! That I do like", Dinah replied. "Used to farm all the time down home in Virginia. Yes, Dinah'll go and hoe the corn and . . ."
Turning to Bert, she grinned. "Are there any watermelons at Meadow Brook?
You and I . . ." Dinah stopped talking.
The Bobbseys looked at one another, wondering what Dinah had in mind.
When she did not tell them, Bert spoke up. "You and I what?" he asked.
Dinah looked at Mrs Bobbsey, then at Bert. "Well, I was a-figurin'", the cook laughed, "that maybe Bert and old Dinah could have a water-melon-eatin' contest. But maybe we'd better not. Bert might get himself sick!"

While attempting to eliminate the blatant racism of the water-melon-stealing incident, the authors could not bring themselves to abandon the watermelon-eating stereotype. Nor did they eliminate the stereotype of the eye-rolling, superstitious blacks.

"That sure is a ghost", whispered Dinah to Martha in the hall above. "Ghosts always lub music", and her big eyes rolled around in that way coloured people have of expressing themselves.

Justification by New "Scientific Theories"

The most critical period to examine for its impact on the development of children's literature and history textbooks is the first quarter of the twentieth century. It was then that many of the earlier "scientific theories" based on racist assumptions made their final breakthrough. A number of these theories still influence the development of social policy affecting the Afro-American. It was the period in which the theory of social Darwinism which celebrated the "survival of the fittest" and the concepts of the "white man's burden" and "manifest destiny" were all advanced to justify colonialist expansion and oppression of people of colour abroad, and quickly utilized to defend racial oppression within the United States.

Having served their uses, these theories faded into the background as the intellectual disciplines projected other racist assumptions that were to have a more lasting effect on the position of the Afro-American. From Columbia University came the doctrines of Ulrich B. Phillips as espoused in his study, *American Negro Slavery: A Survey of the Supply, Employment, and Control of Negro Labor, as Determined by the Plantation Regime*.[3] This study was informed by Phillips' own assumptions that blacks were, by racial quality, "submissive", "light-hearted", "amiable", "ingratiating". Wrote Philips:

On the whole plantations were the best schools yet invented for the mass training of that sort of inert and backward people which the bulk of American Negroes represented.

Also from Columbia University came John Burgess, respected as the dean of academic scholars, with this contribution to racist thought;

A black skin means membership in a race of men which has never created a civilization of any kind. There is something natural in the subordination of an inferior race even to the point of enslavement of the inferior race. . . "It is the white man's duty and his right to hold political power in his own hands".[4]

The newly developed science of sociology ushered in the era of the study of race and culture which contributed to the branding of the Afro-American as intellectually, morally, physically, and biologically inferior.

Robert E. Park was deified by other academics and co-founder of the dominant University of Chicago School of Sociology. He was widely regarded as "a friend of the Negro". It was he who characterized the black as "the lady among the races. . . by natural disposition", neither

an "intellectual" nor an "idealist" or "a frontiersman" but possessed of
a talent for "expression rather than action". And it was he who proposed an "etiquette of race relations". According to Park's premise,
conflict and competition occur whenever large and diverse populations
come into contact. Stabilization occurs when one race becomes dominant and the other accommodates to an inferior position. The etiquette of race relations demanded that a "social distance" be maintained between the races. This would allow them to coexist but not
necessarily on equal terms. It should be noted that Park was the
powerful mentor of Booker T. Washington who, in 1895, allayed the
fears of the South by publicly proclaiming acceptance of political in-
equality and lower economic status for blacks.

The Height of Distortion and Myth

E. B. Reuter, trained by Park, carried racism to even greater heights
in his *American Race Problem*.[5] Reuter asserted: "The status of slavery
lies well within the mores of the Negro race . . . the institution was
usual in many of the African tribes". Reuter further posited that the
"Negro, brought into the New World situation and reduced to perpetual servitude, became very rapidly accommodated to the environment and the status". "The second generation", Reuter maintained,
"accepted the white as superior and the master. They came to expect
mastery and superiority from the white. . . The Negro was thus not
alone a slave in body; he came to be a slave in mind as well". Denying
the existence of institutional racism which enforced the slave status of
the black, and the continued efforts of slaves to secure their own
liberation, Reuter asserts:

Without the appropriate mental attitudes no people can be kept in such
servitude. No slave system can rest alone on the basis of physical force.

After emancipation, Reuter further affirms: "The Negro retained the mental attitudes and behaviour responses appropriate to
that status". According to Reuter, the blacks

were without ancestral pride . . . even a tradition of historic unity or racial
achievements . . . the whole record of the race was one of servile or barbaric
status.

Here, in one influential volume, are expounded all the historical distortions and racial myths that would influence the development of materials dealing with the life, history and culture of the Afro-American in all the future decades: distortion of the African background; distortion of the nature of slavery on the African continent; acceptance by blacks of their slave status; development of a servile personality; and lack of ability to produce substantial achievements.

This volume is still in print, with a 1970 copyright, and with the author saluted on the cover as "one of the most rigorous and critical sociological thinkers of his time".

The black movement for full equality gained momentum in the 1950's and escalated into the decade of the "Searing Sixties". Afro-Americans posed a large political and economic threat, as had their ancestors one hundred years earlier. They proudly celebrated their pride in their African heritage. Black parents pressed demands for reconstruction of school curricula and the elimination of those racist materials which had been damaging their children. It was a heady time for young blacks and a frightening time for those committed to the perpetuation of racism.

Reactions of the Academics

The response from the academic community was not long in coming. Stanley Elkins' *Slavery, A Problem in American and Institutional Life* appeared in 1959, published, appropriately enough . . . by the University of Chicago. After repeating the racist historical myth that "the typical West African tribesman was a distinctly warlike individual", Elkins proceeds to develop the "Sambo" theory in which we perceive the modern reworking of the theme developed earlier by Reuter. "Sambo", submits Elkins, is a uniquely American phenomenon created by the slavery experience. He is the "perceptual child. . .incapable of maturity". Elkins insists that this was the type of personality developed by the Afro-American as an accommodation response to the institution of slavery. He gives as proof of the validity of his argument the overwhelming presence of this type in plantation literature.

Time on the Cross by Robert Fogel and Stanley Engerman attracted unusual attention when it appeared in 1974[6] and was enthusiastically received in some academic quarters. Using the modern science of cliometrics, the authors conducted a study of plantation life and produced a report which repeated the racist myths of an earlier generation. The slaves worked so hard to make plantations successful because their master treated them so well. They also lived materially better than the free farm workers in the South. Daniel Moynihan and Nathan Glazer in *Beyond the Melting Pot*[7] wiped out the entire cultural heritage of the Afro-American with this statement: "He (the Negro) has no values and cultures to guard and protect".

The literary establishment gave overt approval to racist sentiments in literature by the awarding of prestigious prizes. William Styron's *The Confessions of Nat Turner*[8] won the coveted Pulitzer prize in 1968. The award was a clear message to those Afro-Americans who had reacted with justified anger at this derogatory and dehumanizing portrayal of an Afro-American hero in the fight for the liberation of the slaves.

The Cay by Theodore Taylor, dedicated to the memory of Dr. Martin Luther King, appeared in 1969.[9] This story carried the modern version stereotype of the contented slave to the ultimate conclusion: the slave gives his life to save his young master. Timothy, the contented slave, establishes his servile relationship to the young white hero with the very first words he speaks to him: "Young bohss, how are you feelin'?" Timothy is also stereotyped as "the grotesque negro":

His face couldn't have been blacker or his teeth whiter. They made an alabaster trench in his mouth and his pink-purple lips peeled back over them like the meat of a conch shell. He had a big welt like a scar on his left cheek.

Other evidences of racism abound in this highly acclaimed work for children. Timothy is made to reject his African heritage by denying any knowledge about "Afreeca" and expressing lack of interest in that continent. The strong tradition among blacks of lovingly caring for children who are not blood relatives is downgraded by Timothy's casual, unfeeling statement: "I was raised by a woman named Hannah Gumbs". In the African context there would have existed a warm mother-son relationship, and Timothy would not have considered himself an orphan, as is suggested in the text. *The Cay* was given national media exposure in a television version sponsored by the Bell Telephone Company in 1973.

Paula Fox's *The Slave Dancer*[10] won the highly respected Newbery Award for outstanding children's literature in 1973. This book is a good example of the subtle racism which can be detected in children's literature. Skillfully written, it repeats several racist historical myths: Africans were barbarians; they were responsible for selling their own people into slavery; and there were good men engaged in the slave trade "whose hearts weren't in it". The reason for the suicides of the Ibos is attributed to a defect in character rather than that they preferred death instead of enslavement.

The following excerpts are illustrative:

The native chiefs are so greedy for our trade goods, they sell their people cheaper than they ever did to tempt us to run the British blockade.

. . . as everyone knows, our whole country is for the trade, in spite of the scoundrels who fling themselves about at the fate of the poor, poor black fellows. Poor indeed! Living in savagery and ignorance. Think on this—their own chiefs can't wait to throw them in our hold.

I won't have those Ibos. They're soft as melons and kill themselves if they are not watched twenty-four hours a day. I will not put up with those creatures.

CIBC Racism-in-Textbooks Study

Textbook publishers also responded to the demands of the late fifties and the sixties. They produced new history texts which purported to be more accurate depictions of Afro-American life, history and culture. Instead, these materials subtly presented the same recycled racist theories in a form that often, at first reading, appeared to answer the demand of Afro-Americans.

The Council on Interracial Books for Children recently undertook a groundbreaking study of racism in textbooks as it affected the portrayal of the Afro-American and other minorities. An inter-racial team of Afro-American historians, authors, and curriculum experts analysed 13 history texts published since 1970. Their findings were published in 1977 in a book entitled *Stereotypes, Distortions and Omissions in United States History Textbooks*. It is striking evidence of the racism present in the newer textbooks. In the CIBC book, passages from the textbooks are presented in one column, with critiques in the next column and supportive evidence in a third column. It is a handy format for teachers and students. Here are a few examples:

One important thing to remember about slavery is that it was a long and brutal episode in our history. It was a terrible system, basically, but many kinds of slaves, from the most oppressed field hand to the talented cabinet-maker, were able to earn money and buy their freedom. There were also many different masters. There were brutes who beat their slaves, but there were also kind men like George Washington who met their responsibilities well and freed their slaves.[11]

A kind master would often divide his slaves among his children. In his will he would give to his son or daughter one or more slaves to serve them for life.[12]

While appearing to condemn the barbarity of the system, the texts still project the myth that slavery in the hands of the right master was indeed a beneficial institution. The basic principle—that enslavement of another human being is morally wrong—is never addressed.

Why did the slaves so seldom revolt. . . First, the slaves knew that the masters held all the power. . . Also, many slaves had learned the rules of slavery so well they hardly thought of rebelling.[13]

This passage repeats the racist theories first projected in the early 1970's, that the Afro-American had been habituated to slavery and had developed a servile personality. It completely ignores the types of resistance offered by the slaves: rebellions, escapes, suicides, infanticides and murders of overseers.

. . . three and a half million blacks became free men. Many southerners did not know how to live without slaves. Many former slaves did not know how to live without their former masters.[14]

This is a reworking of the "unfit for freedom" theory. Destruction and confusion follow any major war. Such a presentation ignores the achievements of the freed blacks in working to establish civil governments which provided to *all* those democratic rights of suffrage and free education which had been denied slaves.

Actually the delegates to the constitutional convention were more than good politicians, They were really statesmen. A statesman does what is best for his nation. He works unselfishly for the good of all people . . . they must figure out ways to do the most good for the most people without hurting the rights of anybody. . . . The men who wrote our Constitution were able to compromise and solve many big problems.[15]

This passage effectively precludes the development of any understanding by the student that the United States was founded on racist assumptions. Almost half of the framers of the Constitution were slaveholders. The infamous Dred Scott decision of 1857 affirmed that the principles enunciated in the Constitution were not meant to apply to blacks.

Facing the Problem Internationally

The elimination of racism from children's trade books and textbooks requires strategies that will effectively break the cycle by which racist myths are refurbished to match the mood of each succeeding historical period. Much has been written on the disastrous effects of racist materials on white, black and tan children alike. What has not been as generally recognized is that racism in children's materials is not a personal aberration on the part of an individual author but a reflection of the institutionalized racism that pervades every facet of US society. This means, for one thing, challenging the universities which sponsor research based on racist assumptions, which publish this research with academic sanction, and which then proceed to train hundreds of future teachers so that they unquestioningly internalize these values. It means the support and development of writers who are committed to the creation of books that go beyond being merely non-racist; that is, the creation of books that are consciously anti-racist. It also calls for the support and development of minority publishing programmes committed to the portrayal of life, history and culture from a minority's point of view. It requires the development of stringent criteria by which to examine the content of trade books and textbooks. Such criteria should necessarily include an examination of racist assumptions inherent in the treatment of the historical background, characterizations, use of language and terminology, and the culture and traditions of the minority groups presented in the material. Most important of all, the potential users of these materials—parents, teachers and children—must be equipped with the skills and information that will enable them to identify and challenge the racist content of materials.

The exposure of racist scientific theories, the encouragement of writers from minority groups, the formation of criteria to identify racism, and the education of potential users—the CIBC's campaign against racism has included all these aspects. The Council would now like to work with groups in other nations to tackle this problem at an international level.

In addition to our indigenous form of racism we in the United States have also suffered from the importation of *Mary Poppins, Doctor Dolittle, Pippi Longstocking, Little Black Sambo* and, more recently, Roald Dahl's *Charlie and the Chocolate Factory*.[16] For our part, we have exported a great number of racist classics, and modern examples of racism such as *Sounder*[17] and *The Cay*. Since racism is international and is being promoted by multinational corporations which control the publishing world, let us not work in national isolation but develop a truly multinational anti-racist struggle.

Here is a tremendous challenge, but one to which we must be equal. To paraphrase the African proverb, since the coming year of the child is in sight: "Let us be up and doing".

Notes

1. Classics of Children's Literature, Garland Publishing Inc., New York.
2. Whitman Co., Racine, Wisconsin.
3. Louisiana State University Press, Baton Rouge, La, 1966.
4. *Reconstruction and the Constitution*, Scribners, New York, 1902.
5. T. Y. Crowell, New York, 1970 (1st ed. 1924).
6. Little Books, Fort Lee, NJ.
7. MIT Press, Cambridge, Mass., 1965.
8. Random House, New York, 1967.
9. Doubleday & Co. Inc., New York.
10. Bradbury Press, Scarsdale, NY, 1973.
11. Bernard Weisberger & Gerald Hardcastle, *The Impact of Our Past*, McGraw-Hill, New York, 1972, p. 121.
12. Gerald Leinwand. *The Pageant of American History*, Allyn & Bacon, Inc., Boston, Mass., 1975, p. 205.
13. S. Bronz, *The Challenge of America*, Holt, Rinehart & Winston, Inc., New York, 1973, p. 335.
14. *The Pageant . . .*, pp. 281–282.
15. Margaret Branson, *American History for Today*, Ginn & Co., Boston, Mass., 1970, p. 117.
16. Pamela Travers, *Mary Poppins*, Harcourt, Brace, Jovanovich, New York, 1972. Hugh Lofting, *Doctor Dolittle: a Treasury*, Lippincott, New York, 1967. Astrid Lindgren, *Pippi Longstocking*, Penguin, New York, 1977. Helen Bannerman, *Little Black Sambo*, Western Publishing Co., Racine, WI, 1976. Roald Dahl, *Charlie and the Chocolate Factory*, Knopf, New York, 1964. (Dates given are for latest editions.)
17. William Armstrong, Harper & Row, New York, 1969.

3. BLACK PERSPECTIVE IN BOOKS FOR CHILDREN*

Judith Thompson and Gloria Woodard

> I, too, sing American. I am the darker brother.[1]
>
> (America never was America to me)[2]

THESE LINES from two poems by Langston Hughes indicate the dichotomy of American life for black Americans. They suggest what "blackness" should mean in the context of American life, and what it does mean. Neither message is new. Every leading spokesman of every generation of black Americans has revealed the depths of bitterness engendered by the frustration of being the darker brother in a white America. Only recently, however, have we begun to face the difficult fact that "whiteness" is still the major criterion for full participation in American life. W. E. B. DuBois emphasized the extent of this condition when he depicted the black American as born into

> . . . a world which yields him no true self-consciousness, but only lets him see himself through the revelation of the other world. It is a peculiar sensation, this double-consciousness, this sense of looking at one's self through the eyes of others, of measuring one's soul by the tape of a world that looks on in amused contempt and pity.[3]

Our increased awareness of these facts puts a new responsibility on all of us concerned with children's literature. It points to the

---

*Editors' Note: In this article, the use of the masculine pronoun in a generic sense is in accord with the practices of the 1960s—the years when the authors were in collaboration. This usage will be noted in other articles that date from that period, articles by Jessie M. Birtha, Dharathula H. Millender, Paul Deane, and others. And similarly the term "Negro" was widely used in the pre-1970 era, and we leave it to the reader to note the historical time frame for each essay. The term "Black" is not consistently capitalized in this volume when the term refers to African Americans or Afro-Americans. We have not edited the various texts to achieve a uniform style.

necessity to re-examine chilren's books about black Americans, and to begin from a fresh standpoint. We can be glad that the days of direct caricature are behind us, but a less obvious misrepresentation is wide-spread in children's books today. We must ask to what extent and by what means have narrow ethnic attitudes pervaded books about black Americans, even those books specifically written "to further inter-racial harmony"? We must ask whether these books are providing meaningful identification for black children, as well as real insight for white children into the historical, ethnic, and cultural characteristics of black Americans. Finally, we must frankly ask whether the image of the white American has been made to seem more desirable than that of the black American in these books.

The popularized slogans "Black Pride," "Black Power," and "Black is Beautiful" are based on the most universal concern of man: identity. They deal with the eternal questions—who am I, where did I come from, where am I going? Of the two literary genres, fact and fiction, it is the fiction which is too often irrelevant and inadequate as a guide to answering these questions for black children. The histories and biographies are illuminating black experience; the fiction is not. The histories are providing identification and inspiring pride, in self, in ethnic group, in African heritage; the fiction is not.

The research required of a writer of non-fiction partially ex-plains this. It must be granted that to have been, and to be, a black in America is a unique and perhaps unprecedented human and historical experience. As an ex-slave advised Julius Lester in his introduction to *To Be a Slave*, "If you want Negro history, you will have to get it from somebody who wore the shoe and by and by . . . you will get a book."[4] Whether a writer is white or black, if he immerses himself in the history of a period or in the life of a man, he must to some degree "wear the shoe" to report the experience accurately.

Fiction demands a similar kind of "self-consciousness." As James Baldwin puts it, "One writes out of one thing only—one's own experience."[5] The credentials of the writer who undertakes a book about blacks must include a black perspective based on an appreciation of black experience. "Good intentions" are not enough. The writer of books about black children must understand the importance of ethnic consciousness before writing about the goal of ethnic irrelevancy. Conscious of the inequities suffered even after many blacks became "just plain Americans," blacks today refuse to erase the "black" from black American. They refuse to make invisible that one attribute which connotes their unity, culture, and heritage. Certainly, integration and assimilation are not possible until the recognition of and respect for these differences are fully realized.

Hopefully, we can all learn to "wear the shoe," actually or vicariously, but we are not all qualified to write about what we learn. It is this combination of black consciousness and creative ability which will finally result in good books about black children. When a writer lacks these credentials, the result is too often a kind of verbal minstrel show—whites in blackface—rather than the expression of a real or imagined experience derived from wearing the shoe.

Too many of the integrated books or books for "interracial harmony" tend to reinforce the very attitudes they are trying to dispel. In too many of these books the white child dominates the story. He is the controlling factor, the active character. The focus of the story is on his character development. The black child is then necessarily placed in a subservient role. He is the passive character. He is the problem which causes the white child to act. He literally and figuratively waits for the white child to invite him in, to figure things out, to be enlightened. In short, the black child *is* the problem: the white child *has* the problem.

In *Fun for Chris,* by Blossom Randall, Chris the white boy is shown in a fully depicted environment complete with understanding mother, doting grandmother, lovely home, fenced-in backyard with all the childhood toys: swing, sandpile, ladder, etc. Toby, the Negro boy, is a shadow in comparison. We are told he is older than Chris; he refers to a mother for whom he runs errands; he teaches Chris to build sandcastles, and he is, as Chris discovers, "brown all over." Other than these few references to a life, family, and environment of his own, Toby has no identity except as Chris' playmate, as the beneficiary of Chris' largesse, for which he waits every day, sitting outside the gate.

It is not what is said about Toby that raises objections to this book, it is what is omitted. The story gives a white child no insight into the real life of a black child, and it gives a black child no real reflection of himself. The perspective is that of a white world, a world in which the black child is an outsider who endures while the world decides his fate. Told from such a perspective, all the explicit explanations of human equality or racial irrelevancy cannot rise above the implicit inferences of white "superiority."

In many other books for older readers dealing with racial conflicts—in schools, the ghetto, "white" neighborhoods, at the swimming pool, etc.—the implications of white superiority take several forms. In these books, rarely are blacks depicted as effecting the changes that affect them. In fact, the blacks in these stories are represented as ineffective, whether as individuals, American citizens, or an ethnic group. They neither protest, demand, or even suggest that changes be made. Moreover, they are often made to blame themselves rather than society for the various conditions of extreme poverty, segregation, or social ostracism. Nor do these books present a coalition of black and white working to effect changes—a cooperative endeavor based on mutual respect. Instead, the happy ending or successful endeavor is usually due to the intervention of a white benefactor.

In *Call Me Charley*, by Jesse Jackson, the moral is clear. The success of black endeavor is dependent upon the magnanimity of white people. In order to receive the bestowal of this magnanimity, black children must meet certain standards set by a white middle-class society. The index of acceptability is often marked by superficial criteria which are set even higher for blacks, whether they be manners, standards of dress, or speech patterns. It is Charley's mother who instructs her son in the ways of the white world and the role of the black boy in it. These instructions consist of platitudes that are demeaning and repressive:

You'll have to keep out of trouble. It ain't like you were one of the other boys. . . . And watch your manners, boy. Good manners go a long way to help a colored boy get along in this world. You got to keep trying. You got to work harder than anybody else.

By the end of the story, all these platitudes are realized by Charley (with the help of his friend's white liberal parents), and one more "exceptional" Negro has been accepted by the white world.

The perverse relationships that racial discrimination engenders have not been misrepresented in this book or in others with a similar theme. In a climate of prejudice, blacks *do* have to *try harder* and *be better* in order to be accepted into schools, jobs, or neighborhoods. However, by revealing the situation and only obscuring both the real solutions and the real feelings of blacks about these conditions, the various systems of institutionalized discrimination are made to appear inevitable.

In the novel *Tessie*, written by the same author and published last year, a slightly greater sense of "black consciousness" is evinced by the younger generation—Tessie and her friends—while the idea of integration through the acceptance of individual exemplary Negroes is shown as an older-generation viewpoint.

Another facet of the white perspective is seen in the social significance attached to skin pigmentation. The hierarchy, of course, is that white is best and extreme darkness most undesirable.

In *The Empty Schoolhouse*, by Natalie Carlson, the narrator, Emma Royall, makes these remarks about the difference between herself and her sister:

Lullah is the spittin' image of Mama and her kin. Her skin is like coffee and cream mixed together and she has wavy hair to her shoulders. Me, I'm dark as Daddy Jobe and my hair never grew out much longer than he wears his.

That the comparison of these physical differences is not simply an objective appraisal is revealed within a few lines, wherein the emphasis is clearly on self-depreciation (italics added): "Little Jobe looks like me and Daddy Jobe, *but* he's a handsome little boy *all the same*,"—or in spite of the fact that he is dark and has short hair.

The objections are to the subtle and probably unconscious perspective which presents a young black girl in terms of self-hatred and a feeling that white is preferable to dark. On page one, fourteen-year-old Emma introduces herself to us in terms of self-worthlessness: "I always tell myself, since you quit school in the 6th grade, you'll never be anything but a scrub girl at the Magnolia Motel." Her sense of identity is sharply circumscribed by her employment throughout the book; "You'll just have to try to be the best scrub girl there is," she reminds herself repeatedly and in various ways. When the priest conducts the annual blessing of the sugar cane harvest, Emma comments: "It made me feel like I was made special by God and real important to Him even if I was just a scrub girl." Finally, she is overcome by a feeling of nostalgia when her father relates the "good old days" of picking sugarcane: "I wish I'd lived then. . . . I'd be a field hand instead of a scrub girl." Not only is it unrealistic for a young girl to identify herself entirely and on all occasions in terms of her occupation, it is an exaggeration which turns the admirable traits of endurance and perseverance into a mere caricature.

The glorification of poverty has been a familiar theme in children's books throughout the ages. One immediately thinks of Louisa May Alcott's *Little Women* or Dickens' *Christmas Carol* as two examples. Both books provide children with a dramatization of how, with courage and high optimism, people can overcome or cope with the indignities and deprivations that poverty can engender. The writer who undertakes the description of such a situation, however, walks a thin line between developing characters who courageously make the best of a bad situation and characters who, by their reaction to this situation, glamorize abject poverty.

Evan's Corner, by Elizabeth Starr Hill, a book for younger readers, succeeds in walking this line, and the result is an intimate story about a black boy whose yearning to find a corner of his own in the midst of a large family in small quarters is immediately recognized as a universal one. The focus of the story, however, is not on the family's impoverished condition, but on the personal problem of the child and his solution to it. The book reveals a sensitive understanding of children and their need for both a corner and companionship. It also reveals an understanding of the ghetto situation, in which some ingenuity is demanded for one to find a corner of his own.

A book for older readers, *Roosevelt Grady,* by Louisa Shotwell, involves an entire family's search for a corner of its own, a "Promised Land . . . a place where everybody has a chance—a place where everybody can be somebody." It is the story of a black migrant worker's family and its search for security and stability—a job, a home, a school. Admirable qualities such as patience, courage, endurance, and optimism are presented as characteristics of the Grady family. But despite its good intentions, this book reinforces stereotyped beliefs about Negroes as a race, rather than individualized solutions to universal problems. The idea on which the story is based suggests that blacks do not have very high expectations, ambitions, or ideals. Furthermore, the situations the family encounters are always appalling; the response of the characters is inappropriately cheerful. In short, the story depicts people striving for, settling for, and reacting with enthusiasm to subhuman conditions.

At one point in the story, the family finds itself occupying the attic floor of a house "with a roof so low and sloping that most places .. even a nine year old could easily bump his head" and with windows filled with dust and cobwebs, and with drawers and cots to sleep on that "smell of dirty clothes and dust." Stock responses come from each member of the family. From Mama: "Those dormer windows give our attic a real glory." From six year old Matthew, "as he wrinkled up his nose and sniffed at the smell of dirty clothes and fish": "It's a satisfactory smell. I like it."

It is this vast discrepancy between situation and response, between event and reaction, that results in characterization wholly unrealistic. The nine-year-old hero, Roosevelt, responds similarly to an authoritarian, brow-beating teacher: "Maybe she . . . wasn't such a bad teacher after all . . . even if she did teach with a stick . . . . Maybe the Opportunity Class was a good place for bean-pickers. A place where they could find out things. If they asked." These words of apology, justification, and self-recrimination are spoken by a black character, but the words are white. If a black child were to identify with this boy, he would have to incorporate in his perception of life that 1) being beaten or abused by a teacher is an acceptable practice; 2) there is a caste system in our democracy, which, if you are of a minority—bean-picker or black—means there are specially designated, circumscribed facilities for you; and 3) if you don't get an education under these conditions, it's your own fault. You didn't ask the right questions.

At the end of the story, Mama's dream of a Promised Land is supposedly fulfilled in the attainment of a remodeled bus with cold running water and a little potbellied iron stove to keep them through winters known to be so harsh that their white benefactor cautions them: "Nobody has stayed in one of these buses all through to spring, but that's no reason you shouldn't try." The mother's response is not mild relief, but tearful joy: "I like it fine, Roosevelt. . . . All I don't like is thinking about when . . . we have to leave all this behind."

In a land of opportunity and a multi-million dollar economy is it realistic to depict a family finding happiness and fulfillment in the attainment of less than substandard housing? The mother's high optimism should be inspiring; but if the final outcome for this family is considered fortunate, the optimism here borders on simple-mindedness, and the final conclusion the reader makes about these people is the racist platitude: "It sure don't take much to make *them* happy."

A Fair Judgment?

The question sometimes arises as to the legitimacy of any kind of literary judgment which takes sociological or historical factors into account. The British author John Rowe Townsend states that:

to assess books on their racial attitude rather than their literary value, and still more to look on books as ammunition in the battle, is to take a further and still

more dangerous step from literature-as-morality to literature-as-propaganda—
a move toward conditions in which, hitherto, literary art has signally failed to
thrive.[6]

In part, one must agree with Mr. Townsend's thesis. Books
should not be evaluated only in terms of the racial attitudes presented
in them. In fact, it would be better if books were not written for the
sole purpose of presenting certain racial attitudes. When the principal
concern of literature becomes polemics and manifestos, idea replaces
characterization, and the reader leaves the book with a slogan rather
than an experience. And whether that slogan be "Black Power" or
"Brotherhood," the reader will be cheated of sharing the conflicts,
dilemmas, and personal solutions which result from individualized
characterization.

On the other hand, it is precisely because we have failed to
examine our own racial attitudes fully enough that the sociologically
determined stereotype continues to predominate in books about black
children. Such stereotypes are created when the traits assigned to a
character do not derive from the story, but from assumptions about all
members of the community or ethnic group. They produce not only an
inferior literature; they encourage simplistic notions about human
nature and reduce the complexity of personality to a formula.

The very appearance of blacks in American literature has been
historically and culturally determined. The abnormal invisibility of
blacks in American literature corresponds to the invisibility foisted on
them by American society. When blacks were finally represented in
literature, they were presented in terms of the conceptions white
society had of blacks, rather than perceptions of them as individuals.
Thus, blackness is depicted as a stigma, poverty as an inevitable condition to be endured with cheerful optimism, and the solution to racial
discrimination as the independent effort of individual blacks who are
strong enough to pull themselves up by their own bootstraps.

The inferiority complex of an Emma Royall, the limited horizons
of the Gradys, the obsession of Charley's mother with conventions of
acceptability, are realistic in the sense that such distortions of the
healthy personality do in life exist. However, it has not been emphasized that these traits are not inherent; they are not ethnically derived;
they are not natural. The characters in these books fail to show that it
is one's environment which engenders such perverse self-images. It
has not been made clear that the environment itself is unnatural, man-
made.

Unless conscious efforts are made by those who read, review, and publish children's books, blacks will continue to be left out, shaded in, or given a token place outside the mainstream of children's literature. To readjust the balance, black writers, artists, and consultants must become involved in replacing the sociological images with the many and varied self-images of black Americans. The range of individuals within the black culture is as great as that within any other ethnic group. It is those books which give us intimate experience with this great range of characters, all of whom are black, all of whom are different, that will finally further interracial harmony.

To judge literature in terms of the racial attitudes presented in them is actually to judge whether the writer has gone beyond and behind sterotypes, myths, and ideas about blacks, to develop characters whose ethnic, social, cultural, and personal experiences mesh in all the complex ways they do in real life. The literature that will truly give black children a sense of identity will not be literature-as-morality nor literature-as-propaganda, but literature as human experience. To black children, blackness is an intrinsic and desirable component of that human experience.

The better books depict black children as individuals whose identity includes name, home life, family, friends, toys, hobbies, etc. In addition, they are black, American, and first-class citizens. These books lead children naturally to the conclusion that differences—in personality, abilities, background—are desirable among people. Books of this sort which have already been published include the "interracial" *Gabrielle and Selena,* by Peter Desbarats, and *Hooray for Jasper,* by Betty Horvath. Charming and individualized black children are the central characters in the Ezra Jack Keats books, *The Snowy Day, Whistle for Willie, Peter's Chair,* and *A Letter to Amy,* as well as in the books *Sam* and *Big Cowboy Western,* by Ann Herbert Scott, and *What Mary Jo Wanted* and *What Mary Jo Shared,* by Janice May Udry. Books like these, on this level, should be so numerous that children will not be able to browse through a library shelf without finding one there.

One limitation to most of these books, however, is their emphasis on, identification with, and relevance only to middle-class children. For too many black children, they depict an environment removed from their immediate experience. *Stevie,* a recently published book by a young black writer, John Steptoe, provides black ghetto children with identification. The writer simply presents a problem familiar to all children—the intrusion of a younger child on a small

boy's time, friends, and family and his ambivalent feelings about the
situation. To this extent, the book reflects no peculiarly black perspective. Identification for the young black reader rests in the central
character's intimate knowledge of the black subculture—his use of
informal grammar and idiom, his loosely structured family life, his
sophistication and independence in worldly matters, and his brief
sketches of the kinds of good times city children make for themselves—from the familiar game of cowboys and Indians to the less
usual experience remembered nostalgically by Robert: "And that time
we was playin' in the park under the bushes and we found these two
dead rats and one was brown and one was black."

The value of such a book is that it assures the ghettto child that
he, too, is visible—that he is important enough to be reflected in that
literature which has always been made to seem too cultured to admit
him.

Behind the Magic Line, by Betty K. Erwin, and *Soul Brothers and
Sister Lou,* by Kristin Hunter, are among those few books for older
readers (9–16) which reveal, in fictional terms, some degree of black
consciousness. Neither one is entirely successful, but they can be
considered a step from the white perspective of the black condition, to
a black perspective of reality—a view from inside the individual personalities of the characters.

Behind the Magic Line is a humanistic story about a young black
girl, "her dreams and determinations." Throughout the book, there is
an emphasis on black pride and human dignity. Flaws in the book
include underdeveloped characters and Hollywood touches of fortunate coincidences, as well as these overworked ingredients: the fatherless family, the matriarch, the son who is in trouble with the law.
However, this book does attempt to give motivation for each of these
phenomena, motivation which puts the blame not on the individuals,
but on an employment system which perpetuates the fatherless family,
on the traditional tendency to place undue suspicion on members of
the black community and on racist individuals who still think black
means slave. As in *Roosevelt Grady,* the final situation the family finds
itself in is hardly cause for rejoicing, but members of the family seem
to realize this and their reactions are ambivalent.

In *Soul Brothers and Sister Lou,* the ghetto culture is graphically
depicted and the main character and her search for self-identity are
realistic. The drawbacks lie in the one-dimensional treatment of the
minor characters, an unrelenting series of melodramatic situations, a

hastily compiled ending, and a kind of immediacy of response to pleasure and pain that cheats the reader of the experience of real tragedy. These flaws weigh more heavily for some readers than for others, but many readers can use this story as a bridge from pure pulp fiction to the excellent black fiction written for adults.

The timeliness of these books compensates in part for their weaknesses. The relief these books provide from white paternalism, white perspective, and white domination is an important compensation for many black children.

The bulk of that literature which provides identification for black children has so far been confined to the histories, biographies, and autobiographies. To date, informational, biographical, historical, and scientific books are far superior to the fictional works. Documentary materials are now being collected and edited with the young reader in mind. Skillful organization, careful research, and clarity of style may be found in such excellent books as Julius Lester's *To Be a Slave,* Dorothy Sterling's *Tear Down the Walls,* and William L. Katz's *Eyewitness: The Negro in American History.* These books clearly answer the question of black identity, not only for young black readers, but for young readers of every ethnic background, and for us, their older counterparts—uninformed or misinformed as we have been.

In addition to these general histories, many of the recently published biographies of individual black Americans can be highly recommended. These range from the brief biographical sketches designed for middle and upper elementary grades (e.g., *Lift Every Voice,* by Dorothy Sterling and Benjamin Quarles) to such fully developed biographies as *Langston Hughes,* by Milton Meltzer, *Journey Toward Freedom: The Story of Sojourner Truth,* by Jacqueline Bernard, and *Captain of The Planter* by Dorothy Sterling. Fictionalized histories and biographies include Emma Gelder Sterne's *The Long Black Schooner; The Voyage of The Amistad,* Ann Petry's *Tituba of Salem Village,* and *Harriet Tubman: Conductor on the Underground Railroad.* Four anthologies designed for the young adult reader which span history, fiction, and poetry are *Chronicles of Negro Protest,* by Bradford Chambers; *Black on Black: Commentaries by Negro Americans,* edited by Arnold Adoff; *Black Voices: An Anthology of Afro-American Literature,* edited by Abraham Chapman; and *I Am the Darker Brother,* poems by black Americans, edited by Arnold Adoff.

Although the criteria for heroism are indeed variable, in re-evaluating biographies for children, it can readily be seen that the blacks recognized in children's literature in the past were usually those who attained some success by adhering to white values. Today it is important for children to know about Denmark Vesey and W. E. B. DuBois as well as Ralph Bunche, and George Washington Carver. These biographies give children historical perspectives relating to recent human rights movements, and a link to the autobiographical revelations of modern heroes: Malcolm X, Eldridge Cleaver, and Martin Luther King. These books, as well as autobiographies such as Anne Moody's *Coming of Age in Mississippi* (which traces the experiences of a young black girl from her childhood in the South to her activities as a young student in the civil rights movement), show that militancy is not a fad.

The significance of these histories and biographies cannot be stressed enough. The contributions of Afro-Americans to American history have heretofore been distorted or excluded; and can we ever fully realize the loss of identity that generations of blacks have experienced by being deprived first of their original culture and then of any recognition of their contributions to the culture that was thrust upon them? Excellent books such as these recapture to some degree that consciousness of heritage for the present generation of children.

The details of black history cannot be skipped over by any of us concerned with children's literature. The evaluation of children's books implies judgment, and a valid or educated judgment is made from experience. The more profound the experience, the better the judgment. Until now, we have all learned only a portion of our nation's history, but in order to be good book critics as well as whole Americans, we must learn the rest.

Only a detailed knowledge can provide us with the perspective necessary for building totally new understandings and relationships. To quote James Baldwin:

For history . . . is not merely something to be read. And it does not refer merely, or even principally, to the past. On the contrary, the great force of history comes from the fact that we carry it within us, are unconsciously controlled by it in many ways, and history is literally present in all that we do. It could scarcely be otherwise, since it is to history that we owe our frames of reference, our identities, and our aspirations.[7]

Notes

1. Langston Hughes. "I, Too, Sing America," in *The Weary Blues,* Knopf, 1926.

2. Langston Hughes, "Let America Be America Again," *Esquire,* July 1936.
3. W. E. B. Du Bois. "Souls of Black Folk," in *Black Voices,* edited by Abraham Chapman, Mentor, 1968.
4. Julius Lester. *To Be a Slave.* Dial Press, 1968.
5. James Baldwin. "Autobiographical Notes," in *Black Voices, op. cit.*
6. John Rowe Townsend. "Didacticism in Modern Dress," *The Horn Book,* April 1967.
7. James Baldwin. "Unnameable Objects, Unspeakable Crimes," in *Black on Black; Commentaries by Negro Americans,* ed. by Arnold Adoff, Macmillan, 1968.

4. WHAT IS A RACIST BOOK?

Rae Alexander

TO WHAT EXTENT has the resurgence of Black pride and self-awareness been communicated to Black children?

In 1939, Kenneth B. Clark and Mamie P. Clark found that Black children evaluated Blacks negatively and evaluated whites positively. In their monumental study, Black children between the ages of three and seven were presented with a black and a white doll and asked which was "nice," which "looked bad," which they would "like to play with," and which was "the nice color." The Black children invariably preferred the white doll.

Thirty years later, Steven R. Asher and Vernon L. Allen of the University of Wisconsin, substituted puppets for black and white dolls and asked both Black and white children which they preferred. Again, the white puppet was most often preferred and the black puppet most often rejected.

If the studies cited here are valid, Black may be beautiful for contemporary Black youth involved in a new appreciation of Black ethnicity, but apparently the Black Revolution is too new and too tentative for its values to have filtered down to Black children, who are still emotionally and otherwise conditioned by the prevailing white culture.

Books Still Insidious

Based on the books I read in the course of compiling a revision of the NAACP's recommended book list (*Books for Children: Black and White—A Selected Bibliography*), I feel I am in a position to draw this conclusion: Despite the growing number of books depicting the Black experience, the image they give of the Black American is still one of the more insidious influences that hinder the Black child from finding true self-awareness.

In evaluating Black and biracial books for pre-school through sixth-grade levels, a major criterion was that no book would be listed if it was considered likely to communicate to either a Black or a white child a racist concept or cliché about Blacks; or failed to provide some strong characters to serve as role models. Even one such stereotype would be enough to eliminate an otherwise good book. Underlying this criterion was my own experience with many teachers who are insensitive to the racist content of books or who are not equipped to handle such material adequately in their classes. The tragedy is that so many teachers fail to expose racist material for what it is, and they fail to make use of it as a basis for discussing prejudice.

One might say that the basic consideration in my not including a given book in the NAACP list was the pain it might give to even one Black child. Naturally, there were additional criteria. The book must be appropriate for use in (1) an all-Black classroom, (2) an all-white classroom, and (3) an integrated classroom. If a book did not completely satisfy each of these criteria, I excluded it from the bibliography. To illustrate how these standards were applied, I will mention first several books that I did not include in the list and the reasons why.

Marred by Racial Slurs

A number of poignant and stirring stories I did not list because they were marred by racial slurs. Even such an imaginative and exciting story as L. M. Boston's *Treasure of Green Knowe* (Harcourt, Brace & World) I excluded because of a derogatory description of a Black boy's hair. ("Think of Jacob's crinkly hair, hardly the length of a needle. The most she could do with it [in her embroidery] was tediously to make knots.") In contrast, the author writes elsewhere of a white person's "tresses." (". . . he was a vain man with hair he was proud of. . . . There was enough of Caxton's hair to do the whole chimney.")

Not Over Ten Inches High, by Harry Levy (McGraw-Hill Book Co.), is a delightful and charming story. On the first page, one reads, "only a small tuft of kinky hair showed from one end. . . ." In *A Sundae with Judy,* by Frieda Friedman (Scholastic Book Services), the author writes, "She hadn't noticed how dark Barbara and Bob Williams were, or how much Mayling's eyes were slanted. . . ." I do not know whether passages such as those quoted express prejudice on the authors' part, but I do know that in white America this is the

language of racism, and it is what children hear. I freely admit that in
winnowing books, I was primarily concerned with what the child
would be receiving. I was on the child's side, all the way. The Black
child reading passages like those mentioned here surely senses that his
appearance is being unfavorably described, which is hardly conducive
to strengthening self-esteem. One has only to imagine how the child
must feel when such slights are read aloud in the presence of white
classmates. Equally important, how must they condition the white
child's concept of Blacks?

A problem of another kind arose in connection with books that
reflect the recent and entirely well-intentioned emphasis on offering
children material about American life as it really is. One must consider the effect of this realism on the positive self-image we want Black
children to develop. Blacks in the ghetto struggle with life from the
day they are born. It is true that ghetto youngsters often find pallid
fare those books that are favored in the suburbs. However, in assessing
the "realistic" books, the portrayal of ghetto life is often over-
whelmingly negative. There are hurtful parents, broken homes, and
emotionally nonsupportive friends and teachers. These are facts of
life, and the children who face them must cope as best they can. On
the other hand, I believe that the constant exposure of ghetto society
in this light is destructive—both of the Black child's view of himself
and of the white child's understanding.

For essentially this reason, I excluded the much admired books
of Frank Bonham. Two, in particular—*The Nitty Gritty* and *The Mystery of the Fat Cat* (E. P. Dutton)—emphasize a demoralizing, dec-
adent side of Black life, which in these books is always, alas, overcome
only by the direct or indirect intervention of The Man.

For much the same reason, I did not include the autobiography
It's Wings That Make Birds Fly, edited by Sandra Weiner (Pantheon
Books). Ten-year-old Otis tells his story in his own words, which Miss
Weiner recorded. It is a story of a broken home, punitive adults, over-
crowded housing, inadequate play facilities, harassment of younger by
older children, and the eternal benevolence of whites toward Blacks. A
paragraph at the end of the book states that Otis was killed in an
accident while playing in the street.

Portrayals Too Bleak

I do not doubt the human truth of this autobiography, nor, in more
general terms, do I question its social accuracy. But in the unrelieved

bleak and dismal portrayal of lower-class Black life, this book takes no notice of the fact that many poor Blacks do possess personal values, that they have the will and strength to help their children strive to master their environment—qualities that, as it happens, are unnoticed and unsupported by many teachers and administrators. For the young white reader, this book supports rampant stereotypes, but it offers no insight into the "hows" and "whys" of ghetto life. For the young Black reader, the book too strongly affirms that all the Otises of today are doomed from birth.

Of the books that do foster a healthy self-image in the young Black reader, I should like to mention three. *Bimby,* by Peter Burchard (Coward-McCann), is an historical novel set in the Sea Islands, off Georgia, just before the Civil War. Although young Bimby has not experienced slavery directly, it is through the mature wisdom of the old slave Jesse that he comes to understand what it means to be a man, and that he must himself find his own freedom. The author's illustrations enhance the story's underlying wistfulness and sadness. Black youth will find Bimby a strong image with which to identify.

Canalboat to Freedom, by Thomas Fall (Dial press), vividly portrays the life of an ex-slave, Lundius, who risks death to help his Black brothers escape to freedom via the underground railroad. He meets and befriends a white indentured servant named Benja, who is young and inexperienced in the ways of the world. Lundius helps Benja and others in practical, protective ways, but he is also for them a symbol of strength; it is his qualities as a man that so powerfully affect others and that enable Benja to carry on the work of Lundius after he has been killed.

Bimby and *Canalboat to Freedom* stand apart from the general fare of children's books on slavery in three important respects. Bimby and Lundius are luminous, three-dimensional characters, very real and very much alive. Both possess an inner strength that enables them to strike out at the system in a positive way. Both are figures drawn from historical experience, and they will foster respect and pride in Black children today.

Member of the Gang, by Barbara Rinkoff (Crown Publishers), is a story of today. The young Black hero, Woodie Jackson, feels he amounts to little at home, in school, and at the settlement house where he spends his afternoons. His father is hardworking, gruff and stern; his mother is gentle and on the overprotective side. Woodie jumps at the chance to join the Scorpions, because he thinks membership in the gang will make him important to himself and others.

Following the inevitable street clash, arrest, and appearance in Family Court, Woodie is assigned a Black probation officer who gives Woodie the kind of encouragement and support that parents and teachers have failed to provide. Together they build a new perspective on life for Woodie, and for the boy the world takes on a very different meaning. The black and white illustrations by Harold James dramatically interpret Woodie's shifting moods and feelings. The merits of this book are several: there are many Woodie Jacksons in our world, and the author has captured their reality in her central character. While Woodie's parents have negative qualities, the reader is allowed to see that their attitudes are oblique expressions of their concern and love for their son. The Black probation officer projects a strong Black image.

In considering the constructive potential of biracial books for children, one does not ask that they be antiseptic in portraying harsh realities; one hopes that increasingly, authors, Black and white, will foster awareness and sensitivity in their young readers; and, specifically, in the case of Black children, one hopes they will be helped to know better their own strength and power to bring about change.

Postscript

When I prepared the NAACP list, the Newbery Award-winning *Sounder* by William H. Armstrong was unavailable for review. If I were to consider *Sounder* for the list, I would reject it as a racist book. I found *Sounder* offensive and demeaning to Black people. . . .

What the white author of *Sounder* has done to the Black characters is to diminish their role as instruments in effective change. More important, the author has denied Black youth the privilege of having role models with which they can identify and find fulfillment, and on that ground alone the book fails to meet a basic criterion used in selecting the NAACP book list.

The white author of *Sounder* renders the father and boy impotent, much as William Styron portrayed the character of Nat Turner. The mother's character pales against the strong Black women history tells us about—Harriet Tubman, Sojourner Truth. When you study the Black actors in *Sounder,* you wonder how Black people could have survived social genocide since 1619.

5. PORTRAYAL OF THE BLACK IN CHILDREN'S LITERATURE
(Excerpt)

Jessie M. Birtha

> I am only one, But still I am one. I cannot do everything, But still I can do something; And because I cannot do everything I will not refuse to do the something that I can do.

IT WAS WITH THIS QUOTATION from Edward Everett Hale in mind that I accepted the responsibility of addressing librarians on the currently important subject of the "Portrayal of the Black in Children's Literature." Qualifications? I am a children's book selection specialist in The Free Library of Philadelphia, but I have an even more important qualification. I am black.

I would like to share with you, from the viewpoint of a black librarian, some of the background of thought which goes into the selection of children's books relating to black Americans. I shall attempt to help you form some criteria for determining which books are good, which are mediocre, and which, for one reason or another, are not acceptable, and may even be objectionable to the very persons to whom the author may have felt they would have appeal. . . .

Thinking Black

There is a certain corner in North Philadelphia which I pass whenever I travel by bus from my home to the Central Library. There is a brick wall of a store whose front faces the side street. Like almost all surfaces which afford a writing area these days, the wall is covered with graffiti. Standing out among all of the scribbling is stenciled in bold, black letters impossible to overlook: "BLACK IS BEAUTIFUL. BLACK IS A STRUGGLE. JOIN THE STRUGGLE." A few feet farther on the wall one reads: "ARE YOU THINKING BLACK TO-DAY?" I am going to ask you to "think black" with me.

You may have seen the Warren Schloat filmstrip "Growing Up Black" in which several black adolescents express their reactions to the experience of growing up black in America. Although it was not especially emphasized, there was one thing which the youngsters had in common. All had grown up black looking at white faces in their schoolbooks and—if they had access to a library—in their picture books and storybooks. They looked at white faces in magazines and newspaper advertisements and in television commercials. They played with blonde, curly-haired white dolls and paperdolls, or white soldier and sailor toys; they went shopping and bought clothes displayed on white mannequin children. Whenever anything black was shown, it was something either to be laughed at, ridiculed, or had otherwise unfavorable connotations. It was the poet Robert Burns who said, "Oh wad some power the giftie gie us To see oursels as others see us!" For generations the black person has been given the opportunity to see himself as the other race saw him. Needless to say, it has not done too much for the "good neighbor" policy within America.

Twenty years ago, the job of listing the best in children's books would have been comparatively simple. Even during the period called the Negro Renaissance in the 1920s there were few children's books. I recall the joy with which I discovered Jessie Redmond Fausset and the Langston Hughes novels at a time when, had there been children's books, I would have been devouring them. Langston Hughes, Countee Cullen, Claude McKay all held—and will always hold—a special place in my heart. They were about people like me. I could identify with their sentiments and emotions. Yet, I was still hoping that some-where I would come across some stories about Negro children or Negro teenagers. Of course, I still read the stories of white girls going happily off to camp and riding horses and sailing boats. I must have been about twelve when I became fed up with reading about Campfire Girls and Girl Scouts when we did not even have a black Girl Scout troup in town.

Publishers as well as writers have been latecomers to the realization of the need (and market) for books by and about the Negro as well as inter-racial books. They have been unaware or unwilling to include the black segment of the United States population in history or fiction. If America is the melting pot which social studies teachers present to their children, it is a melting pot in which one of the basic ingredeints has been left out of the soup.

As recently as 1967, John Killens, novelist and writer-in-residence at Fisk University, wrote:

The American Negro remains a cultural nonentity as far as books, television, movies and Broadway are concerned. It is as if twenty million Americans do not exist; twenty million people are committed to oblivion. . . . A Negro child can go to school and look into his school books and children's books and come home and watch television and go to an occasional movie, and follow this routine from day to day, month to month, and year to year, and hardly if ever see a reflection of himself. . . .

Since the Kerner Report in 1968 pointed out the facts of racism and prejudice in America, there has been a conscious effort among publishers, authors, illustrators, and librarians to improve the situation. (There have also been opportunists who jump on the bandwagon because writing a black book is the current *thing*. It will sell.) In just two years, the words of John Killens are no longer true. In the fall of 1968 from the sidewalks of New York to the wide spaces of the West, the world of television suddenly became an integrated world. Books with Negro characters and Negro themes became more prevalent.

Book Selection Problems

With the wealth of material available today in trade and library editions and the now popular paperbacks in children's titles, with the increased amount of Federal funds many libraries are receiving to expand their collections, with the expanded racial integration in education and housing bringing different groups of people closer together, it is easy for a librarian to have the best of intentions and still be confused about book selection. Even black people do not always agree on a name acceptable in referring to themselves: Negro, colored, Afro-American, Afram, or black. Some librarians tend to buy any book that appears to be integrated. Others cautiously delay buying until they have seen two or three favorable reviews in outstanding periodicals. I believe that the two most difficult situations for quality book selection about or by the blacks are: (1) a white librarian in an all white area;

and (2) a white librarian in an all black area. The integrated areas in between are not always easy. Sometimes there are repercussions when one least expects a complaint—such as the adult reader who complained about the mother in *The Snowy Day* because she was fat. . . .

Guidelines

There are two questions which a librarian might ask herself when selecting books. First, "How would I feel upon reading this book if I were a black child? Particularly an inner city black child?" Second, "If I were to borrow this book from the library, would I return to get another book like it?" These two questions can help to answer whether this is a suitable book for either a white or a black child. If it contains material inappropriate for a black child, it is also unsuitable for a white child, for the white child would derive from this book a distorted picture of a black child, his emotion, his behavior, his background.

Any book, adult or children's, must first of all meet the essentials of good literature along the lines of plot, content, theme, characterization, style, and format. The *Selection Policies for Children's Books* of The Free Library of Philadelphia includes the following statement under "Factors to Be Considered in the Selection or Rejection of Books."

In judging books, several factors blended with common sense and experience in book selection must be kept in mind: (1) the literary quality of the particular title; (2) suitability in content and vocabulary for children through the eighth grade; (3) need for the subject matter.

Among factors which determine the exclusion of certain books for children are: (1) lack of good taste or sufficient literary merit; (2) an inaccurate, unfair, unhealthy picture of the subject. . . .

Quoting again from The Free Library's book selection policy concerning selection of books according to subject, under "Human Relations" the policy states:

The library considers the removal of prejudice and ignorance regarding racial, ethnic or religious groups of peoples one of its major responsibilities and to this end makes a continuous effort to include in its book collection for children titles which will foster healthy attitudes along these lines. Books on other countries, races, nationalities, and religious groups are carefully selected; and, in general those bearing serious discriminatory remarks or attitudes are not purchased. If possible, books on these subjects are reviewed for accuracy by a member of the particular national, religious, or racial group involved.

Points for Evaluation

I would like to draw from my own experience to cite a few specific points of concern in selecting books with a racial or integrated theme.

1. Approach

Does the author know black people well enough to write about them? Is he, himself, unbiased enough to interpret the content of his book with clarity and meaning? Many white authors fail in this matter without realizing why. An old Indian saying is "Never attempt to judge another man until you have walked in his moccasins." Some of the least successful books about Negroes written by white people have been due to an attempt to write the story from the black point of view. (Some writers have succeeded tremendously: Dorothy Sterling, Frank Bonham, Marguerite De Angeli, all have possessed the necessary understanding of human nature, perceptiveness for locale and relationships, and love of people of all kinds.)

Is the author so involved in conveying this message that the plot is subjugated to his ideas? Is the presentation honest and unsentimental or is it overwritten to prove a point? Does the author realize the true feeling of his subject or is the story the same old story he would have written of a white child, but written with a "color-them-black" slant? Does the book address itself to the white reader, leaving the black reader with a left-out feeling?

2. Style of Writing

Is it dated as far as descriptions, attitudes, or incidents are concerned? This does not refer to a book like Margaret Strachan's *Where Were You That Year?*, about the civil rights voting campaign in Mississippi, but to books which may arouse resentment in the manner in which things are told. A good book may be ruined for a child when he reads accurate descriptions of all characters until he reaches the

black child and reads of his "flashing white teeth" or hears him referred to as "the bug-eyed boy," or if the author assumes that black
children feel that the darker they are, the dumber they are, or if the
author speaks of black people as "darkies."

3. Characterization

Are characters offensively portrayed in any way or are they
shown in a realistic way? Not all Negro characters must of necessity
be good, or exemplary in behavior, but if they are bad or cowardly, is
there reason other than that they are black? Is the hero in the story the
Negro who most nearly resembles white in appearance? Do the characterizations in the book misrepresent the Negro as a person in a
derogatory way which will insult him or give the child who has never
known a black person a mistaken impression of the race? A minor
character represented in an unkind or degrading manner may seem
inconsequential to a white reader, but may cause a black child to reject
any other book by that author. Do the characters act consistently and
normally or do we find a black boy sadly leaning on a fence while his
antagonistic white neighbor paints it black?

4. Language

Dialogue is very close to characterization. How do the characters
speak? Is the language natural and convincing? What about colloquialism and dialect?
Some mention of the Joel Chandler Harris Uncle Remus stories
is appropriate, as they have been victims of condemnation in many
library areas. Few children are capable of reading the written dialect
of the Br'er Rabbit tales. Distinction must be made between Harris's
sincere attempt to preserve consciously the essence and language of
the folk tales of the southern Negro for posterity, and a book which
frames the dialogue of minority groups in dialect, colloquialism, and
broken English as a display of the character's ignorance or intellectual
inferiority.

5. Illustrations

In books for children, illustrations supplement the text in a way
that is not as necessary in most adult books. Many children judge a

book by its illustrations. If these portray abnormally proportioned, repulsive characters following the old stereotypes of books of past decades, children are certain to reject the book. Fortunately, most illustrators today try hard to present a realistic image. Children do not expect every character to be beautiful. In fact, they identify more readily if characters look more like people they are likely to meet in everyday life. Sometimes, illustration errs in subtle ways. A recent picture book tends to perpetuate the feeling of inferiority in children by the fact that all persons in charge, all authority figures, are white.

6. Bias

This refers to bias or prejudice of the author rather than of his characters, unless he is obviously using them to express his own feelings. "Happy plantation books" which picture the Negro as happily accepting his lot in the South fall into this category. The librarian should ask himself if the book is presented in an objectionable manner or whether it instead respects the intelligence of the reader, and allows him to make his own evaluation of the theme, the plot, the characters and their actions, without false or forced moralization on the part of the author. Books selected for purchase should be those which broaden the child's horizons rather than those which direct his viewpoints into narrow channels.

These are some of the points I consider in evaluation of books on blacks and integrated books. I have not touched on non-fiction in a specific way. A great deal could be said concerning selection of non-fiction, but inaccuracies in non-fiction, condescensions and degrading statements, are more readily recognized than in fiction. The sin has been as much one of omission as of improper coloring of facts—and people. Generations of black youngsters grew to adulthood believing that the only part their race played in American history was as slaves, lacking even the initiative to strike a blow on behalf of their own freedom. When the fact recently was established that in the existing histories the black American's participation and contribution had been ignored, a major hurdle was overcome. Hopefully, we will no longer discover books with such questions as "What jobs other than porters can you think of that a Negro in your community can hold?" A sincere effort is now being made to include the black American in his place in history in a way that will foster pride in his own heritage and respect in the eyes of his white classmates.

I could talk with you about awareness and about sensitivity to change in the composition of your library public, in the reading abilities and interests of your library children, but these things, as librarians, you already know. The public library is one segment of the establishment which cannot reject change and remain static, or it signs its own death warrant. Book selection, too, is a changing thing; we are constantly modifying our book selection policy at The Free Library. Our replacement lists are yearly evaluated and changed. We get an increasing demand for books on blacks from our branches in both black and white areas. They ask for histories, black biographies, poetry, integrated picture books, specific people, and events. There is a demand for *Ebony* magazine, even among our youngsters. We find seventh and eighth graders of both races reaching ahead into young adult material for such meaningful titles as *To Sir with Love* (Braithwaite), *Manchild in the Promised Land* (Brown), *A Raisin in the Sun* (Hansberry). . . .

Children's Book Selection "Affects Eternity"

The selection of books for children is one of the most important responsibilities of the librarian, for children's minds are impressionable—ideas, attitudes, and ideals are being formed. The author, the publisher, and the librarian, in their key positions, must join together to help prevent old, time-worn prejudices from being carried forward into new generations. Children need books neither to foster antagonism, hatred, and militancy in the blacks nor to promote guilt feelings or distrust in the whites. This is a NOW generation. They are not responsible for the evils of the past. Children need books through which both blacks and whites can be educated to real life situations through accurate portrayal of life; histories and historical fiction which show the total picture, not a partial picture; and biographies that present people to whom children of all races can look for inspiration to live better lives.

Let us realize that the world is changing at a faster rate than it has at any time since the Great Flood. We can no longer hold fast to our old ideas of right and wrong, or of what is needed or not needed in our field of book selection. The violence, new ideas, unpredictable behavior, and restlessness of black people are all a part of the turbulence of change. The portrayal of the black in children's literature is an important factor in shaping the end result of this change, for everything that a child reads plays its part in forming the adult which he will become. It may be that our real and only hope of survival as an undivided nation lies in our children.

So let us have books chosen by perceptive, understanding librarians, books which can help the black child to realize his identity, his individuality, his proud heritage, and his great potential, books which can help the white child to recognize, understand, and appreciate the tremendous cultural and historical contribution of his fellow Americans. These books should be read by black and white children—not as special books, but because they are good books, meeting the basic criteria of children's literature and the rigid demands of children themselves, and should be presented to children as a part of their normal, everyday reading.

Only when America no longer feels the need of considering the black community as a separate and different part of this country will Americans achieve their true potential as citizens of a great and unified nation.

6. BLACK AND WHITE: AN EXCHANGE

Julius Lester and George Woods

> An article in the *Book Review* last season prompted the
> following letters between Julius Lester, author, and
> George Woods, *The Times'* children's book editor.

April 10, 1970

Dear George:

One of the more pleasant ways I've found of surviving is to read
the newspaper several months after it has come out; thus I have just
read *The New York Times Book Review* of December 7 and your article
on the best books for young readers. I must say that I found some of
the things you said about black books rather disturbing and rather
than keep my comments to myself, I feel warmly enough toward you to
write.

First, to quote you: ". . . I don't like the so-called books for
blacks. . . . They have merit; they're an attempt to right a long-stand-
ing injustice, but it's a stampede that has produced words and pictures
without heart, without soul." You go on to mention the *Black Champions of the Gridiron* as one book of this sort, and, no matter what you
may think of football, the fact remains, that as a black parent, I'm
happy that such a book is available. No, it's not great literature or
anything else, but if my son or daughter becomes interested in football, at least I'll be able to hand them a book that talks of their people
in the sport, instead of a book that pretends that a black man never set
a cleated shoe on the gridiron.

You go on to say that "The best books in this area are about
blacks and for whites. The whites are the ones who need to know the
condition of their fellow humans. The Negro knows his condition. It's
the white who must be brought to sympathy and understanding."
There is one erroneous assumption here which is a rather serious
one—"The Negro knows his condition." If "the Negro" (and we do
prefer to be called blacks) knew his condition, then there would be no

mass sentiment saying that "black is beautiful," or a desire for black studies. Yes, blacks know their condition on a gut level, but to have that articulated, to read about it in a book is to become conscious where before one was unconscious. It is the black writer's job to tell black people about themselves. Too much of black writing has been blacks writing to whites.

A book written by a black for blacks is not, however, closed to whites. And until whites learn to read and understand these kinds of books, there is no possibility of any kind of understanding of blacks by whites. We no longer (and never did) need whites to interpret our lives or our culture. Whites can only give a white interpretation of blacks, which tells us a lot about whites, but nothing about blacks. But, the way it generally turns out is that the white perception of blacks becomes accepted as the thing itself, as black reality. Thus, when the black expression of the black reality begins to get through to whites, whites are angered and uncomprehending, because they have been fed this white fantasy which never had anything to do with us. Whites will never understand the black view of the world until they get it straight from blacks, respect it, and accept it. Could you take seriously a history of Jews written by an Arab? The idea is so ridiculous as to be insulting. No one would bother to buy the book, even if it got published. Yet, whites think nothing of buying a book about blacks written by a white. Indeed, they almost prefer it. After all, blacks are bound to be prejudiced toward their own, aren't they? Sometimes, I'm tempted to write a history of Judaism for children just to get the point across.

I'm not sure I'm being too clear. Basically I'm not sure if you realize that when it comes to books by and about blacks, you need new standards with which to evaluate them. When I review a book about blacks (no matter the race of the author), I ask two questions: "Does it accurately present the black perspective?" "Will it be relevant to black children?" The possibility of a book by a white answering these questions affirmatively is almost nil.

I have been very amused to note the different receptions accorded my own books for young readers, *To Be a Slave* and *Black Folktales*. The former received a fantastic reception. The latter, while being well reviewed, has not been reviewed nearly as extensively and will definitely not be getting any prizes. And the reason to me is clear. The latter is directed totally toward black children. Perhaps it is even one of those books, which in your words, comes "calculatingly from the head." That's what one editor told me. If so, so be it. But *To Be a Slave* was no different. It's just that one is more easily accessible to whites than the other. Whites have to open themselves a little more to dig *Black Folktales*. They have to make an effort. In other words, they have to meet me on my ground, and that is what whites have always been loath to do where blacks are concerned. I'm making the rules now and changing the game a little. So, they want to pick up their marbles and go home.

Both of us find ourselves in a position of being able to influence the thinking of thousands of people. That is an enormous responsibility, as I know you are painfully aware. To discharge such a responsibility requires in each of us the ability to grow, to change, to understand. And that is an ongoing task.

I fear that the two paragraphs you wrote about black books in the 12-7-69 *Book Review* did not reflect the kind of understanding that will eventually get us to that point in history where whites will be able to accept blackness as a good that has value in and of itself and is not the least bit threatening to them, that is, if they are willing to meet the challenge and undergo the changes necessary for them to accept blackness.

Sincerely,
Julius Lester

April 20, 1970

Dear Julius—

I'm glad you feel sufficiently warm towards me to write when something I've said disturbs you. Being able to talk to one another is the important thing; just don't become so outraged with me that you stop talking.

Let me explain my feelings in greater depth: I've got a prejudice—I try not to look at kids as white or black. Sounds very noble of me, but I mean it. I don't want to break kids down into all different kinds. I want kids in general to have good books, something to make them laugh or cry, something they can live inside of for a little while and take some part of its message away with them. I want books to move them for good, make them heroes some day in the future.

In the same article you criticize me for, I said *Sounder* was an outstanding book. Some people tell me it's a book for blacks and black librarians tell be they wonder how they can give such a book to their students when the protagonist is silent and suffers and endures. Those librarians tell me that their kids are activists today and likely to be contemptuous of the book. Just the same it's a great book because somewhere up North, maybe there's a kid brother to one of those snarling white young hoods in Chicago I saw in the paper four or five years ago protesting housing or Civil Rights, who doesn't really know what's going on, but will stick with his older brother because that's his identification. Maybe he'll come across *Sounder* and say "Is that what we did to those people? Humiliate, degrade, cripple and kill, mangle a kid's fingers, put them in jail because they stole to feed a hungry family?" Maybe he won't be in the next mob, shouting epitaphs, throwing rocks.

It's the same with *Jazz Man* for me. The book is filled with the small significant details of real life that are not found in other books, for whites or blacks. It has a woman who walks up five flights of stairs, fast at first, then slower because it's a tough climb for a woman who has worked all day, and there's the thud of a bag of groceries on the kitchen table. There's a world out there that Mr. Middle Class White American doesn't know anything about. And his kids are in danger of growing up to be just like him. Maybe a *Jazz Man* will let him know that there's a hell of a lot going on in the world that's pretty lousy and maybe sometime he'll be able to do something about it.

But let's go a little farther together. I've been talking about fiction mainly. I have no objection to "Black Pride," "Black History," etc. I've seen a hundred titles like them in the past several years. Of course a lot of them are written by whites, but I'm very apprehensive about knowing the color of the author, just as I would be to know about his religion or politics. I judge a book by what it says, by what kind of an effect I think it will have on children—for the better, I hope, always for the better.

If we are arguing specifically about books for the black child to read, to make him aware of his heritage, give him pride, a sense of identification, etc., well, then you are right; we do need those books. But we're being oversold on them.

There's a reluctance on the part of most reviewers to criticize books for and about blacks. I didn't read of anyone knocking *Black Is Beautiful*. I didn't think it was an adequate book in spite of its laudable purpose. Maybe you'll say it makes the black child proud of himself and not damn his color. I don't think it's color that makes a person beautiful or ugly—it's his heart and his soul and his humanity.

As for *Black Folktales,* well, I like it. I didn't think it was as compelling as *To Be a Slave,* but I recognized a strong, masculine voice behind it and that's what I liked about it.

As for *Black Champions of the Gridiron.* Brings me full circle. It's a book that separates us. How would you like to see "White Champions of the Gridiron?" I don't mind anthologies in which four or five of the six players are black just so long as they play a good hardnosed brand of football, but at present it seems we are trading on their blackness.

If it comes to a showdown in this matter between us, you'll probably win. By birth, upbringing, present existence, I'm the product of an all-white world I suppose. But I'm trying to understand and be reasonable. On the other hand, you've had the bad experiences and you know what you're talking about. You've seen the hate and arrogance, suffered the lash and you know what your soul cries for.

Yes, you're right in wanting more books for blacks. I don't want them shut off. I wish they were better and when they're bad I hope we wont't be afraid to say so. But more than anything I still want books that talk about both of us, all of us, as plain people.

I appreciate your having taken the time to call me down. I hope I've said nothing here to make you tune me out.

Best Wishes,
George A. Woods

May 1, 1970

Dear George:

Please don't think that my personal feelings toward you have changed because of our different views on books for black children, etc. I wouldn't have written my previous letter if I hadn't felt that you are one of the few honest people in this business we find ourselves a part of and that you would respond honestly, without any personal animosity toward me.

I guess our basic difference comes around your "prejudice." "I try not to look at kids as white or black. . . . I don't want to break kids down into all different kinds." But the fact remains, whether we like it or not, that kids are black or white, that we live in a world where race has meaning, conferring superiority to white and inferiority to black, and what blacks are now trying to do is to destroy that value system, because that value system destroys them. Because race has been used as a weapon against blacks, blacks must use it as a weapon to free themselves. It is the factor which has oppressed them as people. Thus, there will be books aimed at black children, because, heretofore, the books have all been aimed at white children.

It's strange that whites fear that anything addressed to blacks is an automatic rejection and condemnation of them. That is not necessarily so, unless whites make it so. But whites do not want to acknowledge the fact that if they want to know blacks they will have to immerse themselves in what blacks have to say, and that there is no white Dante who can take them gently by their lily-white hands and lead them on a guided tour of blackness and keep them from getting a little singed by the fires. When I want to know more about the Jewish experience, I read I. B. Singer. There is as yet no black writer who has done for the black experience what Singer has done for the Jewish experience, but he has the advantage of being able to look back, of not having to be involved in a day-to-day battle. The black writer is intimately involved in the process his people are going through—trying to recreate themselves. In this process, there are going to be books by blacks which are bad. There are also going to be some new and exciting ones.

You are right when you say that "color does not make a person beautiful or ugly." In an absolute sense, that is correct. Down here on earth, however, color determines standards of beauty. I don't know if blondes have more fun, but enough people seem to feel that they do so that Clairol isn't about to go out of business. Color has determined not only my standards of beauty, but where I lived, worked, ate and slept, not to mention what neighborhoods I was in after dark. No, color does not have any relation to the inner reality of a person, but, in this society, color has come to be synonymous with the inner reality, whether we like it or not. When I was a kid, I didn't know why white people hated me. They didn't know me, didn't even know my name, but knew that they had something against me. I couldn't close my eyes and say that it didn't matter. It mattered, because whites made it matter.

Ultimately, it is to no one's benefit to be colorblind. Even in the best of all possible worlds I want to be looked upon as a black. Race consciousness does not have to mean conflict and hatred. And, in the battle to see that it doesn't, I must address myself to blacks, to write books that hopefully will give black children the strength and pride that have been deliberately kept from them. It will be a long time before the mass of whites look upon black children as blacks and as individuals. I do not exist in this country as an individual. I am a black. White America has so decreed it, and it could be fatal to ignore the fact. I want black children to have that black sense on which to build. When you come right down to it, they have nothing else.

White writers are so dishonest. Seldom have they written what they could have and should have, which is, the white side of racism. I'd like to see a children's novel about a little white boy who goes with his father to a lynching. Or about a little white kid who goes with his mother to scream at black children on the first day of integration at some southern school. White writers think they can write sympathetic, cloying little books about blacks. Who needs white pity? Whites are not guiltless. Americans love to write about guilt in Germany after Hitler. What about white guilt in America since 1619? After all, I wouldn't be in this predicament if white people had left my great-great-grandparents where they were. There wouldn't be any race problem if whites hadn't created it. Where are the books for children that deal with whites and their racism? They don't exist, because it is easier to be paternalistic than honest.

You shouldn't apologize for being who you are. As long as you and I, as individuals, can talk to each other and know that the other will listen with respect and think about what is being said, things aren't all bad. We're both, in our own ways, trying to deal with the challenge of the sixties and the seventies. There are some, in fact many whites whom I would (and do) "tune out." As this letter should indicate, you are not one of them.

Sincerely,
Julius Lester

Part II

THE ADVENTURES OF
HUCKLEBERRY FINN
AND OTHER EARLY EXAMPLES OF RACISM

7. *HUCKLEBERRY FINN* AND THE TRADITIONS OF BLACKFACE MINSTRELSY

Fredrick Woodard and Donnarae MacCann

SCHOLARS AND OTHER COMMENTATORS have generally maintained that Mark Twain's *The Adventures of Huckleberry Finn* is a broadly humanistic document. Twain's ability as a humorist and stylist, his effective satires and his advocacy—at times—of improved conditions for Black Americans have contributed to this judgment.[1]

However, in spite of the countless analyses of *Huck Finn,* the influence of "blackface minstrelsy" on this story is either barely mentioned or overlooked entirely, even though the tradition of white men blackening up to entertain other whites at the expense of Black people's humanity is at the center of *Huck Finn's* portrayal of Jim and other Blacks. This dimension is important to a full interpretation of the novel and should be considered essential to any classroom analysis of the book.

Minstrel performers were an important cultural influence in the last century. They were featured in circuses and other traveling shows, as well as in the afterpieces and entr'actes of the formal, "high art" theaters. In 1843, four white actors, the Virginia Minstrels, created an entire evening's entertainment of minstrel routines. By the middle of the 19th century more than 100 professional troupes in "blackface" were touring the U.S., with some performing in the White House.[2] According to sociologist Alan Green, the minstrel caricatures were so compelling to white audiences that "anyone after the early 1840s who wished to portray a humorous Negro on the stage had to conform to the minstrelsy pattern, and that included Negroes themselves."[3] By the latter part of the century, guidebooks for amateur performers were available to the general public.[4]

Minstrel actors blackened their faces with burnt cork and wore outlandish costumes. They swaggered about the stage boasting non-sensically about minor accomplishments or fabricating tales of gran-

diose deeds; they had riotous celebrations; they mutilated the English
language; and they quarreled vehemently over trivial issues.

Nineteenth century American minstrelsy drew upon European
traditions of using the mask of blackness to mock individuals or social
forces. The conventions of clowning also played a part, since clowns in
many cultures have blackened or whitened their faces, exaggerated
the appearance of the mouth, eyes and feet, used rustic dialects, and
devised incongruous costumes. Clowns have filled a variety of social
and aesthetic functions, but U.S. blackface performers have been
unique in their singleminded derogation of an oppressed group. In the
U.S., aspects of African American culture were incorporated into the
minstrel routines in a highly distorted form. The resulting ridiculous
or paternalistic portrayals of Black Americans were particularly appealing to the white theater-going audience.

Educators who teach *Huck Finn* as a literary and historical
bench mark need to recognize how Twain used minstrelsy and how he
himself was, to some extent, socialized by it.

Twain called these blackface minstrel routines a "joy." "To my
mind," he said, "minstrelsy was a thoroughly delightful thing, and a
most competent laughter-compeller. . . ." He described the broad dialect as "delightfully and satisfyingly funny."[5] As to the typical violent
quarrels between two minstrel protagonists, Twain wrote:

. . . a delightful jangle of assertion and contradiction would break out between the two; the quarrel would gather emphasis, the voices would grow
louder and louder and more and more energetic and vindictive, and the two
would rise and approach each other, shaking fists and instruments and threatening bloodshed. . . . Sometimes the quarrel would last five minutes, the two
contestants shouting deadly threats in each other's faces with their noses not
six inches apart, the house shrieking with laughter all the while at this *happy
and accurate imitation of the usual and familiar negro quarrel*. . . . [emphasis
added][6]

The notion that these stereotypical portrayals were realistic was
commonplace. Carl Wittke, an early historian of minstrelsy, speaks of
"Jim Crow" Rice, a popular white minstrel performer, as having "unusual powers as a delineator of Negro character."[7] These caricatures,
so enjoyed by whites, moved from the stage to the pages of popular
fiction and, eventually, to radio, movies and TV.

Twain wrote his laudatory remarks about minstrelsy in 1906,

just four years before his death. Like many other authors, he was apparently influenced by this tradition throughout his life, even as he argued for more humane conditions for Black Americans and Africans.

Twain and Stage Performances

Twain's own career as a stage performer gave him a close tie with minstrelsy. Stage performances were a major source of income and status for Twain, and these performances were often based on "readings" of his works, a "lecture" style that was extremely popular at that time. Twain counseled a friend: "Try 'Readings.' They are all the rage now."[8]

Twain's performances point up his willingness to shape his message to his audience. On winning audience approval, Twain himself said: "No man will dare more than I to get it."[9] Following one performance, a Chicago critic wrote: "There is nothing in his lectures, for he very properly sacrifices everything to make his audience roar, and they do."[10]

It is not surprising to find that episodes in *Huck Finn* which read like skits in a minstrel show were probably written after most of the novel was completed, and at a time when Twain was planning a return to the stage with a new tour. These episodes—"King Sollermun," "Balum's Ass," "how a Frenchman doan' talk like a man," Jim's "rescue" by Huck and Tom Sawyer—would fit neatly into a Twain-style lecture tour, and it seems quite likely that they were created with the taste of theater audiences in mind.[11]

The novel's concluding farcical scenes—in which Huck and Tom concoct a nonsensical plan to help Jim, the runaway slave—insured the book's success on and off the stage. As Twain wrote his wife about reading these rescue scenes: "It is the biggest card I've got in my whole repertoire. I always thought so. It went abooming. . . . "[12]

The Minstrel Content

The depiction of Blacks in *Huck Finn* matches those of numerous minstrel plays in which Black characters are portrayed as addlebrained, boastful, superstitious, childish and lazy. These depictions are not used to poke fun at white attitudes about Black people; Jim is portrayed as a kindly comic who *does* act foolishly.

Early in the story, for example, Tom Sawyer moves Jim's hat to a nearby tree branch while he is sleeping. When Jim wakes he claims that witches put him in a trance and rode him over the state; he then elaborates this story several times until he finally claims that witches rode him all over the world and his back was "all over saddleboils."

Throughout the book, Jim is presented as foolish and gullible, given to exaggeration. After Jim and Huck get lost in the fog, an event Jim "painted . . . up considerable," Huck tells Jim their frightening experience was only a dream. Jim believes him, even when he sees evidence that the experience was real:

He had got the dream fixed so strong in his head that he couldn't seem to shake it loose and get the facts back into its place again right away.[13]

Twain has already established that Huck fulfills the role of a youthful, "unreliable" narrator; however, these comments about Jim *seem* accurate because they are backed up by Jim's own befuddled statements and actions. For example, Jim exclaims: "Is I *me*, or who *is* I? Is I heah, or what *is* I? Now dat's what I wants to know."

Similarly, when the Duke and Dauphin come aboard the raft, Huck sees that they are "lowdown humbugs and frauds," but says it "warn't no use to tell Jim," who is childishly proud to serve royalty.

Chapter eight is like a whole series of minstrel routines. First Jim explains how he speculated in stock, but the stock—a cow—died. Then he invested in a banking operation run by a Black swindler and lost more money. He gives his last dime to "Balum's Ass; one er dem chuckleheads, you know. But he's lucky, dey say. . . ." Balum's Ass gives the dime to the church when he hears a preacher say "whoever give to de po' len' to de Lord, en boun' to git his money back a hund'd times."

The closing chapters serve a thematic purpose as Twain strengthens his attacks on the violence and hypocrisy of adult "civilization." Jim is a convenient instrument in the concluding burlesque, but his docile behavior reinforces his role as a dimwit—and hence as an audience pleaser. Jim could have walked away from his confinement many times, but he acts only under the direction of the white children—the implications being that he so dotes on the children that he will sacrifice his survival to their games, that he is helpless without white assistance and that he can think only on a child's level.

The farcical rescue scenes point up the unequal nature of the Huck/Jim relationship, but it is not the only time that Twain treats Huck and Jim as less than equal partners. For example, Huck makes no effort to find Jim after the raft is run down by a steamboat and the two are separated. He doesn't grieve over Jim's apparent death and doesn't express any relief when the two are reunited, although Jim nearly cries because he is so glad to see Huck alive.

Literary critics calling Jim the novel's one and only noble adult are usually focusing on Jim's kindness toward Huck and Tom. With that image in mind, critics credit Twain with a broadly liberal perspective, but in fact, the "sympathy" that *Huck Finn* evokes for Jim is part of what minstrelsy is all about. "Stage Negroes" were shaped by their creators, according to Alan Green, so that they *would* be viewed sympathetically. Who would not feel affection for a "permanently visible and permanently inferior clown who posed no threat and desired nothing more than laughter and applause at his imbecile antics"?[14] Blacks had to be a source of hilarity for whites, says Green, in order for whites to cease feeling guilt and anxiety.

It's true that Jim is admirable because he is not an inveterate schemer, like most of the other people in the book. Jim also often makes more sense than other characters. For instance, when he argues with Huck about how Frenchmen talk, Jim is the more logical. But this debate "plays" like the dialogue in a minstrel show because Jim has the information-base of a child (*i.e.*, Jim believes English to be the world's only language).

African American Speech Ridiculed

When Twain was working on *The Adventures of Tom Sawyer* in 1874, he wrote noted author and editor William Dean Howells, his literary advisor, about his technique: "I amend dialect stuff by talking and talking and *talking* it till it sounds right."[15] The "right" sound, however, was the sound of a white person playing a "stage Negro"—a sound that fit white expectations. The mock Black "dialect" in *Huck Finn* turns the humor into caricature and makes Jim's every appearance stereotypical. Jim's language is largely made up of either so-called nonstandard words or so-called "eye dialect"—words that look peculiar in print, as when "wuz" replaces "was." This eye dialect reinforces the notion that a character is stupid rather than merely poorly educated.

When Huck and Jim are both satirized in the chapter on having

(continued on page 91)

ILLUSTRATIONS

Illustrations in the various editions of *Huckleberry Finn* reflect the artists' interpretations of the text, as well as the publishers' sense of what the public wants. We have collected here an assortment of illustrations originating in different countries and indicating a widespread minstrel influence.

To be sure, Mark Twain had a guiding hand in how the first illustrations by Edward W. Kemble were rendered; thus, the history of the relationship between the author and the illustrator would make an interesting study in itself.* Twain demanded that Kemble attempt to create works of art that would attract interest and maintain a certain lightness of tone and level of entertainment. After some controversy, Kemble produced 174 pen-and ink illustrations that Twain was willing to accept; and for a special "Author's Edition" in 1899, Kemble supplied four new illustrations using what looks like a watercolor technique.

While Kemble established in the first edition a characterization of Jim that suggests a certain degree of ridicule, he also created noticeably derogatory portraits for every adult character who appears in the novel. Thus the slaves, Jim and Nat, are somewhat less isolated in this edition in racial terms. But it was only a few years before subsequent editions included only a small number of the Kemble drawings (about seven or eight and leaving out most of the portraits of townsfolk), or else they included drawings by a newly commissioned illustrator. In many of these later editions, Jim and Nat are pictorially isolated and pictorially stereotyped.

Among the most common types of characterization

---

*Information about the Twain/Kemble relationship is available in Beverly R. David's "The Pictorial *Huckleberry Finn:* Mark Twain and His Illustrator, E. W. Kemble," (*American Quarterly,* October 1979), and in John Hakac's *Huckleberry Finn: More Molecules* (Pecos, Texas, 1962).

are the "stage Negro" and the "primitive." And this is true whether the illustrator is using the conventions of the cartoon or the conventions of realistic drawing. In a German edition, Walter Trier's illustrations of Jim and Nat could almost be mistaken for pictures of Al Jolson doing his minstrel numbers. Trier makes use of a standard minstrel costume (striped pants, vest, oversized shoes), as well as a huge, painted mouth. In another German edition illustrated by Rafaello Busoni, as well as in the Swedish edition illustrated by Eric Palmquist, and the American edition illustrated by David McKay, the mouth and sometimes the eyes are exaggerated. However, these artists use a more naturalistic style of drawing than Trier uses, or the Swiss illustrator, Irma Anita Bebié.

Some explicit minstrel connections can also be seen in an illustration from the *St. Nicholas Magazine* version of *Tom Sawyer, Abroad.* Twain expressed his satisfaction with the magazine illustrations by Dan Beard—illustrations that show Jim in a minstrel interlocutor's top hat and dancing slippers as he sails over the Sahara in a balloon. (Beard had illustrated Twain's *A Connecticut Yankee in King Arthur's Court* in 1889.)

Good illustrators are expected to capture the spirit of a text, to use their own skill and vision to enhance mood, characterization, setting, and theme. The number of stereotypic illustrations in editions of both *Huckleberry Finn* and *Tom Sawyer Abroad* suggest that many illustrators are conscious of stereotyping in the novels. However, it is likely that some artists are responding to a white supremacist milieu and not taking their cues from Mark Twain alone. The important question, regardless of an artist's background, training, or intent, is whether or not illustrations of Black identity are being presented in a uniquely derogatory way. Where illustrations represent elements of the minstrel tradition, they are spin-offs of the "stage Negro" conceptualization in the text. The subtlety of this concept and its mocking reference to Black culture remain a serious literary and social problem.

JIM LISTENING.

IN THE CAVE.

JIM ADVISES A DOCTOR.

Illustrations on these two pages by Edward W. Kemble from the first edition of *The Adventures of Huckleberry Finn* (Webster, 1885).

"They peeped out from behind her." (Illustration by Edward W. Kemble from "Autograph Edition" *Adventures of Huckleberry Finn* (Harper, 1889).

Illustration by Dan Beard from *St. Nicholas Magazine* (February 1894) for *Tom Sawyer Abroad*.

Illustration by David McKay from *Adventures of Huckleberry Finn*, published by Grosset and Dunlap (USA, 1948). (Illustrations from this edition also appear in an edition published in India.)

Illustrations by Eric Palmquist from *Adventures of Huckleberry Finn*, published Bökforlags AB Tiden (Sweden, 1957).

Illustrations on pages 89 and 90 by Walter Trier from *Adventures of Huckleberry Finn*, published originally by Droemersche with permission from Atrium Verlag AG (Zurich).

"a general good time," the language tends to isolate Jim as a fool. Huck reads from books salvaged from a sinking steamboat and we see the highly nonsensical result of his learning experiences in a country school. Jim's garbled impression of the Scriptures is similarly revealed, and there is a nice give-and-take between the two vagabonds throughout the whole scene. But while we can easily laugh at Huck's very human confusion in this episode, it is more difficult to see the human side of Jim because of the exaggerated dialect. For example, Jim says:

A harem's a bo'd'n-house, I reck'n. Mos' likely dey has rackety times in de nussery. En I reck'n de wives quarrels considerable; en dat 'crease de racket. Yet dey say Sollermun de wises' man dat ever liv'. I doan' take no stock in dat. Bekase why: would a wise man want to live in de mids' er sich a blimblammin' all de time?[16]

The Aborted Anti-Slavery Storyline

Jim's attempt to escape slavery contributes a strong element of suspense in the early part of the novel, and Twain has an opportunity to comment on that institution. To a certain degree Twain offers a comic/serious protest against slavery, although we must remember that this issue had been decided by the Civil War some 20 years earlier. There are some brilliantly ironic stabs at slavery, but the plot line that focuses on Jim's escape is scuttled when the Duke/Dauphin burlesque takes over. This plot change occurs at the very moment Jim and Huck might have escaped in a newly acquired canoe. Instead, Huck goes in search of strawberries and then performs one of the most illogical acts in the story: he brings the false Duke and Dauphin to the raft he and Jim are living on. If the original plot line had remained important, good-hearted Huck *might* have sympathized with the desperate con men and he *might* have rowed them to some safer location, but it is hard to believe that he would suddenly contradict all his efforts to keep Jim out of sight.

Twain scholar Henry Nash Smith argues that the escape plan is aborted because Huck and Jim are virtually the captives of the Duke and Dauphin.[17] The text does not support this thesis, however, since Huck and Jim ignore several opportunities to follow through with their original plan while the Duke and Dauphin are working their confidence tricks on the river towns.

When Tom Sawyer reenters the story, Huck helps him carry out the farcical, futile escape plan. Because Jim's escape is not actually a high priority, Tom and Huck play at heroics based upon Tom's favorite adventure stories, affording Twain an opportunity to satirize such tales. When the boys actually release Jim, armed slavehunters are on the premises and the "rescue" has no chance of success. "The unhappy truth about the ending," writes Leo Marx in *The American Scholar,* ". . . is that the author, having revealed the tawdry nature of the culture of the great valley, yielded to its essential complacency."[18]

Jim is, in fact, finally free because his owner dies and frees him in her will. Thus his liberator turns out to be a slaveholder, the very sort, writes Leo Marx, "whose inhumanity first made the attempted escape necessary."[19]

The fact that Huck decides to "go to hell" rather than turn Jim in—to make, in other words, an eternal sacrifice for Jim—is often treated by critics as a superb evocation of anti-slavery sentiment. But to reach this interpretation, readers must not only ignore the characterization of Jim; they must also arbitrarily withdraw their attention from Twain's thematic and narrative compromises throughout the last fifth of the novel. Since Huck's concern for Jim all but disappears in the farcical "rescue" sequence, and since it is finally a slaveholder who is presented as the true rescuer, the "going to hell" pronouncement seems more closely related to Twain's many satirical commentaries on religion than to an overriding interest in the slave question. (In the incomplete novel "Tom Sawyer's Conspiracy," Twain uses Tom and Huck brilliantly as a means of debunking religion, while Jim is again a minstrel side-kick.)

Because *Huck Finn* is very contradictory as an anti-slavery work, it is important for readers, and for teachers especially, to examine the larger context of the "freedom" theme. This means pinpointing the text's cultural biases—the white supremacist beliefs which infuse the novel and which are not difficult to discover in a close reading. Notions of racial and cultural superiority appear in *Huck Finn* in the various ways that Twain undercuts Jim's humanity: in the minstrel routines with Huck as the "straight man," in the generalities about Blacks as unreliable, primitive and slow-witted, in the absence of appropriate adult/child roles, in Jim's vulnerability to juvenile trickery, and in the burlesqued speech patterns.

The Term "Nigger"

One of the most controversial aspects of *Huck Finn* is Twain's use of the term "nigger." As with every detail of the novel, the term needs to be examined in relation to its context. Huck uses "nigger" as it was used by white people to ridicule Blacks. When Huck says, "It was fifteen minutes before I could work myself up to go and humble myself to a nigger," he is rising slightly above his cultural conditioning by making an apology, but at the same time the reader sees him caught up in that bigoted culture by his use of a label that whites understood as pejorative.

A serious problem arises, however, in the fact that Jim refers to himself and other Blacks as "niggers," but the self-effacement inherent in his use of this term is not presented as a Black survival tactic. If Twain did not recognize the Black American use of such language as part of the "mask" worn to disarm whites, he was, like Huck, caught unwittingly in the bigoted system that he could not always transcend. If he understood this strategy, but left out any hint of this awareness in order to please a white audience, then he compromised his literary integrity.

These are necessary distinctions for sophisticated adult readers, but most young readers cannot be expected to make such distinctions. Children cannot usually respond to such loaded words with detachment and historical perspective. Whatever the purpose and effect of the term "nigger" for Twain's original white audience, its appearance in a classroom today tends to reinforce racism, inducing embarrassment and anger for Blacks and feelings of superiority and/or acts of harassment by whites.

It is important here to note Twain's use of irony. Some statements which seem blatantly racist are the most highly ironic. For instance, when Huck responds to Aunt Sally's query about an accident, "Anybody hu't?" with the statement, "No'm. Killed a nigger," a double layer of irony strengthens Twain's commentary. Aunt Sally replies, "Well, it's lucky; because sometimes people do get hurt," and the reader can easily discern the social conditioning behind Huck's denial of Black humanity, as well as the extraordinary indifference that makes Aunt Sally's idea of "luck" a bitterly ironic indictment of slavery. Similarly, one of the most potent comments on slavery occurs when Jim threatens to steal his own children and Huck responds:

Here was this nigger which I had as good as helped to run away, coming right out flatfooted and saying he would steal his children—children that belonged to a man I didn't even know; a man that hadn't ever done me no harm.[20]

These ironic, "topsy-turvy" features are perhaps the easiest to teach in an English class.

Twain's Perspective

When looking at *Huck Finn,* it is important to consider Twain's upbringing and milieu. Twain himself emphasized the importance of
early "training." Significantly, he lamented the fact that his mother
would never abandon her support of slavery, but he defended her by
saying, "Manifestly, training and association can accomplish strange
miracles."[21] Huck himself emphasizes the importance of how people
are "brung up." Tom was not "brung up" to free a "nigger" unless
that slave was already legally free; the Dauphin was not "brung up" to
deliver lines from Shakespeare properly; and kings, says Huck, "are a
mighty ornery lot. It's the way they're raised." While Twain was in
some respects a renegade, he was also "brung up" in a period in which
opposition to slavery was a controversial position, and in which sensitivity to other issues of racial injustice was severely limited. In his
autobiography, he writes:

I was not aware that there was anything wrong about [slavery in my schoolboy
days]. . . . No one arraigned it in my hearing; the local papers said nothing
against it; the local pulpit taught us that God approved it; if the slaves themselves had any aversion to slavery they were wise and said nothing.[22]

When Twain first went to New York in his late teens, he was
apparently shocked by the sight of Blacks who were not slaves and
wrote his mother:

I reckon I had better black my face, for in these Eastern States niggers are
considerably better than white people.[23]

Several years later, when the Civil War broke out, Twain's
sympathies were with the South, and he enlisted in the Confederate
Army. His decision to quit after two weeks of soldiering seems to have
had more to do with a new job opportunity out West than with any
change of heart about the justice of the Confederate cause.[24]

Slavery aside, Twain's writings include many statements about
Black Americans which reflect the prevailing white racist attitudes of
the 19th century. In his autobiography, he mentions Uncle Dan'l, a
slave on his uncle's farm, as the "real Jim." Uncle Dan'l, says Twain,
was patient, friendly and loyal, "traits which were his birthright."[25]
In *Huck Finn,* the racial bias of the statement that Jim was "white

inside" is so extreme that it seems ironical. Yet, when Jim is commended as an "uncommon nigger," this is not unlike Twain's praise of
his own butler as no "commonplace coon."[26] (William Dean Howells
provides some insight on Twain's attitudes in this regard when he
writes that Twain preferred Black or Asian butlers "because he said
he could not bear to order a white man about."[27])

Twain amused colleagues by using the same caricatured speech
he ascribed to Jim. He wrote his publisher:

I's gwyne to sen' you di stuff jis' as she stan', now; an' you an' Misto Howls kin
weed out enuff o'dem 93,000 words fer to crowd de book down to *one* book; or
you kin shove in enuff er dat ole Contrib-Club truck fer to swell her up en
bust her in two an' make *two* books outen her. . . . I don't want none er dat rot
what is in de small envolups to go in, 'cepp'n jis' what Misto Howls *say* shel go
in.[28]

Those claiming that Twain became a staunch advocate of social
justice for Blacks usually cite his essay titled, "The United States of
Lyncherdom," written in 1901. However, Twain decided not to publish this anti-lynching essay in the *North American Review*, as he
originally intended, because "I shouldn't have even half a friend left
down there [in the South], after it issued from the press."[29] Instead,
he chose to bury his indignation by placing the manuscript with papers
he designated for posthumous publication.

Moreover, the essay's content, not Twain's timidity, is the
important problem. It reveals Twain's deep-seated prejudice rather
than his "de-southernization," which it is said to represent. Twain
condemns lynching primarily because it is not due process, but he
ignores the principle of due process in his discussion of a particular
case. His arguments are based upon an unsupported presumption of
Black guilt. He writes: "I will not dwell upon the provocation which
moved the [lynchers] to those crimes . . . ; the only question is, *does
the assassin take the law into his own hands?*" And, in arguing that
lynching is not a deterrent to crime, Twain supports the very myth
that the KKK promulgated to justify its attacks—that Blacks threatened white women. He writes:

. . . one much talked-of outrage and murder committed by a negro will upset
the disturbed intellects of several other negroes and produce a series of the
very tragedies the community would so strenuously wish to prevent; . . . in a
word, the lynchers are themselves the worst enemies of their women.[30]

Twain's Ambivalence

Like many of his white contemporaries, Twain clearly had ambivalent attitudes about Blacks. On the one hand, we see his efforts to help Black college students financially, to aid a Black college, to publicly support the reputation of Black leader Frederick Douglass and to speak out boldly and progressively (*e.g.*, there is a "reparation due," said Twain, "from every white to every black man"[31]). Yet he could not shake off some persistent white supremacist notions. In *Huck Finn*, Twain's ambivalence is recorded in the degrading minstrel elements on the one hand and in the antislavery theme on the other. (We must remember that the period following the Civil War and the abolition of slavery was one of intense racial conflict in this country as repressive forces sought to reinstate the "benefits" of slavery. Repressive "Jim Crow" laws, exploitative practices, terrorist activities designed to deprive Blacks of their voting and other civil rights—all were part of the climate in which Twain lived and wrote. These historical realities should be included in any classroom discussions of the work.)

Twain specialists have not generally provided much help to those concerned about the book's biases. For instance, Charles Neider, in his Introduction to *The Selected Letters of Mark Twain*, notes the offensive racism of Twain's frontier humor, but this does not prevent him from calling Twain the "Lincoln of our literature" and the "Shakespeare of our humor."[32] Perspective has quite a lot to do with what is classified as comic, and there are basic questions that cannot be passed over. Funny to whom? Funny at whose expense?

In *The Grotesque Essence: Plays from the American Minstrel Stage*, Gary Engle refers to minstrelsy as cruel, grotesque, monstrous and racist, and says it caricatures Blacks as "lazy, ignorant, illiterate, hedonistic, vain, often immoral, fatalistic and gauche." But, in spite of this, he calls Jim a "sympathetically drawn version of the minstrel clown."[33] Engle justifies minstrelsy by claiming that it purged the "American common man" of insecurity and blessed him with the "laughter of affirmation"—"By laughing at a fool, a nation can safely and beneficially laugh at itself."[34] Clearly, he is viewing the nation as a white society exclusively.

Consistent Characterization in Three Novels

It deepens our understanding of *Huckleberry Finn* when we examine both the literary and cultural continuity in the three novels that feature Huck, Jim, and Tom in prominent roles. Many critics regard the two sequels to *Huckleberry Finn*—the published book, *Tom Sawyer Abroad* and the incomplete manuscript, "Tom Sawyer's Conspiracy"— as artistically negligible. But the minstrel tradition is strong in each characterization of Jim. This makes the three works culturally unified and, in a literary sense, comparable.

Tom Sawyer Abroad was written in 1892 and published first in a serialized format in 1893–94 in the children's periodical, *St. Nicholas Magazine*.[35] As Huck and Jim went down the river in *Huckleberry Finn,* stopping at various river towns in accordance with the burlesque routines or the social comments that Twain wanted to insert in the narrative, so in *Tom Sawyer Abroad*, Huck, Tom and Jim float across the Sahara Desert in a balloon and touch down intermittently to observe human foolishness and cruelty. Each chapter is structured in a way that includes a debate about maps, time zones, historical events, and so on. Tom is usually on one side of the controversy, displaying his provincial schooling; Huck and Jim on the other, representing the unschooled. To an even greater extent than in *Huckleberry Finn,* Jim is depicted as a child playing with other children, not as an adult; (no mention is made of Jim as a father, husband, laborer, etc.). But since Huck and Jim take the same side in most arguments, there is built into the action of the novel a natural parallel between the two characterizations and it is easy to see how the comparable humanity of Black people and white people might have been spontaneously evoked had not the stereotyping of minstrelsy intervened. Unfortunately, the white child, Huck, is presented as distinctly superior to the Black ex-slave by means of several "stage Negro" conventions.

First, Jim becomes totally addlebrained in the midst of any excitement. Jim can operate the balloon mechanism as easily as Tom or Huck, but after seeing a lion, "Jim had clean lost his head, and said he had forgot how."[36] When the three travelers sight a mirage, Huck is puzzled, but "Jim was trembling all over, and so scared he couldn't speak. . . ."[37] In another encounter with lions,

Jim lost his head, straight off—he always done it whenever he got excited and scared, and so now, 'stead of just easing the ladder up from the ground a little, so the animals couldn't reach it, he turned on a raft of power, and we went whizzing up and was dangling in the sky before he got his wits together and seen what a foolish thing he was doing. Then he stopped her, but had clean forgot what to do next. . . .[38]

Jim is bug-eyed and stupefied when he faces anything unfamiliar or contrary to his expectations; Huck searches calmly for an explanation, but has only the evidence of his senses to work with; Tom instantly dredges up facts from a school lesson (often only half learned) or fanciful explanations gleaned from *The Arabian Nights.*

A second minstrel device is the use of dialogues and monologues about the Bible (as Twain used the "King Sollermun" dialogue with similar effect in *Huckleberry Finn*). Now Jim is trying to explain the Great Desert, the Lord's "mistake":

I b'lieve it uz jes' like when you's buildin' a house; dey's allays a lot o' truck en rubbish lef' over. What does you do wid it? Doan' you take en k'yart it off en dump it onto a ole vacant back lot? 'Course. Now, den, it's my opinion hit was jes' like dat. . . . He measure out some rocks en yearth en san', en stick 'em together en say 'Dat's Germany,' en pas'e a label on it en set it out to dry; en measure out some mo' rocks en yearth en san', en stick 'em together, en say, 'Dat's de United States,' en pas'e a label on it and set *it* out to dry. . . . Den He notice dat whilst He's cal'lated de yearth en de rocks jes' right, dey's a mos' turrible lot o' san' lef' over. . .[39]

Monologues of this sort are similar to the standard, nonsensical "Sermons" of the minstrel show; and Jim is as much the "blackface" clown here as when he breaks down and cries at the sight of Moses' Egypt. ("He was a Presbyterian, and had a most deep respect for Moses, which was a Presbyterian too, [Huck] said.")

The vast difference in the dialects of Jim and Huck are illustrated by the two quotes, a difference marking the influence of the "stage Negro" tradition in all the novels.

Twain's consistent treatment of Black characterization over a twenty-year period belies the claims made about an increasingly liberal outlook. And this consistency also points to the reason why some interpretations of *Huckleberry Finn* are extremely hard to accept. For example, Daniel Hoffman maintains that Jim wears a minstrel mask only when affected by the slave environment or by Tom's mentality. On the raft, says Hoffman, "he lives in his intrinsic human dignity . . . with Huck." In *Form and Fable in American Fiction,* Hoffman argues that Jim ourgrows the stereotypes, as "Mark Twain began with all the stereotypes of racial character in his mind," and then outgrew them. As evidence, this critic asks us to examine Jim's belief in magic and notice how he becomes gradually a successful magician or shaman. This success is said to give Jim "moral energy." His super-natural power as interpreter of the oracles of nature," makes him the "hero of his own magic."[40] But in the actual text of *Huckleberry Finn* all this "power" consists of is the power to cure snakebite (a cure that Jim helps along with large drafts of whiskey), and the power to predict a storm.

The notion that Jim is connected first with one kind of voodoo (drawing conclusions first from a hair-ball from the fourth stomach of an ox) and then with a more advanced kind (as an interpreter of dreams and as a predictor of the weather) is purely Hoffman's invention. It illustrates the kind of weak logic that critics sometimes employ in their efforts to minimize the minstrel connections. The theory that Jim gradually gains power and moral status as a medicine man becomes thoroughly implausible when Jim is analyzed in the three novels in which he has a major role. The discreteness of each work does not include a marked variation in the depiction of Jim. Hoffman links Jim's alleged growth beyond stereotypes with Twain's growth beyond stereotypes. But any such claim on behalf of Twain is contradicted by the texts that followed: *Tom Sawyer Abroad* and "Tom Sawyer's Conspiracy."

It is impossible to predict what Twain might have ended up with in "Tom Sawyer's Conspiracy," the manuscript he worked on between 1897 and 1900, but the existing evidence does not point to a more liberal book. More than 30,000 words of the narrative were written (*Tom Sawyer Abroad* was 40,000 words), and a few additional pages could have ended it, according to Walter Blair, editor of the 1969 University of California Press edition. Blair speculates that Twain felt, finally, that the book was merely an echo of his earlier work.[41] Slavery is again central to the plot (the conflict is between abolitionists and "pater-rollers"—the vigilante squads that prevented slave escapes), and the Duke and Dauphin reappear. Jim's characterization is again reminiscent of "blackface" performers, and the minstrel "things" in Aunt Polly's garret enable Tom to blacken his face and impersonate an escaping slave.

As in *Tom Sawyer Abroad,* Huck describes arguments between Tom and Jim, with Tom making elaborate references to the fiction he had read. Jim plays the part of the long-suffering fool and lets the children put his life in jeopardy, as in the last chapters of *Huckleberry Finn.*

Huck in his role as narrator, again serves Twain's ironic purposes, but the irony does not negate or offset the stereotyping of Jim. For example, Huck gives a tongue-in-cheek description of Jim as "mumbling to himself, the way a nigger does," and adds the comment, "it's the best way, to let a nigger or a child go on and grumble itself out, then it's satisfied."[42] But Jim's behavior throughout coincides with childishness, as, for example, when he approves of Tom's dangerous and idiotic "conspiracy"; ("he said it was splendid, and believed that it was the best conspiracy that ever was, and was coming along judicious and satisfactory").[43]

The two later Huck/Tom/Jim novels are not widely studied, and would not be pertinent to this discussion of *Huckleberry Finn* if it were not for the light they shed on inconsistencies in Mark Twain scholarship. In critiques of *Huckleberry Finn*, the minstrel element is either denied or glossed over. In critiques of the sequels, this feature is more widely acknowledged, but often unexplored. Kenneth S. Lynn writes about *Tom Sawyer Abroad*: ". . . the compassionate figure of the slave in *Huckleberry Finn* is barely recognizable in the minstrel-show darky of the later book."[44] Yet a point by point comparison of Jim's characteristics in the three narratives reveals striking similarities and few differences. The Huck/Tom/Jim books are a unit, and in regard to the characterizations of Jim, a continuous, minstrel-inspired commentary on Black America.

Conclusion

It is unfortunate that in extolling a work of literature, most critics feel they must endorse it in its entirety and, in effect, support its biases. Not surprisingly, Black author Ralph Ellison is one of the few commentators who has been critical of the minstrel tradition in Twain's works. It is Jim's stereotypical minstrel mask, notes Ellison, that makes Huck—not Jim—appear to be the adult on the raft.[45]

Literary historian Donald Gibson made the following statement about teaching *Huck Finn* to high school and college students:

It should be shown to be a novel whose author was not always capable of resisting the temptation to create laughter through compromising his morality and his art. In short the problem of whether to teach the novel will not exist if it is taught in all its complexity of thought and feeling, and if critics and teachers avoid making the same kinds of compromises Mark Twain made.[46]

"All its complexity" must, of necessity, include the book's racism and its ties to the minstrel tradition. If students learn about this aspect of Twain's work, they will increase their capacity to understand *Huck Finn.*

Notes

1. Twain's talent for vernacular innovation, regional portraiture, mythic associations and other novelistic features could be discussed here, but they have been commented upon extensively in works by other critics. The problem in Twain scholarship is to bring about some balance between discussions of craft and discussions of content.

2. Gary D. Engle, *The Grotesque Essence: Plays from the American Minstrel Stage* (Baton Rouge: Louisiana State University Press, 1978), pp. xvi–xvii, xix–xx.

3. Alan W. C. Green, " 'Jim Crow,' 'Zip Coon': The Northern Origins of Negro Minstrelsy," *The Massachusetts Review*, V. 11 (Spring 1970), p. 394.

4. In the partially completed novel "Tom Sawyer's Conspiracy," Tom Sawyer goes to his aunt's garret to find "our old nigger-show things" and plan a "nigger" disguise. Blacking-up kits, as well as performance manuals containing sample skits and lyrics, were widely sold to the general public.

5. Mark Twain, *Mark Twain in Eruption: Hitherto Unpublished Pages About Men and Events,* ed. Bernard De Voto (New York: Harper, 1922), pp. 110, 115.

6. Ibid., p. 113.

7. Carl Wittke, *Tambo and Bones: A History of the American Minstrel Stage* (New York: Greenwood reprint, 1968; original published in 1930), p. 25.

8. Paul Fatout, *Mark Twain on the Lecture Circuit* (Bloomington: Indiana University Press, 1960; reprinted, Gloucester, Mass.: Peter Smith, 1966), p. 190.

9. Justin Kaplan, *Mark Twain and His World* (New York: Simon and Schuster, 1974), p. 69. In the first lectures in 1866, Twain used a mixture of what Kaplan calls delightful "statistics, anecdotes, edification and amusement, humorous reflection delivered after a delicately timed pause, something that passed for moral philosophy, and passages of gorgeous word painting." In 1884, Twain adopted the format Charles Dickens used in public readings. His style became a blend of telling and acting episodes from his books (Kaplan, pp. 68, 128).

10. Fatout, p. 106.

11. The approximate times when different parts of the novel were written are discussed in Walter Blair's "When Was *Huckleberry Finn* Written?" (*American Literature,* March, 1958, pp. 1–25); in David Carkeet's "The Dialects in *Huckleberry Finn"* (*American Literature,* November, 1979, pp. 315–332); in Franklin R. Rogers' *Mark Twain's Burlesque Patterns* (Dallas: Southern Methodist University Press, 1960, pp. 139–140); in Michael Patrick Hearn's *The Annotated Huckleberry Finn* (New York: Potter, 1981), p. 111.

12. Rogers, p. 148.

13. Clemens, Samuel Langhorne (Mark Twain), *Adventures of Huckleberry Finn: An Authoritative Text, Backgrounds and Sources, Criticism,* 2nd edition by Sculley Bradley, Richard Croom Beatty, E. Husdon Long, Thomas Cooley (New York: W. W. Norton, 1977), pp. 71–72.

14. Green, p. 394.

15. Charles Neider, ed., *The Selected Letters of Mark Twain* (New York: Harper & Row, 1982), p. 84.

16. Clemens, p. 65. The dialect in a typical minstrel play reads as follows: "It 'pears dat de Lawd, after he done made Adam and Eve, sot 'em in de Garden ob Edem, dat de Lawd he Tol' em bofe dat dar was a sartain tree and dat dey musn't eat none of eet's fruit. . . ." (William Courtright's *The Complete Minstrel Guide,* Chicago: The Dramatic Publishing Co., 1901, p. 83.)

17. Henry Nash Smith, *Mark Twain: The Development of a Writer* (Cambridge: The Belkap Press of Harvard University Press, 1962), pp. 113–137.

18. Leo Marx, "Mr. Eliot, Mr. Triling, and *Huckleberry Finn,*" *The American Scholar,* V. 22:4 (Autumn 1953), p. 433.

19. Ibid.

20. Clemens, p. 74.

21. Charles Neider, ed., *The Autobiography of Mark Twain: Including Chapters Now Published for the First Time* (New York: Harper & Row, 1959), p. 30.

22. Ibid., p. 6.

23. James M. Cox, *Mark Twain: The Fate of Humor* (Princeton: Princeton University Press, 1966), p. 7.

24. Twain scholar John C. Gerber has explained how Twain tried to justify his withdrawal from the Confederate Army in an essay Twain wrote in 1885 entitled, "The Private History of the Campaign That Failed." Twain introduced fictional content into his explanation that would help him pacify his Southern critics. (See *Mark Twain: Selected Criticism,* ed. by Arthur L. Scott, Dallas: Southern Methodist University Press, 1967, pp. 281–282.)

25. Neider, *Autobiography of Mark Twain,* pp. 5–6.

26. Arthur G. Pettit, *Mark Twain and the South* (Lexington: University of Kentucky Press, 1974), p. 104.

27. William Dean Howells, *My Mark Twain* (New York: Harper, 1910), p. 34.

28. Pettit, p. 128.

29. Kaplan, p. 194.

30. Maxwell Geismar, ed., *Mark Twain and the Three R's: Race, Religion, Revolution— and Related Matters* (Indianapolis/New York: Bobbs-Merrill, 1973), p. 34.

31. Edward Wagenknecht, *Mark Twain: The Man and His Work* (Norman: University of Oklahoma Press, 1967, 3rd ed.), p. 222.

32. Neider, *Selected Letters,* pp. 2, 5.

33. Engle, p. xxvi.

34. Engle, pp. xxvi, xxviii.

35. The latest edition of *Tom Sawyer Abroad, The Works of Mark Twain: The Adventures of Tom Sawyer, Tom Sawyer Abroad, Tom Sawyer, Detective.* Ed. by John C. Gerber, Paul Baender, and Terry Firkins (Berkeley: University of California Press, 1980), is apt to gain in popularity because it contains *Tom Sawyer Abroad* as originally written and edited by Twain, not edited by the *St. Nicholas Magazine* editor, Mary Mapes Dodge. Dodge's extensive bowdlerization weakened the serial manuscript— a draft that was later used for two-thirds of the American edition of the book. (chapters 1–9). Only the British edition contained the original text when first published.

36. Mark Twain. *The Works of Mark Twain: The Adventures of Tom Sawyer, Tom Sawyer Abroad, Tom Sawyer, Detective,* ed. by John C. Gerber, Paul Baender, and Terry Firkins (Berkeley: University of California Press, 1980) p. 284.

37. Ibid., p. 300.

38. Ibid., p. 305.

39. Ibid., pp. 310–311.

40. Daniel Hoffman. *Form and Fable in American Fiction*, (New York: Oxford University Press, 1965) pp. 337–338, 341–342.

41. Mark Twain, *Mark Twain's Hannibal, Huck, and Tom*, ed. by Walter Blair (Berkeley: University of California Press, 1969) p. 162.

42. Ibid., p. 171.

43. Ibid., p. 207.

44. Kenneth S. Lynn. *Mark Twain and Southerwestern Humor*. (Westport, Conn.: Greenwood Press, 1972) p. 245.

45. Ralph Ellison, "Change the Joke and Slip the Yoke," *Partisan Review*, V. 25:2 (Spring 1958), pp. 215–222.

46. Donald Gibson, "Mark Twain's Jim in the Classroom," *English Journal*, V. 57:2 (February 1968). p. 202.

8. MARK TWAIN'S JIM IN THE CLASSROOM

Donald B. Gibson

THE GREAT CONCERN of the Negro in our time with his social image has caused the question to be raised with increasing frequency about whether *Adventures of Huckleberry Finn* should be taught in high school and college. Most teachers would agree that it should be taught: Mark Twain's novel remains one of the mainstays of the English curriculum. I, too, agree that it should not be discarded. At the same time, however, those who oppose its being taught have a case, and people teaching the novel need to pay attention to that case, for opponents of the book have seen something in it which is really there and needs to be dealt with. [1]

The case against the novel centers around the character of Jim. Opponents of the novel feel that Jim is a stereotype, a minstrel show figure, who in his actions and attitudes proves often to be less than human. Such is the case in the first chapters of the book, in which Jim is presented as lacking dignity, as superstitious, ignorant, and comical. Indeed, a slave such as Jim might well in fact have been undignified, superstitious, ignorant, and comical, but the problem is that he is presented as being *nothing but* these things. Consequently, even granted that Jim appears otherwise later in the novel, the fact is that at the beginning of the novel Mark Twain sees Jim as being no different from the "minstrel show nigger" or the comical darky of plantation literature.

The same case can be made about the presentation of Jim during the final chapters of the novel. Whatever happens in the relation between Huck and Jim during the central episodes of the novel, it is clear that Jim (frequently referred to by critics as "Nigger Jim" though he is never once called this in *Huck Finn!*) is seen by Huck and Mark Twain alike as *only* an object and not human, a pasteboard, one-dimensional figure. At the novel's end Tom turns Jim into an unreal object of his imagination. Huck and Jim go along with the farce, and Mark Twain does too, for despite the limitations imposed on him by his choice of point of view, he is always able, when he wants, to indicate disparity between his attitudes and the attitudes of his characters.[2] The tone of the final section suggests that no such disparity exists.

Opponents of the novel also feel that the relation between Jim and Huck is essentially demeaning. Despite Huck's decision to go to hell rather than turn Jim in, a strong point in his favor, he could only assume the role of leader, protector, and provider in relation to a person whom he considered and who considered himself to be his dependent. Thus, the usual roles of child and adult are reversed, and Jim assumes the inferior role.

One need only compare Huck's reactions to every other adult he encounters in the novel to see this. All other adults in Huck's world embody authority, but Jim, stripped of authority and, indeed, masculinity by social consensus, appears to himself and to Huck as less than an adult.[3] Thus, the general social conception of the proper relation between white and black in regard to authority is carried onto the raft and persists even at the very moment Huck decides to go to hell rather than turn Jim in. The very conditions creating the possibility of the decision stem from Huck's authority.

As a corollary to the preceding, no escaped slave, it is argued, would subject himself to domination by a child to the extent of allowing himself to be led deeper and deeper into slave territory and further and further away from freedom on the Illinois shore. Viewed from the perspective outlined here, the journey downriver is more than a failure of execution. It was only possible at all as a result of the reversed child-parent relation between Huck and Jim.

When the relation between the two characters is described by most critics, the irony and ambivalence so often expressed in Huck's attitude toward Jim is generally overlooked. Most critics see a certain progress, a positive development in Huck's character when in the chapter, "Fooling Poor Old Jim," Huck says finally, "It was fifteen minutes before I could work myself up to go and humble myself to a nigger; but I done it, and warn't sorry for it afterward neither." Indeed there does occur development in Huck's character at this point, for presumably he has never before apologized to a "nigger" and was never capable of it. The fact of positive development cannot be denied.

Yet the statement also indicates that despite Huck's moral growth, he continues to see Jim as a "nigger," a "nigger" to whom he feels the personal necessity to apologize. Hence, Huck sees with a certain duality of vision. Jim is at once an individual, a discrete per-

sonality, to whom respect is due—but at the same time a "nigger."
Which view is the true one? Critics almost invariably see the positive
view as the true one. But why, opponents of the novel ask, is the one
view more true than the other?

Moral growth likewise takes place during the central episode of
the novel in which Huck decides to go to hell rather than turn Jim
in—at least within the limitations outlined. The salient issue, however, is that the conflict within Huck between heart and conscience
reflects the same essential conflict in Mark Twain himself, only he did
not resolve it quite so clearly and decisively. As a result, the novel's
ending serves to obviate all that has preceded and Huck's decision
becomes finally meaningless. For those who might have missed the
point, Mark Twain tells us at the end that Jim was free anyway. If
Huck's decision is meaningful in any sense, the fact remains that
Mark Twain specifically intended to undercut its meaningfulness by
telling us that Jim was free all the while.

From this perspective the ending implies Mark Twain's own
personal decision *not* to go to hell, but to set things right, to square
himself with the values of the society which Huck rejects in deciding
to "take up wickedness." The reconciliation means among other
things turning Jim into the stage clown he was at the beginning of the
book. Thus the central episode of the novel is unambiguous only if we
look at it in isolation, apart from the context of the novel.

Further, what is to be made of the episode during which Huck
meets Aunt Sally and explains why it has taken him so long to get to
the Phelps' farm? "We blowed out a cylinder head," Huck says. "Good
gracious! Anybody hurt?" Aunt Sally asks. "No'm. Killed a nigger."
"Well, it's lucky; because sometimes people do get hurt." This passage
could conceivably be described as simply an instance of a failure of
tone, an instance in which Mark Twain sacrifices character for the
sake of humor, for certainly the author at this point intends to ridicule
Huck and Aunt Sally because both assume that a Negro is less than
human. At the same time, however, Huck's feeling here is not the
least bit inconsistent with his character. Though his attitude toward
Jim may change somewhat, there is no reason to feel that he is able to
see a single Negro other than Jim as simply and only a "nigger," and
toward Jim his attitude is at best ambivalent.

Those antagonistic toward the novel ask whether there isn't
something wrong in the view describing Jim as "noble,"[4] as Huck's
"true" father,[5] or as "the conscience of the novel, the spiritual yard-

stick by which all men are measured."[6] These terms are indeed true and fitting insofar as they describe the spiritual man, Jim. But what of the social man? Is Jim a model human being in any but a spiritual way? Such terms do not describe the character fully enough. Is it noble for a man to allow a child to usurp his authority? Is a "true" father one who is led by his child? It is all well and good to see Jim as "white on the inside," but isn't it luxurious indulgence to believe that his spiritual state, given Jim's circumstances, should be so much more important than his social condition? Are his saintliness and nobility so clearly positive qualities in light of the fact that their price is his masculinity?

If we take into account Mark Twain's ambivalence about so many things, examined in detail in Van Wyck Brooks' *The Ordeal of Mark Twain*, it is not surprising to find him seeing Jim at once as human, capable of deep feeling and compassion, of loyalty and sincere friendship, and as simply a character from a minstrel show. It is not surprising to find Mark Twain concerned in this novel with the theme of man's inhumanity to man while at the same time giving tacit approval to the institution of slavery which is the primary cause of Jim's predicament. Of course Huck, incapable as he is of dealing in abstractions, could not very well condemn slavery. But Mark Twain indicates his own feelings and they are that slavery is all right as long as slaves are not treated badly. The Phelps farm, for example, is a happy place. Further, Jim's only justification for running away from Miss Watson is her cruel intention to sell him down the river and separate him from his family. The extreme degree of ambivalence in the novel calls into serious question the adequacy of most criticism about it, for critics habitually treat it as though its meaning were monolithic. Yet we can find the opposite within the novel of nearly every thought, ideal, feeling, or idea presented there.[7]

Hence, it should be acknowledged by those opposed to the novel on the grounds outlined above that if the book says the one thing—Jim is a "stage nigger," etc,—it also says the opposite. Though the descriptive terms applied to Jim by critics do not define him totally, he is in truth morally superior to anyone else in the book (including Huck). If the image of the Negro presented in the book is of importance, the episode in Chapter 6 need be recalled during which Pap describes a Negro who is educated, knows six languages, is a college professor, respected and free. The novel's expression of the value of freedom should also be acknowledged. At least Jim seeks freedom when his condition becomes utterly intolerable. This distinguishes him from

Harriet B. Stowe's long-suffering Uncle Tom, who acquiesces to the
pain, misery, and hardship of his life in hope of a glorious life in
heaven. Though it is sometimes difficult to distinguish between them,
they are not precisely the same person.

The basic problem, the problem underlying the question
whether the novel should be taught, is the matter of how it is taught.
Too often critics and teachers ignore the implications arising from
Mark Twain's ambivalence toward Jim, either through lack of attention to this aspect of the novel's meaning, or through too great commitment to particular critical schemes. A survey of recent criticism of
Huck Finn reveals the operation of one or both of these factors in most
of it. For example, all of the criticism justifying the last section of the
novel ignores or glosses over the problem of the presentation of Jim as
stereotype. Likewise, a significant number of critics seeing the ending
as a limitation of the novel deal with it in terms other than the moral or
sociological.[8] Problems about whether the novel should be taught are
bound to arise if the moral and sociological ramifications of the book
are ignored.

If the novel is taught truly, as it is, rather than as a vehicle for
the practical application of various limiting critical notions, the problem of *whether* it should be taught will not arise. It should not be
presented as simply a great novel by a great author, as non-evaluative
critical approaches usually imply, but as a novel written by a man
limited like the rest of us in his inability to be constantly charitable
and always to think and feel the right thing. It should be presented as
the work of a man whose intentions were in large measure good, but
who was not entirely able to overcome the limitations imposed upon
his sensibilities by a bigoted early environment. It should be shown to
be a novel whose author was not always capable of resisting the temptation to create laughter though compromising his morality and his art.
In short the problem of whether to teach the novel will not exist if it is
taught in all its complexity of thought and feeling, and if critics and
teachers avoid making the same kinds of compromises Mark Twain
made.

Notes

1. Edward Wagenknecht's response to objections to the novel on racial grounds is
characteristic: "When Negroes object to Jim in *Huckleberry Finn*, one can only regret

that they are behaving as stupidly as white folks often do, for surely Jim is one of the noblest characters in American literature." *Mark Twain: The Man and His Work* (Norman: University of Oklahoma Press, 1961), p. 222.

2. One of many such examples occurs in Chapter 22 in which Mark Twain shows Huck's inability to distinguish between illusion and reality at the circus. A more subtle instance occurs in the title of Chapter 8, "I Spare Miss Watson's Jim." The note of condescension is clear.

3. It is significant to note that Jim has been described as Huck's "spiritual" father, his "mother," and even as a homosexual. He is none of these, though he might appear to be because he does not possess the dominant characteristic of masculinity in our society, authority. He is a child and does not have even the limited authority of a mother.

4. Wagenknecht, *op. cit.*

5. Lionel Trilling, Introduction to *The Adventures of Huckleberry Finn* (New York: Rinehart, 1960), p. ix.

6. James M. Cox, "Remarks on the Sad Initiation of Huckleberry Finn," *Sewanee Review*, 62 (Summer 1954) 404. Reprinted in Barry A. Marks' collection of essays, *Mark Twain's Huckleberry Finn* (Boston: D. C. Heath and Co., 1959), p. 73.

7. This statement could be made in relation to the ending which many feel reverses the novel's meaning. But there are more specific examples available. One is Mark Twain's shift in attitude toward the Widow Douglas in the opening pages. At first *she* is seen as Huck's tormentor, then that role is assumed by Miss Watson and the Widow becomes a positive force. Note also Mark Twain's shifting attitude toward Colonel Sherburn from Chapter 21 to Chapter 22.

8. The prominent exception is Leo Marx whose view of the novel and of criticism of it implies the importance of the question dealt with here. Marx specifically refers to Jim at the end of the novel as "the submissive stage Negro," and points to its source as a "lapse of moral vision" on Mark Twain's part. The preceding quoted phrases are implied to have the relation I suggest. "Mr. Eliot, Mr. Trilling, and *Huckelberry Finn*," *American Scholar*, 22 (Autumn 1953) 423–440. Reprinted in Marks, *op. cit.*, p. 53–64.

9. THROUGH A GLASS, DARKLY
(Excerpt)

Dharathula H. Millender

FOR CENTURIES, literature has been valued for introducing readers to each other. Books describe the physical appearance of other people, explain customs, modes, and ways of living, and illustrate graphically how others are supposed to look, live, and seem to be.

Tragically, however, books have often planted false images in the minds of readers. Certainly, much is being said today about the damage the early books about Negro life for children have done to foster misunderstanding between the races. With little or no contact between the races in the early 1900's, books were the only medium of introduction. Yet they often explained customs and modes and ways of living not as they normally were, and often showed grotesque stereotypes in illustrations portrayed as "true" representations but certainly not genuine. They introduced readers to people, but not real people or normal situations. Unfortunately authors seldom knew the subject about which they wrote, and those who did know were seldom allowed to make the introductions. The result was irreparable damage.

Yet one must remember that books are just a mirror of the times. . . they present life as it is interpreted to be by authors who can convince publishers that they have something that will sell. Most authors successful in having stories for children published in the early 1900's had no real way of knowing the Negro about whom they were writing, but they wrote about Negroes, nevertheless, and people believed their farcical presentations. At that time in our country's history, it was accepted that the Negro lived little better than in his plantation days, that he wanted nothing, had nothing, and looked like nothing that resembled other humans of the day.

The Negro author, who could have made a valuable contribution to human relations at that time, writing truthfully and plausibly about his own people, seems to have been unacceptable to most publishers. So separated were the races in the early 1900's that few whites knew that many Negroes lived in much the same way that they themselves lived. Unaware of the Negro society within the crowded ghettoes they did not know that the Negro was trying to provide for his young people many of the same kinds of opportunities and advantages for growth that the whites provided for their youngsters. Few outside the ghetto knew what life went on within the narrow confines of the Negro's partially unimproved area, usually down by the railroad tracks or in the slums of the inner city, which had been destroyed and left by others who had moved on to a second try at decency. Few knew that within such areas the Negro was providing for his youth opportunities for leadership and development, and preparing him to be ready for acceptance when it came; that the Negro was constantly looking up and struggling for a better way of life; or that, without fanfare, the Negro was educating his youth to take jobs that were not even available then . . . but merely hoped for at this point.

Books did not mirror this kind of life, the life that really was, but revealed instead another and alien existence. How different life might have been for all if they had really mirrored the times, and the outside world could have seen in them the struggle of the Negro to survive under tremendous odds . . . ever moving forward with hope when at that time he found most doors closed to him. Many who could have opened those doors were ignorant of the fact that the Negro wanted a chance and was not content to do, be, and want nothing but idleness and pleasure. Without books to reveal the true life and aspirations of the Negro, progress in race relations was set back years. Those who chose to promote the inferiority of the Negro went unchallenged by the masses—who had no way of finding out for themselves.

In the early 1900's publishers, I'm sure, really wanted stories that mirrored the thinking of the day and times. They, too, had little or no contact with Negroes, and were perhaps governed by the way public opinion was shaped by the leading news media of the day. *Scribner's Magazine,* (Vol. XXXIV, Aug., 1903, No. 2) had a story entitled, "The County Fair," by Nelson Lloyd, illustrated by Edwin B. Child. On page 142 of that issue, a "representative" illustration of Negroes was shown. Apparently the reader was to think that these Negroes were on their way to the Fair. Nothing in the story revealed this. Each other illustration, previously shown with its appropriate caption, portrayed the text of the story; yet the grotesque illustration of the Negroes had nothing to do with the story, nor was the picture caption included in this story on "The County Fair." The three horrible, apish-looking, black creatures did have a small boy with them who looked normal. The picture caption was: "Dey's somfin' goin' on."

Typical of the times, the Negro was usually portrayed by whites in books and articles speaking the unknown tongue of a dialect no one but the author understood. Also, typical of the times, the Negro was portrayed as a caricature or joke, as afraid, lazy, docile, and unambitious.

Here again, the news media planted this stereotype, and the books that followed merely mirrored this concept. *Harper's Weekly,* Editorial Section for the week ending May 16, 1903, in its comment on various articles summarized thus: One of the best authorities on Negroes and the Negro problem is Mr. Alfred H. Stone of Greenville, Mississippi, who had many deliverances about the "Southern Blacks." He declares, said *Harper's,* that mulattoes weren't Negroes as such and achieve only because of their Caucasian blood, for the "true Negro," according to Mr. Stone, ". . . is of a contented and happy disposition . . . docile-unambitious . . . with but few wants and those easily satisfied."

About 1903 many articles were written to explain the supremacy of the white man and justify the disenfranchisement of the Negro. True, the 14th Amendment had given the Negro paper citizenship, and the 15th Amendment guaranteed him the right to vote, but there were whites who had to keep before the public the image of his inferiority. Though the Constitution said the Negro was a citizen, he was portrayed, cruelly, as a servant with no real rights; and, there was a school of thought that theorized the Negro, though legally a voter, was not capable of exercising that Constitutionally guaranteed right. The July 18, 1903 (Vol. XLVII) issue of *Harper's,* on the "Negro Problem," reported that Dr. Lyman Abbott, editor of *Outlook,* explained equality of the Negro thus: "Equality does not mean that all men, black and white, are to govern as state executives, as sheriffs, as members of a legislature, or as voters. We are reminded that a boy 16 years of age is equal before the law with a man of 60; but the boy can not vote and the man can." Thus the practice of referring to the Negro always as a "boy" was firmly implanted in the minds of people across the country, and to this very day, to many whites, even the most outstanding educated Negro scholar is still just a boy. Comparably, the Negro woman is a "girl," no matter what her age. The idea of calling all Negro men, even gray-haired old men, "boy," was a carry-over from the days of slavery, and the articles in the early news media insisted that Negroes should not mature to functioning adults, even though they were.

About the time that the 1903 article appeared in *Harper's*, the era of the Negro in the U.S. Congress, State Legislatures, and in high positions in government, had just passed. The molders of public opinion had to eradicate the memory of the fact that the Negro had led commendably . . . even, at one time, signing the paper money issued by the U.S. government before it could be spent. (Blanche K. Bruce, a Negro, was Register of the Treasury under President Garfield).

The white protective societies were flourishing with the old black codes, though supposedly outlawed, to back them up to help "keep the Negro in his place." But, as these societies flourished unchecked, there was a ray of hope for the Negro. White philanthropists and their agencies poured money into the improvement of Negro education in the South . . . a South menaced by the devastating cancer of hatred. This hatred of the Negro was probably fostered by the unspoken realization that the exploitation of the Negro was beating their consciences. As the middle class and poor whites fought to regain some of what they had lost by the ravages of the Civil War, they lashed out openly at the Negro whom they blamed for all their ills. Inwardly, they must have beaten themselves for what they knew they had done to make the situation so bleak. All this was reflected in books and writings of the times for adults, but children got a different kind of story; yet subtly, stories for children added little happiness and joy to the reader's life. Books were mirroring the sadness, frustration, and fear of truth.

In books for children, authors of this frustrated background wrote all sorts of plantation stories and little "ditty" stories purported to show the Negro they told publishers they "knew." Because these authors "played" with them in Alabama, or "grew up" with them on such and such plantation of a relative, they were supposed to know the Negro. Now this was the early 1900's, I must remind you, and down to and through a part of the 1930's we still had only the "plantation" story that showed Negro life to the boys and girls.

The times, certainly, were in turmoil for all people. There was confusion, then a spurt of prosperity, and then depression. All this took its toll. Books were sorely needed about all kinds of children. People wanted books about the Negro, who was really a puzzle to many. The southern white saw the Negro migrate to the north by the thousands. The northern white often met those hordes of people with subtle and open resentment. In the South the Negro was drawing his circle tighter as he kept from the whites his plans to advance above the

menial status of the past to one of leadership and status as the new
citizen he was. In the North the whites pushed the Negro into ghettoes and drew a tight band around that area from which he had few
ways and means at his disposal to escape. So, the Negro closed the
whites out as he made a way of status for himself.

Needed at this point were stories of the happiness within the
Negro communities, north and south. The Negro always found a way
to give hope to his youth and show the brighter side of a very bleak life.
This spirit often gave the outside world the wrong impression. Often
the writings in the journals and news media of the day portrayed the
Negro as always joking and laughing and taking nothing in life seriously. It would be hard to explain the philosophy of life taught
incidentally and sometimes purposefully to the little Negro child and
reemphasized daily as he went out to meet a hostile and fearsome
world. It is almost impossible to explain the humor of the Negro and
what it really means. The impression portrayed in news media and
books of the early times might have mirrored the life and aspirations of
a small percentage of Negroes; yet certainly not the average nor the
whole. Handed down to us, however, were many false stereotypes of
Negro life. The children of the early 1900's are the grandparents who
taught the parents of today, and who are often parents of the open-
minded youth of today who don't want to buy the old half-truths.

The books our grandparents of today read to our parents of today
were what the publishers thought the people wanted to read. The
larger and more established publishers who could afford to gamble on
the market did include a few books about Negro life for children by
authors who were supposed to know the Negro. The stories were
blown up as good literature, and the public accepted them and passed
them down.

A sampling of a few of the books for children might emphasize
what was available.

1890: Pendleton, Louis. *King Tom and the Runaways*. Appleton.
Gr. 7–8. Life in the south before the war—Georgia.

1922: Lindsay, Maud. *Little Missy*. Lothrop. Gr. 4–6. Southern
life before the war—Alabama.

1924: Perkins, L. F. *Colonial Twins of Virginia*. Houghton. Gr.

4–6. Plantation life with a note that the author got her "local color" by staying on a Virginia plantation. (in 1920?).

1929: Bannerman, Helen *Story of Little Black Sambo*. Stokes.

1930: Pyrnelle, L. C. *Diddie, Dumps, and Tot, or Plantation Child Life*. Harpers.

1931: Knox, Rose B. *Miss Jimmy Deane*. Doubleday. Plantation life before the Civil War.

1932–1935: Hogan, Inez. The *Nicodemus* books. Dutton. The *New York Times* in its review stated, ". . . amusing pictures of the little darkey . . . the excellence of the drawings and their humor help to make up for the somewhat commonplace quality of the text." So even then, reviewers realized that they had no stories . . .no real contribution to literature, and that is how they explained it all. . .that the illustrations of the little pickininny would make up for the lack of story.

1935: Credle, Ellis. *Across the Cotton Patch*. Nelson. Gr. . 3–5. Plantation life with "black twins" whose names were "Atlantic" and "Pacific" . . . not even human beings with real children's names.

1936: Bannerman, Helen. *Story of Sambo and the Twins*. Stokes.

1935–1938: Evans, E. K. *Araminta, Araminta's Goat, and Jerome Anthony*. Putnam. City-bred children visit "down home" in the country. These were not the typical plantation stories, and not too bad for the times. This author really seemed to be trying to present the public with acceptable stories.

1937: Braune, Anne. *Honey Chile*. Doubleday. Plantation life again.

1938: Evans, E. K. *Key Corner*. Putnam. The author was trying to show Negro professional life, but the little stereotypes crept in, and it was, I'm sure, unintentional. One writes only what he thinks is so, if he is a sincere writer, and I believe this was a sincere attempt to show that Negroes could be teachers. A new teacher comes to the

Negro school which has had a stern, white one, and this Negro teacher immediately exhibits unconventional behavior . . . she sits on the
desk "swinging her legs like a little girl," doesn't hear giggles and
whispers in the back of the room, and generally shows the laxity
Negroes were said to exhibit. She does bring a better type of education, eventually, for that area and inspires the youth to move up; yet
typically this story, though better than most at that time, had to throw
in subtle untrue stereotypes.

1938: Nolan, E. W. *Shipment for Susannah*. Nelson. Back again
to the plantation.

1938: Lattimore, E. F. *Junior, a Colored Boy of Charleston*.
Harcourt. While this was not a plantation story, the stereotypes that
presented a false image of general Negro life were portrayed . . .
deprivation and lack of a strong father figure are here and were what
the news media of the times portrayed, so one would expect a publisher to accept such a story. The author, I'm sure, was sincere, but
just didn't know enough about many Negro families.

While the Negro was being portrayed on the plantation, or stories of the Civil War life were being rehashed in books, there was just
as little progress in the concepts presented in books about white children. Stories for children were more or less regional, it seemed, and
told of the life of the past, also, with rare exceptions. Stories about
Arizona told of Indians and Mexicans; Arkansas, Ozark Mountain
people; Colorado, ranch life; Idaho, pioneering; Indiana, Quakers,
Dunes, New Harmony; Iowa, farm life; and Kansas, lumbering or the
history of the Kansas territory. Stories about New York and California
included children in modern settings, showing the fascinations of
Hollywood or San Francisco, or the wonders of New York City.

Since books were the only way some children could learn about
the Negro, as they were the one way they could learn about children in
other states, it is unfortunate that stories of plantation life, Civil War
days, deprivation in the South, and general poor living conditions were
the only stories available. White children may have had a rash of
regional stories that also presented life of another day, but they did
have actual contact with all kinds of white children living normal life-
situations in normal family and community settings where there were
laughter and good times. It is a sad commentary, however, that from

the early 1900's up to the 1940's all that seemed known about Negro life was how he had lived on the plantation some 50 years before.

It was the Negro author who was most frustrated during this period. He could and did create, but as he approached publishers with his stories, he was rejected as having nothing of value for the market of that day. Those who wrote for the adult market met with slightly better success, but many manuscripts that could have given a true picture of Negro life went unpublished, while often the manuscripts that showed what people wanted were accepted, though the life was not really that of the average.

Finally the Negro author grew so upset about the image constantly fostered in books and the news media that he found a way to make a contribution. In 1927 a Negro, A. H. Fauset, published *For Freedom* (Franklin Press), a biographical story of the American Negro. Carter G. Woodson published a history of the Negro, incorporating African culture, entitled *Negro Makers of History,* but Dr. Woodson, who promoted the study of Negro History, started an association for the study of Negro Life and History, and had to, also, form his own publishing company (Associated Publishers, still in existence today) so that authentic books about Negro life and history could actually reach the public. After that, more books about the true history and culture of the Negro were published.

In 1933 Charles C. Dawson, a Negro, published a book for young children, *ABC's of Great Negroes,* a series of alphabet pictures of outstanding Negroes, incorporating linoleum cuts with a brief text.

Friendship Press, which today publishes material on the Negro, began as early as 1936 accepting material on the Negro. *We Sing America,* by the Negro, Marion Cuthbert, was one of the contributions of Negro Americans to the culture and development of this country.

Recognizing the frustrations of Negro children in trying vainly to find books with material about their people, a few writers saw that the time was ripe for elementary histories on the Negro for children. Jane D. Shackelford's *Child's Story of the Negro* (Associated Publishers, 1938) filled a great need for children and teachers. After its publication Mrs. Shackelford, who was a teacher in Terre Haute, Indiana, published *My Happy Days,* showing through photographs and some text that some Negro families could live much the same as any other family. This was her sister's family. The sister was a housewife, her husband, a fireman; they lived in a modest, but clean and well-kept home in a Negro neighborhood. The children had what any other family of equal means could afford—nothing elaborate, but a life typical of many other such Negro families. This truly mirrored the times, for though many Negroes didn't fare as well, many lived just as this family lived. (This was my home town. I knew the family and the author.)

Several other books of photographs of Negro life appeared at this time. Stella Sharpe's *Tobe* showed a farm family in North Carolina which, I'm told, presented a true picture of that type of farm life. Books showing the Negro in his school appeared about this time, and added much to the changing concept of the Negro. Many whites did not know that the Negro went to school in the South, which seems hard to believe, but when races are so separated, it is no condemnation that we do not know each other and how each other lives when there are no books to help us.

As publishers began to accept some of the many manuscripts presented them, Negro authors and others kept trying, and with the 1940's more books for children on Negro life succeeded in reaching the public. A few were fictional, but most were nonfiction biographies, probably published in an attempt to show in true lives what had been achieved despite tremendous odds. Or perhaps the publishers were playing it safe in printing mainly true stories. But whatever the reason, the publication of Negro biographies began to dispel many of the myths and stereotypes that had branded the Negro as an inferior non-achiever with few capabilities similar to others, and generally wanting nothing.

Those few fictional works and stories that were published often were objectionable in that they insulted the average Negro who lived just as simply as any other average citizen. The Negro who had little to eat; fought off rats and rodents; froze in unheated, decaying, over-crowded kitchenettes; turned to dope and the cut-throat life of the streets; had no father-figure, but a mother with eight or nine children who turned to Welfare for aid were the types of stories people wanted to read. And isn't this true today? This is the kind of story that gets the rave notices, even today. This kind of story gets in the movies. . . .

10. PORTRAYAL OF THE BLACK IN CHILDREN'S LITERATURE

(Excerpt)

Jessie M. Birtha

. . . LET ME CLEAR UP one question which may be in your mind, as it is the question which I have been asked most often when people approach me on the subject of book selection. "What do you think of *Little Black Sambo?*" I think that the story of *Little Black Sambo* was and is an entertaining story for small children, *but* the development of circumstances concerning the Sambo tradition has been unfortunate. The usefulness of *Little Black Sambo* is dead. The acceptability of *Little Black Sambo* is dead. The story itself is not about an African child. It is about a child in India, and contains little in the slight plot that is objectionable, although as racial sensitivity and pride grew, the book has been dissected and all manner of symbolism attributed to its motivation, including sexual. However, a librarian will never offer this book to a black child if he stops to realize that the name Sambo has been used so often to refer to a Negro in a derogatory sense. Remember that the end man in the minstrel show, the stupid one who was the butt of all the jokes, was Sambo. The ventriloquist's little black, red-lipped dummy was named Sambo. *Webster's Third New International Dictionary* defines Sambo as "Negro, mulatto, perhaps from Kongo *nzambu*, monkey. Often capital: NEGRO—usually used disparagingly."

The argument has been offered, children don't know or care about the background of a name. They only listen to the story. But it has been proved—and experienced—that if a story of this type is used in an integrated story hour or classroom, there is a certain amount of discomfort and—yes, inferiority feeling—for a black child when white classmates look at him and giggle, later teasing him by calling him Sambo. No matter how entertaining a book is, one group of children should never be entertained at the expense of another group's feelings.

The same is true of another once popular classic, *Epaminondas and His Auntie*, by Sara Cone Bryant. The illustrations portraying a stupid, trifling, big-lipped black boy and his equally worthless looking aunty, spoil for Negro children and their parents the same story line which they happily accept when presented in the Lazy Jack version. The two books mentioned were written long ago, but are still available. (A new edition of *Epaminondas* by Eve Merriam, illustrated by Trina Schart Hyman, offers a change from the original edition.)

I am not saying that I advocate destroying all of the existing copies of such books. These books have been classics in children's literature and as such have value for adults in tracing the development of black children's literature. However, I feel that at this time, their existence should be relegated to the historical collection in the children's library. To these, I might add *Dr. Dolittle* and *Mary Poppins* in their original form, and I have never really advocated rewriting a book to improve its acceptability once it has been in circulation. Mark Twain, Booth Tarkington, and Harriet Beecher Stowe's *Uncle Tom's Cabin* may be considered from a somewhat different viewpoint. Children are older when these are read, and should be encouraged to evaluate the stories in the light of the time in which they were written.

Part III

RACISM IN 20TH-CENTURY FICTION AND BIOGRAPHY

11. *WORDS BY HEART:* A BLACK PERSPECTIVE

Rudine Sims

Words by Heart is the latest book honored by the literary establishment even though it perpetuates negative images and stereotypes. An American Book Award nominee and winner of the 1980 International Reading Association's Children's Book Award, it has been praised in many library publications. It joins such books as *The Cay, Sounder* and *The Slave Dancer* in purportedly presenting a sympathetic picture of Blacks even as it misinforms readers and reinforces racist attitudes. Like the other prize winners, it has been honored for the excellence of the author's craft, but it is flawed because it presents an outsider's perspective on Black lives and fails to recognize the political, racial and social realities that shape the Black Experience in this country. And like *The Cay*, it features the death of a "noble" Black man, that very expendable literary creation.

Based on a short story published in 1968, *Words by Heart* shares with other late sixties children's fiction about Blacks the implied purpose of raising the consciousness of white readers to racial injustice. *The Horn Book* suggests that "it dramatizes the Black people's long struggle for equal opportunity and freedom," but the dramatization fails because the statements the book makes about the human condition are fallacious. Unlike books written from a Black perspective—Mildred Taylor's *Roll of Thunder, Hear My Cry*, for example—*Words by Heart*, for all its literary artistry, fails to do more than evoke pity and compassion through heartrending sentimentality. (*School Library Journal* labeled the book "a finely honed heartwrencher.")

On the surface this is a well-written, poignant story, offering such time-honored themes as "Love thy neighbor" and "Overcome evil with good." (See Editor's Note that appears on p. 128.) The Sills family is portrayed as warm, close and strong. The father is, in many ways, admirable—wanting a better life for his family and placing a high value on education. However, the portrait of this Black family, supposedly seen from its center (Lena's point of view), is out of focus. The viewpoint remains that of an ethnocentric outsider. In its totality, the book perpetuates some negative images, some tired stereotypes and some implicit themes that are, from a Black perspective, questionable at the very least. There are both major and minor problems.

One problem, indicative of the book's perspective, is the tendency to associate things black with things negative. There is the minor incident when Ben takes one look at a new kitten and names him Old Nick because he is "a little black devil." There are uninviting descriptions of the Black characters. Ben Sills' hands are "perched on his knees like spiders ready to jump." Lena sees in her reflection "spiky plaits and a rascal face." At the contest, "Then everybody looked at Lena, smiling behind their eyes because she was different and comical looking, oozing like dark dough over the edges of last year's Sunday dress." No matter that *everybody* in this case includes her family, who would hardly view her that way. The rest of the audience is "an orchard of pink-cheeked peaches," and the standard of beauty that is invoked reflects their ethnocentric perspective.

The main problem with Scattercreek, too, seems to have been that it was all Black. While the move west represented potential freedom from the oppression prevalent in the South of that era, the book suggests that Scattercreek also provided refuge, but was inferior because it was an all-Black town. Sills explains that because they could not live in some Southern towns, Black people made "their own communities like Scattercreek, with their own schools and churches and stores. It eases some of the trouble." And "She [Claudie] felt safe when we moved to Scattercreek." But then he says, ". . . it was easier there, but I wasn't proud of myself." Earlier he had said, "I wanted *more* for us than Scattercreek" (emphasis added). What is not clear is what Bethel Springs offers that is more, and why he was not proud to live in an all-Black town. He does cite his right as a U.S. citizen to live where he chooses, but the implication is that he chose an all-white town because there was something shameful about living in an all-Black one. This attitude contrasts to positive descriptions, like those given by Zora Neale Hurston of the richness of life in Eatonville, Florida, the "pure Negro" town in which she was born.

It is through Sills' talks with Lena that the most insidious messages about the nature of racism occur. Sills stubbornly refuses to acknowledge racism as the motivation for the hatred the Haneys—and others—express. There are threats and namecalling, the mysterious death of the Sills' dog, a knife thrust through a fresh loaf of bread the night Lena wins the contest. Yet Sills insists: "This is a good town we've come to . . . they took us in." He attributes whites' behavior to their fear of change or to their hopelessness and frustrations with being poor sharecroppers, rather than to racism. He proposes that the white people's actions be met with understanding: "It's not your place to judge people," he tells Lena. "That's for God." When Sills' wife Claudie urges him to tell Lena about racism and about the family's earlier experiences in the South, Sills softens the telling with the suggestion that the isolation Claudie experiences in a white town exaggerates her fears that those "bad old times" could happen again. Although Ben does recognize that, even in Bethel Springs, some cannot accept them, for the most part Claudie's fears are made to seem almost unreasonable in this "good town." (Moreover, the "bad old times" were hardly past since this story takes place during the period historians call "The Nadir" because it was a time of intensified violence and brutality against Blacks; there is no sense of this reality in the book, however.)

When discussing the family's history and the Black Experience in general, Sills refuses to place the blame where it belongs: "They reconstructed us—one little loss at a time. . . . Somehow we got put in our place again." The anonymous, unspecified forces at work are never labeled, never named. The violence that Black people experienced in the post-Civil War period is only touched on in one brief paragraph and, in fact, some of the historical information given is not correct. (Black people did not, for example, only *begin* to read and write after the Civil War; freed people aside, many slaves learned to read and write, even when it was illegal. And to say about the Civil War, "all those people fighting for our rights," as Sills does, is to minimize the role that Black people played in fighting for their own freedom). The entire section is clearly a contrived bit of writing designed to bring in some historical information.

The most overtly racist behavior comes from unsympathetic characters whose behavior can be "explained away" in large part by their situation or personality traits. The Haneys are stereotypes of poor-white Southerners—lazy, hard-drinking, irresponsible, gun-toting males, dirty children and women kept barefoot, pregnant and silent. Another prejudiced person in the story is Mrs. Chism, the woman for whom both Sills and Haney work and from whom Ben Sills rents his home. She is an eccentric elderly woman—lonely, unhappy, seemingly oblivious to the effects of placing Sills and Haney in competition with each other and indifferent to the effects of her sharp-tongued barbs on other people. Neither her own children nor her neighbors like her, and only one person attends what was meant to be her large and elaborate dinner party. The pompous school teacher at one point asserts the inferiority of Blacks and is disputed by Lena and a white boy whose father then forbids him to associate further with Lena. Predictably in a book of this type, at the end of the story the boy openly and publicly defies his father to befriend Lena's family, an act which lacks credibility. In any case, the portrayal of the "bad guys" as mostly atypical or unlikeable people projects a picture of a utopian town where racism is an aberration.

Moreover, the cumulative picture of Ben Sills is the prototype of the "good Negro"—hard-working, Bible-quoting, understanding, passive, loving and forgiving towards whites, and willing to "wait on the Lord" until whites are ready to accept his family. (Sills' favorite Bible verse is "They that wait upon the Lord shall renew their strength. . . .") Sills lives to serve others—and those others (outside of his family) are white. When Lena asks why her family must always work for others, Sills replies: "What's wrong with working for people? That's what we are here for, to serve each other. . . ." That is a questionable generalization, since no whites "serve" any Blacks in the story. This stereotypic portrait of passivity does not advance the art of writing about the Black Experience, and in the late 1970's it need not have been perpetuated.

The characterization of Sills will be justified by the fact that he had wanted to be a minister, but it is false to equate godliness with passivity. Furthermore, Black ministers have been in the forefront of the struggle for freedom. Dr. Martin Luther King, Jr. was non-violent, but not passive. His counsel was not to "wait on the Lord," but to recognize "why we can't wait."

Many works, both fictional and historical, provide alternative portraits. Nate Shaw's story, told in *All God's Dangers*, and even the popular *Roots*, suggest that Ben Sills is unreal. Even James Weldon Johnson, a staunch integrationist, wrote in 1934 in *Negro Americans, What Now?*, "There come times when the most persistent integrationist becomes an isolationist, when he curses the white world and consigns it to Hell. This tendency toward isolation is strong because it springs from a deep-seated, natural desire—a desire for respite from the unremitting, grueling struggle; for a place in which refuge might be taken." It is the recognition of this truth that is glossed over in the portrait of Ben Sills.

The most disturbing aspect of this book is its ending. Given the characterization of Ben Sills, it is entirely consistent for him to crawl, though fatally wounded, a considerable distance to help Tater, his attacker. (Sills doesn't even try to leave to get help for himself; that option "never occurred to him.") Given the described relationship between Lena and her father, it is also consistent for her to help Tater—for her father's sake and for the sake of her own humanity. But only if one can equate justice with vengeance can the message implicit in Lena's decision to lie about her knowledge of her father's murder be seen as consistent behavior—or acceptable. The message is that if a white boy, as part of his rite of passage into male adulthood, even goes so far as to kill a Black person, the proper Christian response is to "let God handle it." (Can you imagine literary prizes bestowed on a book in which a rotten Black boy murders an angelic white man and is forgiven by the white man's daughter?) That message remains un-tempered despite the intimation that Tater may eventually be healed both physically and morally, and despite the closing scene in which Tater's father silently picks the cotton of the family his son has made fatherless. He knows that the cotton crop represents money the Sills family will need to survive, but the question of whether his helping is motivated by remorse, guilt or a desire to buy Lena's continued silence is left unanswered. Given the characterization of Haney as hate-filled and lacking in hope, Lena's hope that he has acquired a new sense of morality is totally unfounded.

The message is certainly untempered by Claudie's speech to Mrs. Chism and other white town leaders. Says Claudie:

"We know how to earn our keep and we know how to knuckle to you. Only we mean to work and knuckle the way we choose to, and where we choose to. I have two boys coming up to be the same threat to you all that Ben was. You better be ready for them because I'm going to have them ready for you."

The idea that hard work and submission and gradualism will overcome is untenable. Hard work is no threat to people on whom one depends for one's livelihood. Hard work was never a defense against oppression; it is not today. This is an irresponsible message to give to any young readers. In addition, Claudie's dramatic speech misses the point, touched on earlier in the book, that it is Lena's facile mind and her thirst for knowledge that are the real potential threat.

"Love thy neighbor" and "overcome evil with good" are worthwhile themes. In an ideal world, where racial differences don't count, it wouldn't matter which characters exemplify those themes. However, in a book set in the real world, where racial differences *do* count, when the responsibility for loving, forgiving and overcoming evil with good lies solely with the book's Black characters, the action takes on racist overtones. The implication is that white people should be understood and forgiven, even for violent racist acts. In all likelihood, many aware young Black readers will reject this message, and the book with it. They understand that passivity will not cure racism. Others may not be so aware. If they, along with young white readers, come away with the message that passivity is acceptable and that whites are to be forgiven rather than held accountable for racist actions, the damage will be doubly done.

In these troubled times, when the KKK still operates on the assumption that they can threaten and kill with relative impunity, it is important to recognize that *Words by Heart* invokes a third Judeo-Christian tenet—"Thou shalt not kill." A prize-winning book that plays "overcome evil with good" against "thou shalt not kill" has a responsibility to see that the latter receives equal time.

Editor's Note: A plot summary accompanied this article when it was first published, and one may be helpful here. Ben Sills and his family moved in 1910 from Scattercreek, an all-Black town in the South, to Bethel Springs, an otherwise all-white town in the Southwest. Sills' twelve-year-old, Lena, wins a school contest and otherwise displays a quickness of mind that is disquieting to the local residents. While Sills is mending the landowner's fences, he is fatally shot by a poor white sharecropper's son, Tater. Tater is thrown from his horse, and Lena finds her dying father trying to keep the boy alive. Sills extracts a promise from Lena to help Tater and not identify him as her father's murderer.

12. FALSE FLATTERY AND THIN HISTORY: A STUDY OF THREE NOVELS FOR CHILDREN

Opal Moore

> They stood gazing at the artificial Negro as if they were faced with some great mystery, some monument to another's victory that brought them together in their common defeat. They could both feel it dissolving their differences like an action of mercy. . . .
>
> "The Artificial Nigger"
> Flannery O'Connor

IN 1953, FLANNERY O'CONNOR touched upon the odd psychological necessity behind the creation of the cast-in-iron Sambo figurine with its standard matte black face, grinning broad lips, and white eyes. The artificial Negro represented a mass psychological need to reduce Black people to the simple lines of caricature—substitute icon for the living, breathing, complex reality.

It could be argued that the persistence of this image in the conscious and subconscious mind has done more to frustrate the hopes of Black people for mobility and parity than any other single phenomenon. It is both artifact and symbol. It reveals the manner in which Black people have been represented in American historical record—a representation that distorts the meaningful contribution and impact of Black people on American history and society. For O'Connor, the little black figure seemed to exert a strange power over those whites who viewed it, the power to dispel the superficial differences of age, culture, or class and allow them to unite within the myth of their racial superiority.

The struggle against racism could, in large part, be described as a struggle to displode this symbol and its conjunctive myths, to counter their paralyzing effect on Black life in America.

This struggle for control of our representative symbols is a primary distraction in a trilogy of novels for young readers: *Jump Ship to Freedom, War Comes to Willy Freeman,* and *Who Is Carrie?,* created by James Lincoln and Christopher Collier. Apparent in these books is the authors' struggle between what is true, and what is comfortingly familiar. Although intended for children, these three books should be of interest to all who are involved in defining the images of the past and present: to white Americans who have traditionally celebrated their historical triumphs while burying the legacy of American injustice; to Blacks who wish to unearth their history and resurrect those heroes who are obliterated beneath the embarrassments of the nation; to all those with the courage to step outside their own myths.

The artificial "nigger," as in O'Connor's figurine, must be understood. He is not myth, but artifice. He can reveal a white psychology while obscuring Black reality. He is a means of absolution. He is made to grin at the garish absurdity of his own existence as if he were a self-created, insignificant joke, and not the worship stone of racism. He is as real as an idea. And he is not dead.

The flaws in this trilogy of historical novels relate to these questions of history, art, and the substance of an image.

The use of the "Black" narrators in *Jump Ship to Freedom, War Comes to Willy Freeman,* and *Who Is Carrie?* might lead some to automatically assume that these books present a Black perspective on American history, or that they would be especially appropriate for Black children. These are not valid assumptions. Dan Arabus, Willy Freeman, and Carrie, the respective Black protagonists of these novels, offer very little insight into the lives, thoughts, or relationships of Black people living during the Revolutionary War era. Strangely enough, the authors' decision to use "Black" narrators seems to have included only a marginal awareness of the need to construct a textural reality or historical context for these fictional Black youngsters of the late 1700's. In many instances, they seem content to impose upon their Black characters beliefs and habits more typical of the European immigrants of the period.

This tendency is demonstrated in the explanations the authors themselves offer in the Afterword called, "How Much Of This Book Is True?" For example, in *War Comes to Willy Freeman,* the Colliers state that, although they are not certain how people of the period spoke, "we are more sure about the attitudes that Willy and others around her had—the idea that women were inferior to men, blacks to whites, children to adults. Almost all historians agree that such ideas were held by nearly all Americans of the Revolutionary Era." Clearly, the "nearly all" of their reference would have been European/American males who brought these beliefs with them from the "old world." There is no reason to believe that African women considered themselves inferior to men, mentally or physically. In their homelands, although their roles were highly defined, they were often independent agents, accustomed to providing for themselves and their children while still giving respect to their husbands. The weak, dependent, stay-at-home female ideal was a white male notion which was never intended to protect the Black woman and therefore did not hinder her. Black people, on the whole, acknowledged the implications of their captivity (or political powerlessness) and taught their children, not the lesson of inferiority, but the lesson of survival: to defer to forces that might damage or destroy them. The "nearly all" who believed in the inherent inferiority of women were usually men, especially white men. The "nearly all" who believed in the inherent inferiority of Black people were unquestionably "nearly all" white. In *Jump Ship*, the concept of Black inferiority is presented as an idea that Dan Arabus holds true of himself, rather than the propaganda of oppression. In *War*, Willy and her mother are presented as totally accepting of the concept of male superiority. The idea of female inferiority is presented as a concept that women entertained about themselves, rather than the self-serving edict of a male ego. What becomes apparent is that the Colliers have reduced reality to a white and/or male reality.

Another topic that is addressed in the Afterword is the problem of the authors' use of epithets. The Colliers explain that since the words "nigger" and "darky" were frequently used in America, to omit them would be a distortion of history. It is true that the term "nigger" has been used by whites and Blacks alike; it is also true that the use of this word by Blacks occurs in decidedly different contexts, for vastly different purposes, and is nearly always ironic or self-protective—a distinction never made in the Collier books. What is suspect about the abundant use of "nigger" is the apparent contempt for authentic detail in other more significant aspects of these books. The authors seem perfectly willing to sacrifice the consistency of their fictional characterizations for the sake of supporting a stereotypical theme or story line. Given the admission that not much is known of actual speech patterns of that period, and the authors' compromise to a modernized style of speech, the inclusion of "nigger" and "darky" with such oppressive frequency and inaccurate application would appear selective and not merely in the interest of authenticity.

Adherence to a totally white perspective and context exposes the authors' lack of commitment to a broader historical perspective. Presenting this white perspective through Black fictional mouthpieces suggests subterfuge. This narrational device creates conflict within the novels, a tension which subtly alters the meaning of all that is presented—the positive becomes negative, the negative becomes fact.

Sambo On My Mind—Irony and Absolution

"'If I wasn't just a stupid nigger, I'd have seen it before,'" says Dan Arabus (the protagonist in *Jump Ship to Freedom*) in a typical self-evaluation. The decision to utilize Black slaves as narrators in the three "Arabus" novels is the most interesting and perplexing aspect of these Collier books. Perhaps the most disturbing aspect is the careful ambivalence with which the Black characters are presented—a juggling act which alternately validates and discredits them.

In *Jump Ship,* the first of the three novels, we meet Dan Arabus, a brave and self-sufficient 14 year old who seeks to redeem the face value of his dead father's soldier's notes in order to buy himself and his mother out of slavery. In chilren's literature, it is widely accepted that the protagonist will be a likeable, admirable character, somewhat resembling the targeted reader that the reader can identify with. Dan Arabus, with his overriding desire to be free and his willingness to take risks in gaining that freedom, could have been such a character. Unfortunately, he is not. Instead, the authors chose to create an anomaly by imposing upon him a white belief system—the presumption of his own inherent inferiority. On the second page of this story, Dan describes himself as a stupid nigger, an admission which would certainly alienate any young reader, Black or white. The origins of these statements are carefully attributed to a minister, but the minister never appears in the novel and, therefore, his participation is no more than a footnote. At any rate, it is quite clear that Dan agrees with him.

While Dan's derogatory references to himself may have been intended to provide an ironic contrast to the bravery and intelligence of his actions, they, instead, cause him to appear ignoble. It would have been more effective, and less damaging to the reader's ability to care about Dan, if he were confronted with this prejudice in dramatic action, rather than made to present these ideas as his own. A young reader may wonder why Dan has accepted such a self-assessment, but will probably accept his evaluation of himself at face value. The fact that the first of such statements appears on the second page of the book disallows even the possibility that the reader might have developed affinity for the character. Dan's credibility is undermined still further when he presents arguments disputing the "logic" of racism and white supremacy but never approaches self-enlightenment. Consequently, even if the reader could perceive Dan as a character who is confused about the notions imposed upon him by a hostile society, his tendency to overlook the truth of his own observations would surely persuade the reader that Dan is not tragic, just pitifully stupid. Apart from the fact of his captivity, which is not portrayed as particularly cruel (and in spite of which he seems to enjoy amazing mobility), nothing is presented within the book to indicate why Dan has chosen to believe what he does. It might even appear that Dan believes himself to be inferior because he actually *is*. Dan is portrayed as good-hearted but stupid, "nice" yet dishonorable, and the victim of his own ignorance.

It is possible that Dan's negative statements are intended to present his inner conflict—society's teachings of Black inferiority vs. his personal awareness of his father's strength and bravery, the accomplishments of other Black people, etc. But Dan is never presented as a boy with an interior, psychological conflict. He appears comfortable with the idea of his own inferiority; he never rejects these concepts in his mind but repeats them as bland fact. This conflict is, typically, represented through polemic: Dan dispassionately outlines both sides of the issue of his intelligence with only marginal interest:

I wished I'd thought to grease the hinges the night before. . . . If I wasn't so ignorant I might have thought of it. Probably a white boy would have. But I was black and wasn't as smart as white folks. Leastwise, that's what Mr. Leaming, the minister, always said, although when you got down to it, my daddy was pretty smart, and he was black. (2)

Dan's lack of a real inner conflict and his failure to resist the derogatory labels thrust upon him, are responsible for a lack of believability in the character. It is a serious problem within the book, and is a direct result of the authors' failure to permit emotion or response in their characters—an issue to be dealt with later.

The Colliers' use of irony within the novel is abundant. Both verbal and situational irony is employed. Situational irony usually relies upon unreliable narrators—narrators who present the reader with false "facts" or inaccurate interpretations of events due either to their dishonest nature, or through their stupidity. It is expected that the reader will "see through" the device and perceive the truth in spite of the narrator's lack of intelligence. The reader is intended to know more about the narrator's situation than the narrator himself/herself. This device is useful and powerful in some literary situations. But it would not seem advisable to try to convince a reader of the protagonist's intelligence by presenting this character as unreliable due to his or her own stupidity.

But Dan Arabus is unreliable. He consistently distorts his own "reality" by failing to use the facts available to him. Dan declares himself stupid at the same time that he is outwitting his foe. He labels his father a nigger at the precise moment that Mr. Fatherscreft, a friendly Quaker, describes him as a hero. Dan brags about his slave market value in the same breath that he claims his right to freedom so that he may "own" himself. The reader is expected to perceive these contradictions and "realize" Dan's native intelligence. However, Dan's daring adventures—the recovery of his father's notes, his escape from his master's ship, his successful evasion of the traitorous Black slave Big Tom, etc.—cannot disprove Dan's claims to stupidity simply because the structure of the irony will not allow it. The mere fact that Dan cannot perceive what is plainly obvious reinforces his claim to stupidity. It is difficult to admire or identify with this narrator who, at best, inspires pity. Because Dan appears so unintelligent, his ingenuity in escaping dangers seems merely cunning. Dan's adventures provide action and suspense, but do little to mitigate the evidence of his larger stupidity. And there is no neat trick available to contradict the label of "nigger".

Irony in a children's book is not, of itself, objectionable. But the manner in which irony is used here appears to directly contradict the authors' established purpose. It is through the misuse of this literary device that the image of the "stupid nigger" is successfully invoked but never successfully rescinded. For example, Mr. Fatherscreft tries to convince Dan that, based on the bravery of his actions, he could actually be considered intelligent. However, a superficial analysis of the use of language and image in this scene reveals the authors' contradictory use of irony. The language and images associated with Dan countermine Fatherscreft's assertion of Dan's intelligence:

I scratched my head. "I'm blamed if I can see how that could happen sir," I said. . . . (113)

I was beginning to feel pretty stupid. . . .(113)

I scratched my head again, feeling more stupid. "I don't rightly know," I finally said. . . . (114)

Once Mr. Fatherscreft spelled it out point by point like that, I could understand it. "If I wasn't just a stupid nigger, I'd have seen it before," I said. (116)

The repetition of negative terms and images in reference to the narrator transforms him, in direct contrast to the regal and fatherly image of Fatherscreft, into a head-scratching, open-mouthed imitation of the Stepin Fetchit model. And it should be noted that in juxtaposition to this image of Dan is the depiction of the unseen but ever present white "heroes"—the founding fathers. In rather exalted language, the reader sees the magnitude of their preoccupations:

The greatest men from twelve of the thirteen states are gathered in Philadelphia to try to write a constitution. . . . (113)

Some of us are especially worried about the black people of America. Many of us want slavery abolished. (114)

Emphasis is placed upon the idea that Mr. Fatherscreft, and other white men, believe in the equality of Black people and oppose their enslavement. It is not unintentional that it is the slave, Dan Arabus, who has initiated the issue of his inferiority and who, almost single-handedly, has promoted himself as stupid, ignorant, and unworthy. It becomes clear that Dan's self-derogation has been contrived for the pay-off of this "high" irony. However, such use of irony takes dangerous liberty with history and misrepresents the struggle of Black people to retain their dignity while seeking equality.

It becomes evident that no white character in the book has disparaged Blacks to the extent that Dan has belittled them. Even

Captain Ivers, the "evil" slaveholder, never deprecates Dan's mental capacity or implies that he is inherently inferior. Heightening the irony of this situation, when Mr. Fatherscreft informs Dan that he is wrong to consider himself "just a stupid nigger," Dan balks and responds as if the thought of his own human worth (in spite of his bid for freedom) had never occurred to him:

It confused me. When you figured you was one kind of person all your life, it's hard to start thinking of yourself as another kind. I reckoned I'd have to think about it some more. (116,117)

This creates ancillary questions of logic and motivation—why does Dan seek his freedom if he has never considered himself as worthy as the people who hold him in bondage?

The Colliers effectively absolve white people of the psychological burden of a racist system by saddling their ignoble "hero" with the blame of his own dehumanization. There is little sense of Black people as constituting a self-protecting community, as resisting the mentally and emotionally debilitating effects of slavery. There is no indication of the role that family played in maintaining a sense of self. The characterization of Dan maintains a distance between the reader and the narrator. The likeable Fatherscreft is portrayed as a white man weary from the work of encouraging Black people to accept their human worth, and fighting for their salvation and liberty. In fact, the reader is more likely to identify with Mr. Fatherscreft who poignantly dies on his journey to strike "the best bargain he can" for Blacks. The reader's relationship with Dan is more likely to be that of judgmental observer rather than participant. This psychological distance is not likely to foster a clear understanding of the social politics of the period. Dan is never allowed to become a person, nor even a viable fictional character, but remains a pawn who is manipulated to his own dishonor and, by extension, the dishonor of the Black people of his period.

Dan's manipulation as a fictional character is one thing. However, similar compromises for the sake of irony are evident in the treatment of historical incident. For example, even though Dan is a slave, the condition of slavery is downplayed throughout the novel. It is later trivialized in a scene where Mr. Fatherscreft dies and entrusts Dan to deliver to the men of the Constitutional Convention the terms of his future enslavement. When Dan foregoes the opportunity to escape into free territory and "chooses" to deliver this compromising message, his decision creates in the novel the ultimate irony: that a slave would have voluntarily delivered the slave compromise. But the reader will surely infer from this that Dan's quest for freedom is not so urgent after all, and not the best means by which to free his mother. It is more important that he not break his word to a dead man. Black historical figures are dealt with in a similar fashion.

The Collier novels introduce three Black characters based on real historical figures—Jack Arabus (Dan's father), Black Sam Fraunces (a businessman), and Jordan Freeman (Willy's father). However, the racial make-up of Sam Fraunces, a renowned restauranteur of the period, is made a constant point of contention and Jordan Freeman is only summarily dealt with, leaving Jack Arabus as the primary Black individual of accomplishment to be featured in the three novels. The narrator describes his father as "a great hero." However, Dan considers his father a hero, not because he served with distinction in the Revolutionary War (fighting for his own and his family's freedom) but because he once assisted George Washington across a shallow river, thereby preventing the general from getting his feet wet. Even though it may be understood that this is the type of picturesque incident that a child would remember and enlarge upon, the fact is, the actual accomplishments of this man are withheld from the reader until much later. Through the unreliability of the narrator, Arabus is not made to appear heroic, but ironic.

It is Mr. Fatherscreft who reveals Jack Arabus' actual accomplishment. He explains to Dan that his father's real heroism involved his suing of Captain Ivers, his former owner, for his freedom. His victory guaranteed, at least in theory, that Black slaves who fought in their master's stead, would not be cheated of their freedom (if they survived). Fatherscreft's admiration for Arabus is undermined by specious language placed in the mouth of Dan:

. . . But for a black man to sue a white man, just like he was as good as anybody, why, that was a terrible daring thing to do.

The indulgent tone of this statement alters the superficial meaning of Dan's words like a pat on the head. The ambiguity here could go unnoticed but Arabus' heroic stature is further compromised when Dan exclaims, "Was my daddy the first nig—. . . Negro who did something like this?" This "slip of the tongue" is, of course, no slip. The timing is impeccable. Prior to this scene, Dan frequently refers to himself as a "nigger," but never even thought of his father in this manner. Because this slip is not consistent with Dan's earlier perceptions or statements concerning his father, it seems to stand out as the authors' insertion of a timeworn qualifier: but he's still a "nigger." The use of Dan in stating this qualifier is diversion. Dan's references to his father provide a counterpoint of "misstatements." These responses are almost comic in their exaggeration, reducing the Quaker's sincere words of praise for Arabus to the level of indulgence that adults lavish on the helpless. Dan's comment, "just like he was as good as anybody" cues the reader that, in Dan's opinion, Arabus was in fact *not* as good as anybody. Through Dan, the reader will surely perceive that a man cannot be a "nigger" and a hero at the same time.

Dan is manipulated to discredit himself and, in the process, all that he represents. The portions of historical record that are introduced into the novels and pertain to Blacks seem to self-destruct. Jack Arabus, a man of high accomplishment, is tentatively depicted as brave and admirable. But this view is then invalidated. Establishing a fact or character and then dismantling it through the use of irony, inconsistency, insinuation, or just plain slapstick is a pattern in the Collier novels. The very people with whom the authors purport to sympathize are discredited.

What results from these books is the reincarnation of the image of Sambo, and all of his made-in-America progeny. The artificial "nigger" is not dead but lives between the lines of false flattery and thin history.

Character vs. Caricature

A good deal of the difficulty with the use of irony in the "Arabus" books is directly attributable to the authors' use of caricature as a substitute for true character delineation. The one-dimensionality of Dan Arabus, Willy, and Carrie does not bear the weight of the novels' indulgence in ironic contradiction. Moreover, because these characters are denied serious treatment, the impact of the historical issues in the three novels—denial of human freedom based on color, the daily peril of Black life, the hypocrisy that was built into the foundations of American democracy, the anonymity of being Black in America—the substance of these issues is frequently not apparent. The lack of character depth is largely due to the authors' refusal to reveal the natural responses or emotions of the narrators. They are stilted and bloodless, merely "reporting" on their activities. The combined effect of the flat style of writing and the unresponsive narrators is deadly.

In *Jump Ship to Freedom*, when Mr. Fatherscreft explains to Dan the manner in which Black people will be compromised by the formation of the new government, the expected reactions of anger, indignation, desperation, or even fear, do not occur in Dan's thoughts and are not reflected in his actions.

(Mr. Few) and Mr. Fatherscreft was bargaining out what would happen to us black people if a new constitution got written. It was sort of queer that it was all going to be decided by white folks . . . but we had to be thankful that at least there was some white people around like Mr. Fatherscreft. . . . (139)

After a discussion of the Fugitive Slave Law which would enforce the return of escaped slaves from free territory and threaten the freedom of free Black persons, Dan responds:

Oh, it made me sad and sick to think of it. But there wasn't anything I could do about it. . . . I tell you, I was pretty mixed up in my feelings. . . . (139)

Anger is circumvented by gratitude. Determination to be free is undermined by an emphasis on Dan's feelings of helplessness (reinforcing the belief that Black people have merely waited for their freedom to be granted to them by benevolent whites). Flat and ineffective language such as "it was queer" and "pretty mixed up" are supposed to represent the quaint simplicity of the uneducated slave's expressive capacity. However, lack of education or vocabulary should not eliminate the complexity of Dan's feelings. The device of the authors that denies Dan any range in his verbal expression also denies him the depth of his emotions. There is nothing in Dan's reported thoughts or actions to indicate his feelings of betrayal as white men barter him like beads.

The minimization of central, emotion-laden issues by denial of narrator response is a consistent feature of the Collier novels. For example, in *War Comes to Willy Freeman,* two Black soldiers suspect that Willy, despite her short hair, is not a boy. To test their theory, one reaches out and grabs her breasts. Neither Willy nor her mother makes any protest or comment. Willy says to the reader:

It gave me a queer, dirty feeling to have him mess with my body like that. . . .
(11)

After a few seconds of this, Willy's father steps through the door and
saves the day. The scene is intended to emphasize the passive roles
that women were expected to play and their utter helplessness and
defenselessness against men during that period. However, the authors'
theme does not accommodate the demands of reality. No Black mother, who would certainly be familiar with the threat of rape and be
accustomed to looking out for her own and her children's survival,
would allow her daughter to be handled without even a verbal protest.
And, again, there is the ineffectual, non-committal language and denial of real emotion. Instead of making some move to free herself from
the soldier's grasp, or expressing shock, disbelief, anger (any of the
possible reactions a young girl coming into womanhood would be likely
to have) she responds by considering how "queer" it feels. Furthermore, after the soldiers leave, there is no further mention of the
incident by Willy *or* her parents. Willy, apparently, has learned nothing from this, and neither will the reader.

In *War,* the spectre of rape is, again, obliquely broached when
Willy encounters a group of idle white soldiers who also suspect her
gender. The rape is clumsily diverted but, rather than consider the
perilous nature of her existence as a Black woman or come to some
conclusions about the base nature of a society which victimizes her
both sexually and racially, the incident is transformed into a bad joke.
Willy reveals two roasted potatoes she has been storing underneath
her shirt, convincing the men that these were her "breasts." The
reader is expected to believe that such a group of men would be so
easily fooled or so polite they would not check for themselves (after all,
the Black soldiers did so). After her escape, Willy simplistically concludes, "It was pretty clear that I'd better go on being a boy for a
while," (77) suggesting that a Black boy would not have comparable
dangers to face but, more importantly, diverting the attention of the
reader away from the real issue. At the same time, the reader is
encouraged to laugh at Willy's peril and its deeper implications. It is
routine in the "Arabus" novels for the authors to introduce serious
topics but then decline to deal with them.

In *War,* the issues of sexism and racism are obfuscated when
Willy seems to have no response to her own victimization. The sin-
gling out of Black women for sexual assault is suggested, but then

avoided with a slapstick gambit or example of male bravado and ter-
ritoriality. The wartime sacrifices made by Black soldiers—men who
would be rewarded only with the deeper entrenchment of the institution of slavery—is never explored. Willy witnesses the death of her
father, a violent death by bayonet, but does not grieve for him or
consider the worthless sacrifice of his life. Throughout the book, she
merely represents the image of his death by flinging open her arms in a
simpleminded imitation of his death pose—a coyness in the writing
that is inappropriate to the subject.

In *Who Is Carrie?*, the title character's search for her identity is
reduced to the activity of wondering who her parents are. Though her
search, on this level, is not an unimportant search for a child, Carrie
never achieves the symbolic level of her search—the larger issue of
Black heritage. Despite the use of the institution of slavery as a back-
drop for action, no mention whatsoever is made of the origins of these
slaves. In fact, their African origins are never made apparent. Questions of where they come from, how they came to be in America, what
it must have meant for Black African men and women (with memories
of Africa intact) to live here in chains, questions regarding the meaning of freedom or why it is so ardently sought by Dan, Willy, and
Carrie—these questions are never raised or answered.

The one-dimensionality of the characters is further accomplished through a paucity of physical description, or in some instances,
a distortion of cultural detail. For example, Dan describes his father as
"tall and stern"—a typical, Victorian/Puritan "father-type" description, not designed to make Jack Arabus visual. The 12-year-old
female, Willy Freeman, (mistakeable for a boy even though she has
breasts) is said to have short hair. In *Who Is Carrie?*, the physical
appearance of the Black characters is pretty much a mystery except for
references to their ability to blush. In the latter example, it is probable
that the use of the term "blush" has less to do with the cast of their
complexions as with the authors' contentment to "describe" Black
characters in non-descriptive terms.

It is important to note that the white characters are given no
more depth of treatment than the Black; however, this does not justify
the practice. Their failure to resemble reality serves only to minimize
the seriousness of what they represent, further convincing the reader
that slavery and all of its results are playful and non-fatal. In all three
novels, for example, Captain Ivers is a stereotypical "bad guy" who
attempts awful crimes against the Black narrators but is always

thwarted by the "good guys." Ivers is exaggeratedly portrayed as a man with no human feeling. The effect is that he becomes, not fictional, but "fantastic"—someone more evil than anyone the reader is likely to have encountered, someone unusual, monstrous and aberrant. To demonstrate that Ivers is not like real people, when Capt. Ivers' nephew, Birdsey, is killed at sea because Ivers failed to jettison cargo to lighten the vessel, Dan reports that Ivers merely read a scripture from the Bible but exhibited no remorse or sorrow. In *War,* Ivers denies medical attention to Willy's mother (causing her death), beats Willy with a whip, then goes after her uncle with a gun. This simplification of Captain Ivers to a cipher of evil misrepresents the real issue and fails to acknowledge the complicity of "normal" white people in the institutionalization of racial exclusion and the exploitation of Black people. The non-serious treatment which satisfies itself with simple caricature creates a paralysis of meaning in material which should not require the superficial "Hollywood-style" chase scene to inspire suspense, drama, and action.

This non-serious attitude extends even to the fictional names which are sometimes facetious and designed to exploit the familiarity of stereotype. For example, in *Jump Ship,* a Black slave who hates Black people is named, (what else) Big Tom. The kind Quaker's name includes the root word "Father"—and Mr. Fatherscreft is clearly intended to personify the "great white father" stereotype. It is all rather tongue-in-cheek, each of the images bearing its own disclaimer.

Each of the "Arabus" novels purports to offer the point of view of a young Black slave caught between a conflict of idealism and expedience—the cruel irony of the Revolutionary War period when Thomas Jefferson and others were expounding upon the concepts of equality, while the substructure of the slave system was being buttressed to withstand the next century of Black servitude. Given the impact of that hypocrisy on the current status of Black people, this material represents more than just an interesting plotline for a writer of light historical fiction to exploit. An understanding of the dynamics of American politics and social thought during the Revolutionary War period is essential to the formulation of a progressive self-concept for modern Americans. The decision of the Collier brothers to represent Black people during this crucial point in American history assumes an unusual burden of responsibility, if only because the Black perspective is not commonly acknowledged as significant, nor is it commonly available to the young student of history. Unfortunately, the conceptual promise of these novels is never fulfilled. Rather than explore the perspective of a Black slave, the books seem to illustrate a tug-of-war of conscience extant in contemporary white America.

Jump Ship to Freedom, War Comes to Willy Freeman, and *Who Is Carrie?* have, if nothing else, pointed up the need for good historical fiction. Young readers require a sense of story and adventure, as well as a sense of the philosophical and moral conflicts of our history. An honest exploration of history through the eyes of the disfranchised might do much to cure the blindside that continues to hamper the intellectual integration of modern America. The disappointment of these three books is the realization that they provide little depth, human complexity, or insight. They introduce no new heroes. The novels conjure the ugly familiar, failing to break new ground.

13. *THE CAY:* RACISM STILL REWARDED

Albert V. Schwartz

RATHER THAN PRAISE for literary achievement on behalf of "brotherhood," *The Cay* by Theodore Taylor (Doubleday 1969) should be castigated as an adventure story for white colonialists to add to their racist mythology. That the major review publications[1] and the five organizations[2] that gave it literary awards—one even for "brotherhood"—so totally misinterpreted *The Cay*'s meaning supports the charge that children's book publishing is indeed a racist institution.

The Cay is the story of the initiation of a white upper-middle-class boy into his superior role in a colonialist, sexist, racist society. Colonialist, because the people of Curaçao and most other people of the Caribbean Isles, where the story is set, are "owned" by outside white powers, which is taken for granted by the author as an acceptable way of life. Sexist, because the only woman in the story is a weak, subservient mother, whose very weakness sets in motion the boy's adventures. Racist, because the white boy is master, and the Black man is subservient throughout the story. It is incredible that in a book for children today, any writer would be so racially insensitive as to put a Black man in the role of subservience to a white boy—a servant who risks his life for the boy and, in the end, sacrifices his life so the white boy may live.

Specifically, the story is about eleven-year-old Phillip Enright, who is marooned on a small island (a cay) with an elderly West Indian, Timothy (no last name). Phillip, who relates the tale, has been living in the Caribbean because his father is an oil refining expert on loan to Royal Dutch Shell from a U.S. company.

The first half of the book sets Phillip up as a young Southern cracker. The reader knows from the outset that the boy's bigoted remarks are deliberate and that the author will slap Phillip down. Phillip early in the book declares that his mother was brought up in Virginia and that "she didn't like them." The "them" are Black people. Of the Black Timothy, says Phillip "[his] smell was different and strong." The Black man's appearance, says Phillip, "is very much like the men I'd seen in jungle pictures. Flat nose and heavy lips." Phillip recoils from the touch of Timothy.

Midway in the book Phillip undergoes a conversion—or so the author would like the reader to believe. This is the "character growth" of young Phillip that is supposed to contribute to the literature espousing "brotherhood." If Phillip's racist attitudes were to undergo substantive change, were Phillip really to have his consciousness raised and grow in human understanding as a result of his close association with Timothy—all well and good. But this just doesn't happen. All that changes in Phillip's growth is a shift in the direction of his racism.

Binnie Tate in an article dealing with authenticity and the Black experiences in children's books (*School Library Journal,* October 1970) states that, from the Black point of view, "the author fails in his attempt to show Phillip's growth in human understanding."

Phillip's "conversion" stems from loss of eyesight after he is shipwrecked, and he comes to depend on Timothy for help and protection. The conversion comes when Phillip—remember, now he is blind—lies down next to Timothy and says, "[Timothy] felt neither white or Black." Soon he is saying that Timothy is "kind and strong." Then comes the question: "Timothy, are you still black?"

Elsewhere in *Interracial Books for Children,* Ray Anthony Shepard contrasts the interpretations of the Black experience by two author/illustrators, one white and the other Black. Mr. Shepard makes the point that the stories of the white author/illustrator are oriented toward the liberal insistence on human similarities and sameness, whereas the Black author/illustrator celebrates the ethnic differences of Blacks.

In this light, consider the implications of Phillip's question to Timothy: "Are you still black?" Phillip is really saying that in order for him to have warm feelings toward a person, that person must be white. Instead of having Timothy answer loud and clear, "No, I am not white, I am Black," he has Timothy disappearing into anonymity.

True to the liberal absurdities of a bygone age, the *New York Times* book review of *The Cay* made this comment on Phillip's question: "Phillip . . . realized that racial consciousness is merely a product of sight." What a racially unaware remark that is!

One thing we are certain about. Phillip won't grow up to march with a Martin Luther King (to whose memory *The Cay* is dedicated). On the contrary, Phillip will return to the Islands and, following in his father's footsteps, he will become a leader in the system that exploits the "natives."

Near the story's end, when Phillip has successfully fulfilled his initiation, he puts on a verbal blackface: "Dis b'dat outrageous cay, oh, Timothy?" In the end, the white boy is given control even of the Black man's language!

We will be hearing a lot in the months and years to come about "Black language." One thing Black language is *not* is verbal blackface, and that is the use of apostrophes and abbreviated word forms to stereotype the language of America's non-white minorities and, to some extent, its lower-class whites. The use of apostrophes and abbreviated word forms is a shoddy literary device used to connote inferior status under the guise of authenticity.

We have said very little about the Black servant. At the story's beginning and through to its conclusion, Timothy is very much the invisible man. We know more about him by omission than by commission. We know that he is good, kind, generous, resourceful and happy. We know that he is well schooled in oppression and colonialism. He is very much aware that the system dictates he call a white boy "Young bahs." Only when the white boy no longer is afraid of his servant is Timothy given permission (which is granted, not assumed) to call the white boy by his first name. Phillip at eleven knows much history. The considerably older Timothy knows no history. When asked about Africa, Timothy answers: "I 'ave no recollection o' anythin' 'cept dese islands. 'Tis pure outrageous, but I do not remember anythin' 'bout a place called Afre-ca."

Outrageous? Yes. What should outrage all of us is that the book's author, its editor, and its publisher should foist upon our children such an image of a Black man today!

Not only is Timothy denied his color by the act of a white boy's "conversion." He is denied parents, family, children. He is denied all social ties except one, and that single tie is with a white boy, for whom in the end he is denied his life.

Notes

1. Marilyn B. Singer, *School Library Journal;* Paul Heins, *The Horn Book;* Polly Goodwin, *Book World;* Charles Dorsey, *New York Times.*
2. Jane Addams Book Award, Lewis Carroll Shelf Award, Commonwealth Club of California Literature Award, Southern California Children's Literature Award, Woodward School Annual Book Award.

14. *SOUNDER*: A BLACK OR A WHITE TALE?

Albert V. Schwartz

IN A RECENT EXCHANGE of letters with George Woods, the *New York Times* children's book editor, Julius Lester, wrote: "When I review a book about blacks (no matter the race of the author), I ask two questions: "Does it accurately present the black perspective?" "Will it be relevant to black children?"

Since the book *Sounder* by William H. Armstrong (Harper and Row) has achieved prominence as the 1970 recipient of the coveted John Newbery Medal award for the year's most distinguished book for children published in the United States, it merits literary analysis from many points of view. Lester's two questions represent an ideological approach, and it is from this approach that I wish to analyze *Sounder*.

Shelton L. Root, Jr., reviewing the book for *Elementary English* (May 1970), states: "As important literary social commentary, *Sounder* cannot be faulted." Root feels that the injustices of the story will leave the reader "both indignant and guilty." This commentary is typical of the reviews that have appeared by white critics for white audiences. Surely this response by white people played a paramount role in the book's selection for the Newbery Medal.

Whose Story Is It?

Mr. Armstrong states in his Author's Note that the actual story was told to him by a teacher, "a gray-haired black man." The note continues: "It is the black man's story, not mine . . . It was history—his history." Thus the author claims authentic Black history originating in the perception and intelligence and "soul" of the Black teacher, casting the white author in an entirely passive role as the tale is written. This claim, while undoubtedly made in good faith, does not bear up under examination.

Tom Feelings, in the Spring 1970 issue of *Interracial Books for*

Children, questioned whether a Black man could freely talk to a member of his oppressors at the time the story was first told. Mr. Feelings stated that a story of the Black Experience must come directly from one who has lived it. Authenticity or syntheticness would hinge upon that life experience.

Style—White and Black

The style of *Sounder* is white fundamentalist; the words, imagery, and philosophy are simple, direct, and interwoven into the story are occasional religious tales offering hope of a "heavenly sanctuary." By contrast, the Negro Spirituals—"Swing Low, Sweet Chariot" and "Steal Away to Jesus"—embody a struggle for freedom and a hope for a better life here on earth. The music of Sounder's family is more the "white spiritual" than "blues." Black language, a vital and historic means of communication for the creation of a story of Black people, is totally absent.

Whose fault is this? Did the Black teacher talk the language he thought the white man understood? Would it be that the white man who listened failed to hear the subtle tones that were spoken to him? Or is it possible that *Sounder* is a highly commercial package at this time in synthetic garb?

No Name, Except for the Dog

Why is no one in the sharecropper's family identified by a name, except the dog, Sounder? The mother is simply "mother," the father, "father," and the youth, "boy."

This would be an acceptable literary device in the hands of a Black author. For a white author to resort to it immediately raises the issue of white supremacy. Within the white world, deep-seated prejudice has long denied human individualization to the Black person. At the time of the story's historical setting, white people avoided calling Black people by their names; usually they substituted such terms as uncle, auntie, boy, Sambo; or they called every Black person by the same name. The absence of name helped to avoid the use of the polite salutation.

In *Sounder,* did the Black storyteller really narrate the story

without names? Or was the unconscious racism of the white tran-
scriber of the tale actively at work?

Suffering, but Silent

Within the institution of white supremacy, Black people are supposed
to express no resentment and suffer in silence. Black militancy today
is forcing whites to consider Blacks as human beings, but at the time
the story took place, white people assumed that Blacks were incapable
of such a human emotion as suffering. In the literature of the Southern Tradition, Black people suffered, if at all, in silence.

In *Sounder,* only the dog expresses reaction and bitterness. The
author actually calls the dog a "human animal." When the father is
taken away by the sheriff, the dog angrily rushes in pursuit, and by
that expressive act risks its life and is shot. The mother, the boy, and
the other children say and do nothing. They are impotent, or at least
made so, by the teller of the story. What if the boy had reacted and
expressed anger, as he probably did in actual life? Then the writer
might have had to deal with Black "activism"—perhaps even a Black
Panther. While this might have intrigued the literary creative taste of
a Black writer, one can see why a white author would hesitate to
construct a forceful anti-white image.

Compare the forceful reaction of the children when their dog is
taken away! The innuendo here seems to be that Black children care
more about their animals than their parents. Or is it that the institution of white supremacy permits Black children to show human response to animals only?

W. E. B. Du Bois wrote *The Souls of Black Folk* in the same
historical setting as *Sounder.* Here is how Du Bois presented the Black
sharecropper: "I see now that ragged black man sitting on a log,
aimlessly whittling a stick. He muttered to me with the murmur of
many ages, when he said: "White man sit down whole year; Nigger
work day and night and make crop; Nigger hardly gits bread and meat;
white man sitting down gits it all. *It's wrong.*"

Never once in *Sounder* do you meet the white owner of the land.
The oppression results from the poverty of the land and the cruelty of
the penal institution. Yet the father is crushed, not by the mean prison
guard, but by a chance "act of God."

True to the white Southern fundamentalism of the author, the "boy" meets up with no activist. His hope lies in getting an education. Suddenly, after his father is taken from him, the boy manages to go to school, where he studies the words of Montaigne. "Only the unwise think that what has changed is dead," says that author.

These words the boy is to contemplate "years later, walking the earth as a man." The message for the Black youth in the story is from Montaigne! What irrelevance!

Sounder's family is isolated; there is no relationship with other Black people, except an occasional preacher. The Bible stories the Black mother tells are exclusively white Baptist fundamentalism—and very racist. Her Bible stories have none of the qualities of Black biblical interpretation, and so we hear the mother telling her son: "Some people is born to keep. Some is born to lose. *We was born to lose,* I reckon." [Italics added]

The mother in the story is the Black stereotype of the Southern Tradition. Toward her children she shows no true feeling, no true compassion—strictly a Southern interpretation of Black motherhood. After her son makes great sacrifices to go to school, she even discourages him from going. After he has searched for his dog for hours, she admonishes him coldly: "You're hungry, child. *Feed yourself.*" This mother is divested of "soul," a quality a Black writer today would assuredly have given her.

When Lerone Bennett, Jr. wrote a criticism of William Styron's *The Confessions of Nat Turner,* he made this statement about white writers emasculating Black families: "First of all, and most important of all, there is a pattern of emasculation, which mirrors America's ancient and manic pattern of de-balling black men. There is a second pattern, which again mirrors the white man's praxis, a pattern of destructuring the black family. . . ." Bennett's statement applies equally to *Sounder.*

In the light of an analysis of *Sounder,* I, for one, respond negatively to the two questions posed by Lester: "Does it accurately present the black perspective?" and "Will it be relevant to black children?" I wholeheartedly affirm Lester's next contention: "The possibility of a book by a white answering these questions affirmatively is nil."

15. THE "REAL" DOCTOR DOLITTLE

Isabelle Suhl

THIS IS THE YEAR of Doctor Dolittle. Movie producers, book publishers, manufacturers, promoters and publicists, headed by Christopher Lofting, second son and sole literary heir of Hugh Lofting, are trying to turn the little Doctor into a new Davy Crockett. Many adults, writing reviews of the film or of the many new versions and adaptations of the stories, deplore these efforts, worry that success may spoil Doctor Dolittle and take comfort from the fact that children can still discover the "real Doctor Dolittle" in the original books with Hugh Lofting's own illustrations.

Who is the "real" Doctor Dolittle? And what manner of man is his creator, Hugh Lofting, who for more than forty years has been hailed as a genius and his books as "classics" by teachers, librarians and children's book reviewers? Rarely has a word of criticism of him or his books been heard. As a result of careful examination of four of the most popular of these books, I charge that the "real" Doctor Dolittle is in essence the personification of the Great White Father Nobly Bearing the White Man's Burden and that his creator was a white racist and chauvinist, guilty of almost every prejudice known to modern white Western man, especially to an Englishman growing up in the last years of the Victorian age, when the British Empire was at its zenith. These attitudes permeate the books I read and are reflected in the plots and actions of the stories, in the characterizations of both animals and people as well as in the language that the characters use. Editing out a few racial epithets will not, in my view, make the books less chauvinistic.

Consider the situation in *The Voyages of Doctor Dolittle*, the second of the books published (1922) and winner of the 1923 Newbery Medal as "the most distinguished contribution to children's literature" in that year. In this story Doctor Dolittle, accompanied by Prince Bumpo, ten-year-old Tommy Stubbins, Polynesia the parrot, Chee-Chee the monkey and Jip the dog, arrives on Spidermonkey Island off the coast of Brazil in search of the "Red Indian" Long Arrow, the world's greatest naturalist. On his first day on the island, Doctor

Dolittle rescues Long Arrow and a group of Indians entombed in a cave and brings fire to the heretofore fireless Indians of Popsipetel. This makes him so popular that he is constantly followed about by crowds of admirers. After his fire-making feat, this childlike people expected him to "be continually doing magic." He continues to solve problem after problem for the Indians. In consequence of his good deeds they ask the "Mighty One" to become "not merely the Chief of the Popsipetels . . . but to be . . . the King of the whole of Spidermonkey Island." Reluctantly he accepts, and with elaborate and fitting ceremony he is crowned King Jong.

Brings White Man's Blessings

He becomes, of course, the hardest-working, most democratic king in all history and brings his new subjects many of the blessings of white civilization—proper sewerage, garbage collection, a pure water-supply system, etc. He locates iron and copper mines and shows the Indians how to use metal. He holds court in the morning to settle all kinds of disputes, teaches to thousands in the afternoon and visits sick patients in the evening. The Doctor would like to go home, but the tradition of noblesse oblige hinders him. He realizes that "these people have come to rely on me for a great number of things. We found them ignorant of much that white people enjoy. And we have, one might say, changed the current of their lives considerably. . . . I cannot close my eyes to what might happen if I should leave these people and run away. They would probably go back to their old habits and customs: wars, superstitions, devil-worship and what not; and many of the new things we have taught them might be put to improper use and make their condition, then, worse by far than that in which we found them. . . . They are, as it were, my children. . . . I've got to stay."

His animal friends have different ideas. Polynesia the parrot "had grown very tired of the Indians and she made no secret of it. 'The very idea,' she said . . . 'the idea of the famous John Dolittle spending his valuable life waiting on these greasy natives!—Why, it's preposterous!' " When Polynesia gets an idea, she acts on it. In a matter of a few days she works out all the details of their departure, comes up with all the answers to the Doctor's objections and even succeeds in getting Long Arrow to urge the Doctor to leave. With that the Doctor gives in. Laying his crown on the beach where his "poor children" will find it and know he has gone, he heads back for England to carry on his "proper work" of taking care of the animals of the world.

Kingdom of Fantippo

This adventure with the Indians was not the Doctor's first experience at playing the Great White Father to ignorant natives. In *Doctor Dolittle's Post Office*, he served a somewhat similar function for the West African kingdom of Fantippo. This book was the third to be published (1923), but in time it takes place between the events in *The Story of Doctor Dolittle* and the events in *The Voyages*. In this story, he does not become a king, but he does more for that country while he is there than had ever been accomplished by the reigning African king. The Doctor's contribution is neatly summed up at the end of the book:

People who have written the history of the Kingdom of Fantippo all devote several chapters to a mysterious white man who in a very short space of time made enormous improvements in the mail, the communications, the shipping, the commerce, the education and the general prosperity of the country. Indeed it was through John Dolittle's quiet influence that King Koko's reign came to be looked upon as the Golden Age in Fantippan history. A wooden statue still stands in the market-place to his memory.

The pre-Dolittle years of King Koko's reign were not so "golden." In those days he occasionally made war on other African tribes and took many prisoners. Some he sold as slaves to white traders if they offered him especially high prices; others he kept for himself "because he liked to have strong men at his court." He greatly admired the ways of the "civilized world" and tried to copy and compete with it. That was how he had come to set up a post office in the first place, a most unusual thing to find "in a savage African kingdom." There were many false starts before he got it functioning. Then one day a "white man explained to him a new craze for stamp collecting that was sweeping over the civilized world," and that was his undoing. He immediately shifted from selling stamps for mailing purposes to selling stamps for stamp collections. It was a profitable business for his kingdom, but "the Fantippo mail service was neglected and became very bad." That is why he had to invite Doctor Dolittle to come to Fantippo and "arrange the post office for him and put it in order so it would work properly."

African King Ludicrous

The King is depicted, both in text and drawings, as a ludicrous figure. A very vain man, he always insisted—before, during and after the Doctor's sojourn in Fantippo—that the stamps for the post office "must all have my beautiful face upon them, and no other." He was usually found "sitting at the palace door, sucking a lollipop—for he, like all Fantippos, was very fond of sweetmeats." When he wasn't sucking one, he used it as a "quizzing glass" to peer through in the "elegant manner" of white men. "But constant lollipops had ruined his figure and made him dreadfully stout. However, as fatness was considered a sign of greatness in Fantippo, he didn't mind that." When Doctor Dolittle was ready to inaugurate his foreign mail service, it was King Koko who brought the first letter to be sent off by the Swallow Mail. And to whom did he send it? A friend of his "who runs a shoe-shine parlor in Alabama!" Even after Doctor Dolittle's departure from Fantippo, "the excellent postal service continued. . . . The stamps with Koko's face on them were as various and as beautiful as ever," including one special one that showed "His Majesty inspecting his new ships through a lollipop-quizzing glass."

Characters All Childlike

The other African characters in this book fare no better than Koko from the pen of Mr. Lofting. They emerge as quaint, comic, childlike figures with simple minds and ridiculous customs and funny-sounding names such as Chief Nyam-Nyam, King Kakaboochi or the Emir of Ellebubu. "Now the peoples of West Africa," says Lofting, "have curious tastes in dress. They love bright things." On the other hand, because the weather is hot in Fantippo, the "black men" there wear only a string of beads. That is why the Fantippo postman's uniform ends up being "a smart cap, a string of beads and a mail bag." The Postmaster-General was "a very grand man, who wore two strings of beads, a postman's cap and no mail bag." To make the post office operate properly, Doctor Dolittle has to get to it by nine o'clock every morning, because if he didn't "the postmen didn't start working."

The animals, too, feel superior to the African people. The Pushmi-Pullyu tells a story about a tribe of ostrich hunters, the Badamoshis, who, "like most savage peoples, are very superstitious. And they are terribly afraid . . . of anything they can't understand. Nearly everything they can't understand they think is a devil." He also complained of the mean, "underhanded and deceitful" methods that "black peoples" used in hunting wild animals. Cheapside the Cockney sparrow is downright insulting. He calls the Fantippans "these bloomin' 'eathens" and derides their town because it isn't like London. He refers to King Koko variously as King Cocoanut or Cocoabutter and to the town as Fantipsy. He preferred the company of two Cockney lighthouse keepers to the Fantippans. He said that "the faces of those two Cockney seamen were the best scenery he had looked on since he had come to Africa."

Most Outrageous Character

In *The Voyages,* Chee-Chee the monkey returns from Africa and recounts how he escaped from Africa by disguising himself as a girl dressed in clothes he had stolen from "a fashionable black lady." The idea had come to him when he saw "a lot of people, black and white, getting on a ship that was coming to England." One of the children of a "big family of funny people" reminded him of a cousin of his. " 'That girl,' he said to himself, 'looks just as much like a monkey as I look like a girl.' "

The most famous of all Lofting's African characters is Prince Bumpo. He is at the same time his most outrageous creation, but apparently he was dear to the author's heart because he is one of the few human characters to appear in several books. He first appeared in *The Story of Doctor Dolittle* and reappears as a major character in *The Voyages* and as a minor one in *Doctor Dolittle's Zoo.*

Color Change Episode

It is in *The Story of Doctor Dolittle* that the objectionable episode about turning Prince Bumpo white occurs. Briefly, for anyone who is not

familiar with it, the story is this. Doctor Dolittle and his animal
friends are on their way home after curing the sick monkeys of Africa
when they are captured for the second time by the King of the
Jolliginki, Prince Bumpo's father. Polynesia the parrot slips out of
prison, sees Bumpo in the garden reading fairy tales and overhears him
say, "If I were only a white prince!" She tells Bumpo that a famous
wizard, John Dolittle, is in his father's prison. "Go to him, brave
Bumpo, secretly . . . and behold, thou shalt be made the whitest
prince that ever won fair lady!" Then she rushes back to the Doctor
and convinces him that if they are to succeed in escaping prison he
must fulfill her promise, no matter what tricks are necessary to do it.
Bumpo arrives as planned and begs the Doctor to turn him white so
that he can return to The Sleeping Beauty who spurned him because
he was black. The Doctor concocts a mixture of liquids which turn the
Prince's face white. In gratitude, Prince Bumpo lets them out of
prison and gives them a ship in which to sail away.

　　This summary merely suggests the objectionable nature of the
episode. It must be read in full to understand the depths of Lofting's
racism. Every line is replete with insults and ridicule. Of course, this
is not the only racist incident in the book. There are many others. The
treatment of Bumpo's parents, the king and queen, is as bad as any
described earlier. It is impossible for Lofting to depict Africans, be
they kings, princes or ordinary people, with dignity and genuine
human qualities. The thought obviously never crossed his mind. To
him they are only vehicles for so-called humor.

　　I asked a Negro friend, who is very much concerned about the
portrayal of black characters in children's books, to read *The Story of
Doctor Dolittle* and give me her reaction to it. Her response was so
revealing and thought-provoking that I am including a portion of it
here in her own words.

In this book, black people are projected as being extremely gullible, naive,
basically ignorant and certainly inferior. This is, of course, personified in
Prince Bumpo's desire to 'become white.' He is willing to sell out everything—
even his father's authority—to 'become white.' For only if he becomes white
will he be able to achieve true and lasting happiness. There is no happiness to
be found in his blackness—in his natural state.

Doctor Dolittle does indeed turn Bumpo white, but does Bumpo ask how—
and for how long? What of the effects on his skin? We are given the answer—

of course Bumpo cannot ever be turned white permanently. Is this not a symbolic way of saying that the black man can never be turned 'white'; that is, he can never be expected to acquire the virtues, the acculturation, the degree of intelligence, refinement of feelings, etc., that are the white man's 'natural endowment.' Is not Bumpo's a futile search? Is not the black man's quest of today also equally futile in light of the attitudes expressed in *Doctor Dolittle* about Bumpo and the king and queen? Is not the book's . . . great success a very subtle reaffirmation of the basic concept of white superiority?

Bumpo Appears Again

If the characterization of Bumpo is bad in *The Story of Doctor Dolittle*, I maintain that it is worse in *The Voyages*. Even defenders of Hugh Lofting have had to denounce the racism of the white prince episode, but I have yet to see or hear any serious criticism of *The Voyages*. This book is, apparently, sacrosanct because it is a Newbery Award winner. I would like, therefore, to turn now to the treatment of Bumpo in this book.

Early in the story, Polynesia the parrot returns to Doctor Dolittle's household after an absence of five years in Africa. One of the first questions the Doctor asks her is about Bumpo. Polynesia informs him that Bumpo is now in England, studying at Oxford University. The Doctor is naturally surprised. Polynesia adds, "He was scared to death to come. . . . He thought he was going to be eaten by white cannibals or something. You know what those niggers are—that ignorant!" [This quotation is taken from page 36 of the official Lippincott edition. The copy I used was the 35th impression, bought in 1965 for a branch of the New York Public Library. In the paperback edition published by Dell in November, 1967, the word "nigger" has been changed to "native."] Polynesia continues her insulting explanation of why Bumpo came to England. Then the Doctor asks, "And The Sleeping Beauty?—did he ever find her?"

'Well, he brought back something which he *said* was The Sleeping Beauty. Myself, I think it was an albino nigeress. . . .'

'And tell me, did he remain white?'

'Only for about three months,' said the parrot. '. . . It was just as well. He was so conspicuous in his bathing-suit the way he was, with his face white and the rest of him black.'

Insults Not Reproved

I must interject one comment here. Polynesia speaks in this insulting way about Bumpo and also directly to his face on many occasions in all the books in which they are together, and never does the "good, kind" Doctor object or reprove her for even her bad manners, to say nothing of her degrading attitude.

Shortly after this conversation, the Doctor decides to go on the voyage to Spidermonkey Island, described earlier. He is looking for just the right person to be the third man of his crew. One day when he is on the ship preparing for the journey, a visitor appears on the gangplank. He "was a most extraordinary-looking black man." He "was dressed in a fashionable frock coat with an enormous bright red cravat. On his head was a straw hat with a gay band; and over this he held a large green umbrella. He was very smart in every respect except his feet. He wore no shoes or socks." Who is this apparition of sartorial splendor? Why, of course, none other than "Bumpo Kahbooboo, Crown Prince of Jolliginki"! (In both name and attire, does he not call to mind that other Lippincott "classic" *Little Black Sambo?*) He has come to offer himself as the much needed third crewman. When the Doctor asks what will happen to his studies and his university career, he replies that he had intended to take a three-month "absconsion" anyway and that by going with the Doctor he will not be neglecting his "edification" since the Doctor is a man of "great studiosity." So the Doctor agrees to take him along.

Prince Turned Cook

From this point on, both in *The Voyages* and *Doctor Dolittle's Zoo*, Bumpo speaks only in malapropisms—once more, the ridiculous African trying to be white, this time by unsuccessfully imitating the speech pattern of a cultured, educated Englishman.

On first glance the interracial nature of the crew might be construed as a positive contribution to race relations, but the opposite is true. Once the voyage is underway, Bumpo, African prince and

Oxford scholar, is consigned to the stereotyped role of cook for the rest of the crew. Despite his age and college training, he is, at best, only on a par with ten-year-old Stubbins, the other crewman. On Spider-monkey Island, both of them help with the teaching of the Indians, but just "simple arithmetic and easy things like that." Only the Doctor can teach the advanced subjects.

In his characterization of Bumpo, Lofting has missed few of the colonial Englishman's views of the "savage" nature of Africans. In tense, dangerous situations Bumpo is seen as a man of great brawn, little brain and brute violence. He is ready to resort to murder to save his friends. When an obstreperous able seaman turns up as a stow-away who has been eating up the ship's store of salt beef, Bumpo suggests to Polynesia that while the seaman is asleep, they "strike him on the head with some heavy object and push him through a port-hole into the sea. . . ." Polynesia vetoes the idea, saying, "No, we'd get into trouble. We're not in Jolliginki now, you know—worse luck!" In *Doctor Dolittle's Zoo*, the Doctor is just about to be kicked by a man named Throgmorton. Bumpo rushes to the rescue and lifts the man up "like a doll." Fortunately, the Doctor intervenes just in time. "For the Crown Prince of the Jollinginki was apparently just on the point of knocking Mr. Throgmorton's brains out on his own doorstep." Bumpo begs to be allowed to eliminate this "useless" man, but the Doctor refuses. "You're not in Africa, now Bumpo. Put him down. . . ." On another occasion in *The Voyages* he threatens to "choke the life out of" a Spanish taximan if he refuses to obey certain orders. There is even one suggestion of cannibalism as a solution to a problem. Polynesia worries that they have no money with which to replace the salt beef the stowaway ate. "'Would it not be good political economy,' Bumpo whispered back, 'if we salted the able seaman and ate him instead?'" Polynesia again reminds him that they are not in Jolliginki, and be-sides, "those things are not done on white men's ships."

Extravagant praise has been heaped on Lofting's illustrations. Many are, indeed, delightful, but in my estimation, all the drawings of Africans are as insulting and offensive as the text. They are nothing more than grotesque caricatures. In combination with the text, they serve no other purpose than to make children laugh at those silly, funny-looking black people.

The Dolittle books have already had a long life and a wide cir-culation which is rapidly growing wider. Several million have been sold in English alone. *The Story of Doctor Dolittle* was published in

1920, went into twenty-three printings in ten years and has been translated into twelve languages. It is now in its 52nd printing in the official Lippincott edition. Only recently Dell-Mayflower published it in its "complete and original text," but without any Lofting illustrations. Lippincott keeps all twelve titles in print, and Dell has so far reprinted the first five books in paperback in a boxed set and as separate books to sell at the very accessible price of 60 cents per book. All twelve titles have appeared on numerous lists of recommended books for children, including one published by A Special Committee of the National Congress of Parents and Teachers and the Children's Service Division of the American Library Association, *Let's Read Together: Books for Family Enjoyment* (2nd edition, 1964). At least two prominent list makers have excluded all the titles from their lists. Nancy Larrick does not include them in either her *Parent's Guide to Children's Reading* (Revised edition, 1964) or *A Teacher's Guide to Children's Books* (1960). Josette Frank of the Child Study Association has dropped them from her latest edition (1968) of *Your Child's Reading Today.*

Lippincott's Treasury

Of all the many new Dolittle books issued by several publishers to tie in with the release of the movie last December, I wish to comment on only one, Lippincott's *Doctor Dolittle: A Treasury.* The publisher's foreword describes at great length their pride in being the publisher of the Dolittle books and their responsibility to make sure these books are "always readily available to all children everywhere" and "to preserve the heritage of Hugh Lofting as he left it." They claim the purpose of the *Treasury* is to "bring more children . . . to Doctor Dolittle than could the twelve separate books" and "to serve as an invitation to the later . . . reading of the twelve original volumes." They further assert that the material in the *Treasury* is "just as Hugh Lofting wrote it." This is not exactly truthful. The book contains excerpts from eight of the twelve Dolittle titles and was very carefully edited by Miss Olga Fricker, sister of the late Mrs. Hugh Lofting. Nowhere in any of the selections does Bumpo appear, although the distorted portrait of Bumpo still appears on the reproduction of the original title page of *The Story of Doctor Dolittle,* which is included. That whole book has been reduced to fifteen pages. The largest excerpt is of *The Voyages*

(104 pages), but no longer is there a "third man" in the crew. Where the excerpt chosen makes it necessary, Bumpo's original role is assigned to one of the other characters, animal or human. Miss Fricker seems to understand better than her publisher that it is no longer possible to publish a Lofting story "just as he wrote it."

All adults who have any connection with the world of books for any age level are dedicated to the idea that good books, especially great creative literature, can have a profound and positive influence on the lives of their readers. Many of us are especially dedicated to providing books for children that are literary and imaginative in form and that in content promote and foster better understanding among peoples. If good books can help combat racial prejudice, as many of us believe they can, then is it not also true that some books can and do promote and foster racial prejudice? Must we not then be as willing to combat such books as we are to promote the others, even if those books have been called "classics"?

This well may be the Year of Doctor Dolittle, but it is also the Year of the Riot Commission's report to the President, in which white racism was clearly and sharply charged with being the main cause of last summer's race riots. In the light of that report and of the earlier Supreme Court decision on desegregation of schools, which pointed out that making white children feel superior to black children was as damaging to white children as the reverse was true for black children, what justification can be found by anyone—and I ask this particularly of those adults who still defend Lofting—to perpetuate the racist Dolittle books? How many more generations of black children must be insulted by them and how many more white children allowed to be infected with their message of white superiority?

When will we ever learn?

16. THE PERSISTENCE OF UNCLE TOM: AN EXAMINATION OF THE IMAGE OF THE NEGRO IN CHILDREN'S FICTION SERIES

Paul C. Deane

BETTE BANNER PREER believes that since about 1940, and definitely since 1945, the Negro in children's fiction has been losing his stereotype.

The familiar Negro character who is too meek, too lax, too superstitious, too eager to be content with "leftovers" which society has to offer, is slipping into the background. . . . In the earlier books there was a definite attempt to show the Negro boy and girl content with his lot in life, accepting defeat, unambitious, menial, inferior in all respects. [1]

What she says may be true of certain children's books; hopefully it is. But she does not read the series, and that fact is especially significant, for the fiction series—the Bobbsey Twins, the Hardy Boys, Tom Swift, and the like—by any standard, dominate children's reading from grade two to grade six, when children are between seven and twelve. Inexpensive enough to be bought by children themselves, readily available in Five-and-Ten's, supermarkets, and drug stores, and widely traded, they have a huge reading public, the extent of which can only be guessed. They are also the one major kind of children's reading designed to be read by children themselves, and not by adults; hence adult censorship and expurgation are not generally possible.

During the entire history of the children's series since 1899 (the year that the Rover Boys first appeared), the image of the Negro has not changed. He lost his dialect in the 1950s, and certain descriptive or identifying words with unpleasant connotations ceased being used at about the same time. But these are superficial changes; his position in society, his general character, and his personality have never really varied.

The change in the use of dialect is dramatically revealed in the

Bobbsey Twins. Since the series began in 1912, the Bobbsey family has had Dinah, a cook, maid, and mammy, and her husband, Sam, a handyman and driver. When the family visited Washington in 1919, Dinah's dialect was as strong as that of Uncle Remus: "What's aa dish yeah I heah Nan say?. . . . What you gone and done to yo' l'il broth' an' sistah?" Sam's is identical: "I'll put back de hay fo' yo' all. 'Tain't much, an' it won't take me long." By 1953 Sam was speaking quite differently: "Well, I don't know. . . . Folks say that if a horseshoe is thrown so that it lands with the two ends pointing toward you, that means good luck." (*The Horseshoe Riddle,* p. 1). When the Bobbseys went to Pilgrim Rock in 1956, Dinah used the phrase "mighty careful"; that was as close as she ever came to dialect again. Clearly, phonetic spelling had disappeared; both Dinah and Sam put g's on words ending in *ing;* "yo" has become "you"; *d*'s are now *th*'s.

Until the 1950s, when agitation for civil rights became a major issue in the United States, the Negro in children's fiction always spoke in dialect. In the earliest series with which this study was concerned, The Rover Boys, the Rover family had a negro servant, Alexander Pop. Aleck never lost his dialect or even modified it ("yo' is a sight fo' soah eyes, deed yo' is," he says in *The Rover Boys in the Mountains*), despite his having lived in the North for decades. The dialect seems an element of race, not geography. When the Rover Boys actually went into the South (*The Rover Boys in Southern Waters*), they found that all Negroes used dialect. Almost a quarter of a century later in 1924 (*The Rover Boys Shipwrecked*), Aleck was saying, "Can't say as I's much younger, but I ce'tainly doan feel no older."

The Tom Swift series introduced a comic Negro, Eradicate Andrew Jackson Abraham Lincoln Sampson, always called Eradicate, because he eradicated dirt. Like the Rover Boys, the Tom Swift series lasted until 1930, and as long as Eradicate was in it, he spoke dialect: "Suffin's gwine t' happen," he says early in *Tom Swift and His Motorcycle* (1910); later he adds, "I trabled all ober and I couldn't get no jobs." By 1928, Eradicate declares: "An' ef I kotches de feller what done planted it I—" (*Tom Swift and His Talking Pictures*).

Eva Knox Evans discovered that even Negro children are conditioned to expect Negroes to speak in dialect in the pages of book. Her book *Araminta's Goat* was read to her kindergarten class as she was writing it; not until the final book appeared could the class see that Araminta was a Negro: the illustrations revealed the fact. The children protested that Araminta did not speak as Negroes are supposed to speak in books. When it was pointed out that the class, all of whom were Negro, did not speak in dialect, they answered that in books colored people do.[2] Other writers, Adelaide Rowell, for instance, feel that "dialect is the folk flavor in the speech of all people of all nations."[3] Since the early 1940s, controversy has existed over dialect in juvenile literature. It is practically gone from series books, and since its use in these books was almost invariably degrading—it was a source of humor and an indication of inferiority—one is inclined to applaud its passing.

The Bobbsey Twins began two years after Tom Swift, in 1912, and introduced Sam and Dinah immediately. Their dialect lasted until the year 1950, when a new version of volume two, *In the Country,* rewritten and published in that year presented Dinah suddenly without dialect; in fact, her speech in general underwent a considerable transformation: her grammar also improved. By 1953 her speech was indistinguishable from that of white characters. Negro dialect is heavy in *Bunny Brown and His Sister Sue in the Sunny South* and in *Grace Harlowe's Overland Riders Among the Kentucky Mountaineers,* both published in 1921. In the former, Bunny and Sue meet a porter on the train who tells them, "De do' am done closed," and a Negro woman at their destination warns a boy playing in the street by saying, "Dat freshy l'il niggar suah will be splatter-dashed." On Grace Harlowe's trip South, she and the Overland Riders pick up Washington Washington, whose dialect is incredible: "He war peekin' at yuh-all, an' when he seed ah sawed him, he snooked an' ah didn't sawed him no moah." His speech is twice imitated by Emma Dean, who also shies a pebble at him. In both cases, fun is made of him because of his manner of speaking.

Negroes in the Hardy Boys books *Hunting for Hidden Gold* (1928), *The Sinister Sign Post* (1936), *A Figure in Hiding* (1937), and *The Twisted Claw* (1939) all speak in dialect; all of Sue Barton's Negro patients in *Visiting Nurse* (1938) do also; and in the Nancy Drew series, Negroes, when they appeared, spoke in dialect through the 1940s and as late as *The Mystery of the Tolling Bell* (1946).

If his speech has undergone change and improvement in the last seventeen years, the Negro's position, his role in society, his character and personality have not. In the first volume of the Bobbsey Twins, Flossie has a Negro doll named Jujub!; she used to explain to her friends, "He doesn't really belong to the family, you know." Indeed, so secure were authors and publishers of series that children would recognize Negroes by their jobs that they often did not bother identifying the race. In *The Twisted Claw,* a Hardy Boys mystery, for example, a Negro is merely called "the porter," but the work he does, his dialect, and the fact that he calls Joe and Frank "massa" meant that no one was expected to miss the point. This situation occurs under identical conditions in another Hardy Boys book, *Hunting for Hidden Gold.*

Negroes have remained servants and slaves, always in inferior positions. They are porters in Herbert Payson's Boy Scout series, the Hardy Boys, and Nancy Drew; they are maids and cooks in the Bobbsey Twins (in volume one, Sam and Dinah lived "in some pleasant rooms over the stable"); they are handymen and butlers in the Rover Boys; and they are mammies in Bunny Brown and the Bobbsey Twins; in the Grace Harlowe series they are ineffectual servants, ranch hands in the Honey Bunch books, laborers and cleaners in Tom Swift; Negroes are elevator operators and grease monkeys in the Rover Boys books; they are washroom attendants in Nancy Drew and Don Sturdy books. As late as 1953, Sam was still saying, "I can help my folks [i.e., the Bobbseys] in and out of coaches." Dinah was called "the faithful servant" in 1942 (*Land of Cotton*), and when the Bobbseys go South to visit Colonel Perry, they find that "everyone was fond of the 'master,'" as he was affectionately called; they also learn that "We all depend on [Mammy] Liza here at Great Oaks." Bunny Brown and his sister, Sue, also find a mammy, Mammy Jackson in *The Sunny South.* Both Don Sturdy (*Port of Lost Ships*) and the Rover Boys (*In New York*) were called "boss" and Tom Swift was "Massa Tom" all through his series.

As Negroes are awarded inferior social and occupational status, so are they supplied with traits of character and personality calculated to develop their inferiority further. By way of example, when Sue Barton takes a job as a visiting nurse, she is sent, in chapter eleven, to Harlem. "You'll love working with colored people," she is told. "They're so willing to cooperate, and so eager to learn." Sue concludes that "she was not there to exploit the colored people, or to be grandly feudal, but to help them stand on their own feet." Yet she persists in treating the families to whom she is assigned like children or babies, and they respond by saying, "Yes, ma'am. Thank you, ma'am." On the Bobbsey Twins' trip South in 1942, they found that all Negroes "had a respectful word or smile for Colonel Perry."

If they appear as subservient to Whites, Negroes are also presented as lazy, ignorant, good natured, cowardly; they are consistently patronized. In *Sue Barton, Visiting Nurse* they have "enchanting black babies." Dinah smiles and grins through fifty-eight volumes of the Bobbsey Twins: *In the Country* shows her as "full of fun"; the Twins are carried to bed in *Land of Cotton* by "a smiling Negro butler"; and when they awaken next day, "one thing that interested the Bobbseys was the large number of Negroes they saw about the place. All looked healthy and happy"; the face of Dinah's Aunt Emma "was crisscrossed with wrinkles that made it seem as if she were smiling all the time." Bunny Brown and Sue, also visiting in the sunny South, meet "a fat, jolly-looking colored woman," Mammy Jackson; and their father says, "I'll see if I can get one of these easy-going colored boys to drive me uptown." A Negro applicant for a housemaid's position in *Nancy Drew and the Mystery Inn* arrives "dirty, slovenly in appearance and [with] an unpleasant way of shuffling her feet when she walked . . . answered in an unsatisfactory manner." Washington Washington in the Grace Harlowe book *Among the Kentucky Mountaineers* is the most offensive portrait of a Negro in any series. He is dirty and refuses to wash; he is futile and stupid in emergencies; throughout the book he is an abject coward. Aleck Pop, the Rover Boys' servant, is invariably fooled by plays on words and by the most basic references, his ignorance being revealed thereby. And Eradicate Sampson in the Tom Swift series is so abysmally stupid as to be only a caricatured comic fool.

None of these pictures of the Negro is improved by the terms which, until the 1940s, were liberally applied to him. They shock a modern reader, but the completely matter-of-fact tone with which they are delivered suggests that they were taken for granted by writers and readers. "Nigger" is quite common. It may be used as part of a phrase, such as "nigger in the woodpile," as it is in *The Boy Scouts at the Panama-Pacific Exposition,* or directly applied to a Negro, as in *Don Sturdy in Lion Land,* and in the Tom Swift series, where Eradicate calls himself "nigger" frequently; the term may be found as "They told us you had to make them work like niggers" in *The Rover Boys on Land and Sea;* when Bunny Brown is in the sunny South, a Negro woman refers to a young Negro boy as "dat fresh l'il nigger."

Sometimes the word is used in dialect, as "niggah," the manner used by Washington Washington to refer to himself in *Among the Kentucky Mountaineers.* A Negro is called "darky" twice in *Bunny Brown and His Sister Sue in the Sunny South* and twice in *Tom Swift and His Motor Cycle,* where he is also called "coon" twice, and he is a "black rascal" in *Tom Swift and His Airship.* An amazing irony arises in *The Bobbsey Twins in the Country,* as that book was rewritten in 1950 to bring it up to date, according to the author's claim in the Preface: in the revision, dialect was practically removed, but in one scene, a pigeon is described as making a noise like "see-de-coon, see-de-coon." Negro children are referred to as "pickaninnies" in the Grace Harlowe series.

Other means of debasing the Negro's status are accomplished by the use of certain stereotypes, a device which further equates all Negroes. The majority of Negro women, for example, are fat: Dinah and her Aunt Emma, Mammy Jackson, are only two. Dinah and Sam have "kinky heads" in *The Bobbsey Twins at the Seashore,* and they love watermelon. Eradicate Sampson carries a razor as a weapon of defense in *Tom Swift and His Airship.* Washington Washington plays the harmonica.

There are three notable exceptions to what has been said—the number is absurdly small; one is an attempt to remove some of the onerous clichés mentioned above; one other, an attempt to individualize the Negro by making him a villain. The first occurs in *Sue Barton, Visiting Nurse,* "All the apartments [of Negroes] were clean. . . . They had a tradition of cleanliness and were proud of it. An apartment was seldom cluttered . . . no speck of dust lingered anywhere." After the Hardy Boys are attacked by three criminals in *Hunting for Hidden Gold,* suddenly two Negroes appear: the same criminals had earlier run over their chickens. One is "an enormous Negro"; he and his friend proceed to beat up the hoodlums; throughout the scene they act fearlessly and with considerable ability. The only use of Negroes as villains occurs in a late Tom Swift book, *Tom Swift and His Talking Pictures* (1928). There Tom is captured by two Negroes and taken to see some movie moguls who wish to steal Tom's television machine. They speak well, without dialect—in fact, their language is superior to that of the heroes. Tom is so struck by the fact that "the language of the Negroes was above the average"—note the assumption, however—that he comments on it: "They did not talk like poor old Eradicate. Rather their talk was that of the man who has seen service in wealthy families." (Note also that although they can learn from Whites, Negroes are still servants.)

Only one attempt is made to portray the Negro's housing situation realistically. This occurs in *Sue Barton, Visiting Nurse:* "The moment a Negro family moved into a tenement, the rent would go up."

In general, then, the Negro, with one exception, is never presented in a children's series as bad, so of course, he can never really be good. Never is he allowed to develop as a real character, a real person; instead he is revealed always as a century-old cliché.

Children, as Ruth Viguers points out in her contribution to *A Critical History of Children's Literature,* are not aware of racial, national, or religious intolerance; economic and social fears that create intolerance in the world of adults are not natural in the world of children. Clearly, however, children may take attitudes and prejudices that they see displayed, and as Spencer Brown put it, children's books may become a "fertile breeding ground for prejudice through stereotypes."[4] Eleanor Nolen is even wiser in pointing out that the prejudices and attitudes a child forms through reading may be more serious than actual contacts with minority races. The child, for example, may never know a Negro except through the pages of a book. "The place to combat race prejudice is with the child's first books and first social relationships."[5] Except for removing dialect, the series books are maintaining the traditional image of the Negro.

Notes

1. Bette Banner Preer, "Guidance in Democratic Living through Juvenile Fiction," *Wilson Library Bulletin,* XXII (May 1948), 680.
2. Eva Knox Evans, "The Negro in Children's Fiction," *Publishers' Weekly,* CXL (October 18, 1941), 650.
3. "Negro Dialect in Children's Books," *Publishers' Weekly,* CXL (October 18, 1941), 1556.
4. Spencer Brown, "The Dilemma of Liberal Censorship," *The Education Digest* XXX (September 1964), 4–6.
5. Eleanor W. Nolen, "The Colored Child in Contemporary Literature," *The Horn Book,* XVIII (September–October 1942), 349.

17. RACISM IN PRIZE-WINNING BIOGRAPHICAL WORKS

Donnarae MacCann

THE NEWBERY PRIZE in children's literature was awarded in 1951 to the fictionalized biography *Amos Fortune, Free Man* (1950) by Elizabeth Yates. Reviewers stressed the book's "deep religious feeling" and "deep, serene faith," but their evaluations would have been more credible had they stressed the book's ethnocentricity. A strikingly overt white supremacist attitude characterizes the book throughout. (It may be helpful to note here that the terms "racism" and "white supremacy" are used broadly to designate discriminatory thoughts and actions, although in a technical sense the term "racism" connotes a supposed culture/genetic tie, and the term "white supremacy" connotes the tradition of Euro-American white dominance over non-white populations.)

The narrative presents the life story of Amos Fortune, a slave in New England during the 1700's who late in life buys his own freedom. Beginning with the chapter on Amos' capture in Africa we find the author claiming a divine intervention on behalf of the slavers. Amos' docility is described as if it were a demand of God: he prayed and "the voice of the land gave answer. . . ." This "voice of the land" told him as he rode down a river in chains that "this was the time of birth, the time of renewal." Its inspiration made him go to sleep rather than make the rescue attempt that Ms. Yates says would have had a fair chance of success.

Describing this capture later on, Amos makes the divine intervention even more explicit: "My hand was restrained [from resisting and killing the slaver] and I'm glad that it was, for the years between have shown me that it does a man no good to be free until he knows how to live, how to walk in step with God."

Throughout the biography Africa is depicted as a pagan country, as a place where one could not possibly "walk in step with God." Amos is even described as feeling somewhat elated by the opportunity to leave his homeland. The author tells how he suffers from the hunger and wounds inflicted on him, and then how another sensation takes over:

> But more than all that he felt something expanding within him: a strange feeling that rose to meet the new world his eyes were absorbing. It was as far from elation as it was from fear, yet it was a compound of each. He who had known nothing but jungle now found wonder stirring in him that there was a world beyond.

This confused idea, that slavery was beneficial because it led Africans to Christianity and a "new world," runs through the entire narrative. (It's hard to see how Amos' experiences in American churches provided any illustration of genuine Christianity. He was forced to sit in special segregated sections of the church all his life; and when, at the age of 78, he was permitted to join a local church, a church elder commented: "What a pity he isn't white. . . . He could do much for the church.")

The author's descriptions are condescending, but beyond that they make the African appear almost sub-human. For example, after the captives have been waiting for just three weeks in dug-out pits, receiving rations once a day, the author says "they had turned into merchandise . . . and stood in a long patient row, like animals trained at last to obey commands." In a few more weeks they are said to have lost their power of speech as well as memory. After Amos is shown attempting to communicate with his tribesmen, the author explains their failure to respond:

> They had been made to forget—not only that they were At-mun-shi but that they were men. They made sounds to each other in the darkness of the hold, but they were only sounds, they had no meaning.

In a very short time the captives supposedly lost even their ability to recognize Amos, their chief.

Nowhere is there shown any typical human behavior—conversation, memory, speculations about the future, worry about family members left behind, plans for escape. Nor is the reader given any of the factual, well-documented information about slave resistance involving such tactics as mutiny and suicide.

When information about Amos' tribe is given, it is on a superficial level and in conformity with stereotypes. For example, the author explains that it was the tradition in this tribe to look up to "someone older and wiser as a protector." At the time of capture they "ran across the clearing trying to reach their chief who stood above them in strength and power, symbolizing protection. . . . They knew that he would care for them."

There is no context provided in which the reader can understand this tradition in relation to other complex traditions, religious beliefs, economic necessities, historical evolution and so on. Dependency on a leader is a characteristic seen in total isolation, and in this way given an exaggerated importance that supports the stereotype of alleged African childishness and immaturity.

Descriptions of Amos after his arrival in America make him appear animal-like or sub-human also. His owner's wife "bade the boy come and like an obedient dog he followed her out of the room." He "squatted on the floor and grinned up at her." His owner discusses with his wife the possibility of giving Amos his freedom, but remarks: ". . . in his untamed state it would not be well to give it to him too soon. . . . He is part animal now. What would he do but run wild?"

Later in the story Amos is shown to behave in a childish manner. For example, when he recognizes the financial need of a white customer, he offers him money asking only for his customer's "go-to-Meeting-hat in exchange." The customer was "glad to have his [clothes] press cleared of useless clutter." Then Amos prays "Thank you kindly, Lord, . . . for all my fine clothes. Violet's going to be mighty proud when she sees me in them. . . ." The original owner of the clothes describes Amos in these terms: "[The clothes] caught his fancy like a child's. But that's what they are, those black people, nothing but children. It's a good thing for them the whites took them over." The author never refutes nor discusses this statement nor treats it with irony. It is left as if it were part of the author's own impression of Amos.

George M. Fredrickson, in *The Black Image in the White Mind,* shows the 19th century stereotype of the black American to have included these traits: docility, submissiveness, loyalty, cheerfulness, childishness. In addition, blacks were supposedly musical and "peculiarly susceptible to religious experience."[1] Strangely enough, a contradictory set of traits was attributed to them at the same time. Professor Fredrickson notes that the attitude toward the free Negro in the North also resembled the attitude held toward drunkards and infidels. One colonial journalist was referring to blacks when he wrote: "There is a point beyond which the peace of society cannot permit the increase of the elements of commotion."[2]

In Ms. Yates' characterization of Amos, he manifests an exaggerated degree of submissiveness long after he is free. At one point, when attempting to buy the freedom of his second wife, Amos plays no part in the bargaining at all; rather he thinks: "nor was it for him to question Mr. Bowers' decision." This submission earned Amos the prefix "Mr.," which by the end of his life often "dignified his name." "He had won his way to equality by work well done and a life well lived." The idea that some people must *win* equality, that only their docility and hard labor will achieve for them the right to the title "Mr.," is one of the most racist concepts in the book.

The stereotype of perpetual cheerfulness is created by repeated references to singing, dancing and smiling. Perhaps the most absurd example is when Amos stands upon the auction block; according to the author, "It amused him to hear himself described and he grinned broadly as he listened to the auctioneer's words."

Attitudes ascribed to Amos about freedom and slavery seem contradictory. The At-mun-shi tribe was said to cherish freedom, and yet we are told that the Quaker family that first owned Amos periodically offered him his freedom over a fifteen-year period and he always turned the offer down. This is hard to comprehend since Amos at the same time advised his fellow Africans to "wait for the free day" rather than plot to achieve their freedom. What "free day" did he have in mind?

As an explanation, the author tells us that Amos' attitude was different from the attitude of other blacks, a contrast which may have seemed commendable to white readers at the time this biography was written. "It [the white man's attitude toward Amos' skin color] did not trouble or vex him the way it did some of the other slaves with whom he met and talked. It puzzled him. But then, there were many things to puzzle a man." Amos seems to classify racism alongside the "puzzles" of nature, as if it were just an oddity and not a moral and social evil.

A similar false estimate of slavery is presented when one of Amos' owners dies and the widow, in addition to granting Amos immediate freedom, suggests that he establish the owner's tanning business as his own. Although Amos had been literally slaving over this business for years, he "smiled with delight," but refused; ". . . he had his own pride and he would accept nothing without fair payment." There is no mention of the fact, and apparently no realization, that Amos' whole life and labor had already been given in "fair" payment—that more had been given than could ever be repaid.

As the Revolutionary War approaches, slavery is never discussed as a contradiction to the spirit of that colonial rebellion. Rather Amos is given by the author the warped view that freedom is something you buy with money.

Amos knew he was never too old to wage his own war for freedom in his own way, not with guns or valor but hard-earned coinage, buying manumission and giving it before it was too late for one he loved to die in honor.

Perhaps what basically underlies the contradictions about freedom in this biography is the conviction that dignity and status can be found only in association with the white community and culture. Ms. Yates writes:

As the working member of the Copeland family, Amos had his own dignity. Apart, he would endure the separateness he knew many of his African friends endured because of their lack of status in the white man's world.

To say that slavery in a white family is more dignified than freedom, that it is preferable to "lack of status" as defined by slave-holders— this argument has more than one destructive element. It claims a false dependence on whites, and even worse, it suggests a denial of black identity.

Rejection of identity appears in various ways throughout the book. One instance is the scene where Amos notices his old age. He sees his image in a looking-glass, and his look of surprise is interpreted in these words: "Perhaps he thought he was white until he saw himself in the mirror," Mrs. Richardson shook her head. "Perhaps, but it's more than that." The author never rejects the racist implications of this appraisal. She merely uses the incident as a plot point, for Amos had been searching for the sister captured with him in Africa and realizes now that the search is hopeless—his sister has inevitably grown old like himself.

Several chapters describe Amos' relationships with a destitute black family. He wants to offer financial assistance, but his wife Violet says they are "shiftless" and wants the children to work rather than receive charity. (*What* work would be given to children to support a

family of six, and with what remuneration is never discussed.) In the
end, with the family broken up and one child dead, it is suggested that
this was all God's will, that Violet was right and was in fact under
divine guidance.

The author describes the child's death scene in purely positive
terms: "Peace dwelt in her face, a smile hovered over her lips. . . ."
Then Violet says to Amos, "You've set Polly free to die happy." Free in
this case is freedom from poverty, the condition this child is forced to
die out of, since Violet made it impossible for Amos to help her family
while there was still hope for its survival.

The author's statements about this whole series of events reveal
an attitude that stems from the 19th century. Referring to the failure
of New England abolitionists to carry through the reforms they supposedly advocated, George Fredrickson writes:

In refusing to [acknowledge] . . . that most blacks in the North as well as in
the South were so acted upon that there was comparatively little they could do
to improve their own situation in the ways that whites recommended, the
abolitionists revealed how their underlying commitment to an individualistic
philosophy of moral reform prevented them from perceiving the full dimensions of the American race problem.[3]

"Moral reform" in this context refers primarily to economic
progress, to the accumulation of wealth through industrious competition with your neighbor. Amos Fortune's wife Violet is made the
mouthpiece for this philosophy when she insists that the problem in
Polly's family is "shiftlessness." The author then emphasizes the point
by making Violet's decisions appear God-sent. Amos represents this
viewpoint when, at nearly sixty years of age, he agrees to buy himself
and is glad that his freedom is "achieved by his own efforts and not
through the kindness of any man."

Perhaps something should be said here about the words put into
the mouths of historical characters in children's books. Many biographical works for children are given the same kind of fictional treatment we find in *Amos Fortune, Free Man*. Events are presented as
direct happenings and it is the author's prerogative to imagine what
the characters would say and do in the face of these happenings. The
genre includes this technique as a legitimate literary device, but this
doesn't mean total license for the author. The conversations invented
must be credible in view of what is known about the historical period

and event. The author has the responsibility to show, with as little distortion as possible, what it felt like to live under certain conditions. Furthermore, authors must make their own response to attitudes and happenings clear. The narrator's voice adds a great sense of legitimacy to the ideas presented to a child audience, whether the work is a fictionalized biography or a biographical novel. The shades of difference between these genres is slight, and to the child reader probably non-existent. Therefore the writer for children needs to be in some respects the kind of teacher described by Jeanne Walton in the *Interracial Books for Children Bulletin* ". . . the teacher needs to accept whatever children have to express, but she must let children know where she stands. She cannot be detached or uncommitted."[4]

In *Amos Fortune, Free Man,* even if the sayings attributed to the hero could be documented as fact, we are left with these sayings unchallenged and unexplained by the author. Her position seems to be one of support for the ideas voiced by Amos and other characters—the idea that slavery can be legitimate, that blacks are childish, foolishly docile, passive, submissive, dependent, easily turned into speechless "merchandise," unequal unless they earn equality.

But the author is not alone in supporting these assumptions. The history of the book—its reception over the past thirty years— indicates that thousands of librarians, critics, and educators have supported them also. Ms. Yates was apparently a very accurate representative of her times.

The question now should be, where does the book stand today? Is it placed on lists of recommended books? Is it retained in children's collections or moved to research libraries dealing with American social history? Unfortunately, it is not considered a mere artifact for scholars. It is still referred to as a "heroic saga" in the New York Public Library's bibliography, "The Black Experience in Children's Books" (latest edition, 1984). And it is now marketed like a classic of popular culture with a kit that includes a filmstrip (with disc or cassette), paper or hardcover editions of the biography, and a teacher's guide (Miller-Brody Productions). The National Council of Teachers of English included the book on its list, "Negro Literature for High School Students" (1968), but the annotation mentioned that Amos was perhaps reminiscent of "Uncle Tom"—i.e. he was characterized as "too forgiving."

Another prize-winning book about slavery is a biographical novel, *I, Juan de Pareja* by Elizabeth Borton de Treviño. It was published fifteen years after *Amos Fortune, Free Man,* yet it expresses the same white perspective and contains many of the same attitudes.

Only the setting is different: slavery in Spain rather than America. Juan de Pareja served in the household and studio of the Spanish court painter Velazquez, and his story is cast as a first person account of what slave life was like. Having the protagonist narrate his own story increases the illusion of authenticity, and the author's views reach the child with considerable intensity. Amos Fortune was made to speak for himself often in the Yates book, but now all the ideas are presented as personal drama and with a sense of immediacy.

A few quotations will show the general position the author takes toward slavery. As in the Amos Fortune book, we find the idea that liberation is something that must be earned—unless of course one belongs to the ruling class in the first place. The slave, Juan, receives his freedom after nearly a lifetime of servitude to Velazquez, and this is how he describes the event:

I seized his hand, to carry it to my lips.

"No, no," cried Master, snatching his hand back. "You owe me no gratitude, my good friend. The contrary. I am ashamed that in my selfish preoccupations I did not long ago give you what you have earned so well and what I know you will grace with your many virtues."

In several passages religion is used to rationalize and render less offensive the institution of slavery. For example, a church friar tells Juan there is much good that he can do in the world and Juan disputes this because of his slave status:

"I am only a slave . . . a servant," I complained, feeling sorry for myself.

"Who is not?" asked Brother Isidro, briskly. "Do not we all serve? In any case, we should. That is nothing to be ashamed of; it is our duty."

Later in the story Juan describes the dwarfs kept at court to amuse the king and relates this conversation with one of them:

"We are brothers," he used to say to me in his strange, deep voice like a man's, "you and I, because we are enslaved by reason of the way we were born. You were born strong, a fine normal being, but black. I was born as I am, a man in the body of a little creeping child. Why did God put this burden on us, Juanico?"

"To make us humble, maybe. Our Lord was despised and rejected, you remember. He himself told us so. And He said, 'He who exalts himself shall be brought low, and he who humbles himself shall be lifted up.'"

The self-defamation in this passage is never refuted. Indeed, the author supports and rationalizes it with an inappropriate line of Scripture—inappropriate because humility has meaning as a virtue only when exercised voluntarily. Under the institution of slavery, where a person's life is not his own, humility cannot be the same as when expressed voluntarily by Jesus.

The author depicts Juan's enslaved life as one of bliss after he arrives at the house of Velazquez. Freedom, she claims, is not important to him. He was mistreated by a gypsy during his journey to the city of his new owner and therefore says: "Freedom? I had had a taste of it on the road, and it was cruel to a black boy."

There is just one exception to Juan's good estimate of slavery as a way of life, and this has to do with painting. "I had not really been sad to be a slave, except for not being able to paint. Every life has some drawbacks."

Is giving up an entire life of free choice and action just one of those little "drawbacks" that everyone must experience? This suggestion resembles Amos Fortune's alleged view of racism as just one of those "puzzles" of which there are many "to puzzle a man."

Contentment in slavery is referred to numerous times in this story of Pareja: ". . . in all except that little nagging wish to paint, I was content, having every reason to look forward to a pleasant and comfortable life." If slavery is this satisfying, or as the writer says, something God ordains to make us more humble, the child reader must wonder why people have been so disturbed about it, have argued against it so vehemently, gone to war over it.

But only the illegality of painting by slaves disturbed Juan. It was strictly forbidden under Spanish law for a slave to engage in the arts, and Pareja is in anguish over this throughout much of the story. Finally, after Juan confesses he has broken this law, the painter Murillo tells him that the law is morally invalid anyway. Juan then comments on Murillo's attitude:

In his simplicity, he saw intent as the very essence of the law and could not accept the idea that I had been at fault.

Murillo asks Juan:

"Is it a *sin*, then, to paint?"
"But I am a slave!"
"Is it a sin, then, to be a slave?"
"No. It is an injustice. But I am a religious man. I do not expect justice here on earth, but only in heaven. And I am not a rebellious slave. I love Master and Mistress."

This is a classic example of white perspective: the claim that blacks have no expectation of justice or a good life here on earth; that they are entirely forgiving, even loving the slaver. In particular cases this affectionate bond may have developed, but to generalize in this way about Pareja, without any documentary evidence, is to distort history. The author cannot know that Pareja "loved Master and Mistress," and since it was not customary or natural for the slave to love the slaver, the reader's encounter here is simply with a bias on the side of the slaver.

The most tragic thing about this book is the author's failure to deal with slavery realistically. She doesn't even seem to be aware of what it is—aware that it denies people their inherent right to make choices, to express their own talents and individuality freely, to have relationships with equals. Neither Velazquez nor Pareja seem to be conscious of the injustice in their relationship, to see that a normal human association cannot be based on domination.

Juan isn't freed at all until a dramatic complication arises which forces Velazquez to grant it. His slave has been caught red-handed, breaking the law against painting, and only the sudden granting of Juan's freedom will enable Velazquez to keep him from being taken away and prosecuted. By making Pareja his assistant, Velazquez in effect keeps him performing the same service he has been performing as a slave for years. The king assures Juan after Velazquez' death that the great artist regretted not giving Juan his freedom sooner. And Juan is willing, according to the author, to think of it as just an oversight! "I never held it against him that he had been forgetful."

At the end of the book, the author's Afterword includes this statement:

. . . the threads of the lives of Velazquez and Pareja are weak and broken; very little, for certain, is known about them. . . .

Facts of which I am certain are the bonds of deep respect and affection which united Velazquez to his sovereign, and, with equal strength, to his slave, whom he freed and named his assistant.

This claim would have more credibility if the novel contained some awareness of how respect and affection depend, at the most fundamental level, upon a respect for human rights. The provision of food and shelter says little about a deep consideration of others, for these essentials are no more than what a household pet receives. The assertion in the Afterword that "those two [Velazquez and Pareja] . . . began in youth as master and slave . . . and ended as equals and as friends" is not supported in the preceding 176 pages, for Velazquez never respects Pareja sufficiently to be sensitive to his needs or wishes. He frees him only under the stress of circumstances. He sees Juan's "place" as that of a slave and nothing more. The author clearly intends to show how black and white can live together happily and peaceably; but she never suggests that it is only without slavery or domination that this is possible. Equality is mentioned in the last sentence of the Afterword, but never even glimpsed in the course of the novel itself, never shown as something valued by the major characters. In this account of a master-slave relationship, Velazquez can do no wrong, and his domination of Pareja is therefore presented to the young reader as acceptable.

Books like *Amos Fortune, Free Man* and *I, Juan de Pareja* may conceivably be useful to scholars in tracing the varied manifestations of racism. But why do librarians still call them good reading for children?

Notes

1. Fredrickson, George M. *The Black Image in the White Mind, The Debate on Afro-American Character and Destiny, 1817–1914.* Harper, 1971, p. 103–106.
2. *Ibid,* p. 8.
3. *Ibid,* p. 40.
4. Walton, Jeanne. "The American Negro in Children's Literature," in *Interracial Books for Children Bulletin,* Vol. 1, No. 4, Fall, 1967, p. 6.

Part IV

RACISM IN CONTEMPORARY PICTURE BOOKS

18. PICTURE BOOKS: THE UN-TEXT*

Opal Moore

THE VISUAL IMAGE is the most engaging of sensory messages, imprinting its outlines upon the subconscious like an acid etch. The imprint is often indelible—defying the forgetfulness of the conscious mind. Experiments in subliminal suggestion in advertising offer proof of the lingering and insidious power of even the most fleeting visual image to influence decision-making. On an even more mundane level, common phrases such as "I'll believe it when I see it" demonstrate how closely we all tend to equate reality and credibility with our capacity to "see" a particular thing. (We also tend to discredit those things that we cannot perceive with our eyes.)

With this in mind, it would seem reasonable to expect visual messages and nuances in children's books to receive greater attention than they now receive. This is particularly important for picture books aimed at the young child. Pictures are the primary message vehicle, and texts tend to be extremely minimal.

Concern over the implied messages of images is not new. The struggle against racism in this country has included the reform of inaccurate and derogatory images of Blacks as portrayed by whites in media and literature. And the fight goes on. I am suggesting, however, that like racism in other aspects of our lives, the negative aspects of imaging Blacks and other minorities may be slipping underground. That is, the effects may seem less disturbing to the eye, but they are no less real and certainly no less potent. Pictures are a message shorthand to be "read" in a matter of moments. Their messages, missed by the censoring process of critical analysis, can find their way unobstructed to the uncritical subconscious. Once planted there, this "message" is not something as tangible or arguable as an idea, but is

---

Editors' Note: Ben's Trumpet was an American Library Association Caldecott Honor Book. The illustrator of *Big Sixteen* was an "Honor" recipient for her version of *Little Red Riding Hood* (1983). The prestige connected with these awards can be expected to increase the influence of these books.

immoveable assumption. Needless to say, the assumptions that we harbor establish the basis for much of our thinking, reasoning and behavior.

This awareness of pictorial learning is not new, but should be given more attention when we evaluate literature for a child audience, an audience that is substantially Black, Hispanic, Asian, and Native American, as well as white. It is often on the level of suggestion (nuance) that the works of white writers are flawed, because it is at this level that such authors 1) fail to acknowledge the power and investment of an image, and 2) fail to question their own ingrained assumptions regarding cultures they are unfamiliar with, assumptions that derive from the accumulated racist images of this society.

It is at the level of pictorial suggestion that two books for young children, *Ben's Trumpet* by Rachel Isadora, and *Big Sixteen*, by Mary Calhoun (illustrated by Trina Schart Hyman) provide serious problems in terms of their portrayals of Black images and reality.

Ben's Trumpet tells the story of a young Black boy, Ben, who wants to play the trumpet. From his fire escape he can hear the jazz music of the trumpet player at the Zig Zag Club and, totally enamored, he begins to "play" an imaginary instrument since he is too poor to own a real one. Ben plays and plays. He plays for everyone in his family (and I must digress here to say that at this point there is a tangible "gap" in the text where the author fails to indicate what Ben's family thinks of him and/or his activity, but I will come back to this). Finally, when he plays for some neighborhood children, they ridicule him because his horn is not real. Ben becomes very sad and discouraged and it appears that he will abandon his imaginary horn. But finally a jazz man from the club notices him and offers him a real horn upon which to practice. This is the simple story of the text. But there is a second story, a pictorial story decidedly outside the text.

The bulk of the praise lavished on *Ben's Trumpet* has been due to the technical strength and sophistication of the illustrations. They alternate like jazz riffs between hard-edged, rhythmic, pulsating geometric creations, slick stagey silhouettes, and softer, more "realistic" drawings representing Ben at home. The praise of reviewers has been in response to the ingenious design of the overall book, its pacing, and the daring experimentation and sophistication of Isadora's bold abstracts. The images of Ben's home life, which were intended as soft, mellow interludes, did not elicit much reviewer comment, but these are the images which contain the subtext (or what could be referred to as the "subliminal text") of Ben's story—a second story narrated through a subtle accumulation of visual messages that reverberate beyond the deceptively simple plot.

The author's depiction of Ben at home, and her simultaneous refusal to deal with the responsibility of portraying a Black child in his home environment, is the disturbing note in a work which, on the whole, is an unusual blend of simplicity and sophistication. It appears that, in order to create or exaggerate the pathos of Ben (his poverty, his lack of a real horn, etc.), the author has drawn a picture of a child in isolation—not the imagined or psychological isolation of a child struggling with his ambition—but real isolation, hard-edged and relentless. The ironies of Ben's life are effectively pointed up, not explicitly in the textual material, but through the juxtaposing of text against image. For example, while the text reads (innocuously) "Ben played for his mother, grandmother, and baby brother, his father, uncles and. . . .", the illustrations show Ben as a kind of outsider within his own home. The rooms contain idle, isolated people: mother is engrossed in a newspaper, father, uncle, and friends play cards for money (with depressing seriousness), grandmother stares dispassionately out of a window. All are seemingly unaware of Ben's presence and each other's. Even baby brother seems overwhelmed by the lethal lethargy of home, and as he sits nude and unattended on a blanket, staring out from the page, even he appears unaware of Ben (who is prancing beside him on the sofa playing his horn). The entire family seems stratified and isolated from each other. There is no indication of human feeling, life or energy in these depictions; they are in stark contrast to the movement, life, and vibrancy of the all-over-the-page pictorial jazz motifs which hint at the liveliness of Ben's imagination and the improved quality of life away from home. The text neatly avoids accusing the family of insensitivity; it is left to the illustrations to render that message. Only through the pictures do we understand why the simple teasing of other children is so devastating and disheartening to Ben—the final straw! (Significantly, some reviewers referred to these children as Ben's friends. But, within the story, the children are strangers to Ben, who apparently has no friends—a sad state of affairs.)

A further irony is seen in the soft-edged, grainy pictures of home, which are meant to be the mellow interlude of the jazz solo, but are, in fact, the really hard times of Ben's life. The linear abstractions depicting the flashy, unfathomable world of the Zig Zag Club are suddenly, by contrast, imbued with all the warmth, love and embracing qualities missing at home. And if all this were not enough, Ben sits discouraged and forlorn on a stoop, while on the steps above him a couple embraces, further emphasizing the idea that Ben is outside his own world. He is estranged from the companionship of peers, he misses the supportiveness that should comprise a definition of home, and as yet he is too young for a sexual union.

A story which would appear at first glance to be merely the story of a poor young Black boy's desire to become a musician is transformed through textual lapses and strong graphic images into a disconcerting picture of a boy who, although he has a family (father, mother, siblings and extended family members), suffers due to this family's mysterious lack of human feeling. It is an image which invites the smear of generalization. Interpretation of the visual material is inevitable due to the lack of specifics in the text, and a number of things are suggested: that there is "sickness" or inadequacy in the Black family; that a lack of material wealth equates with a lack of familial love, caring, and responsiveness. There is the image of idleness (no one is shown engaged in any mode of work or gainful activity aside from the musician in the nightclub). And most painfully, there is the notion that Ben must sever himself from his family in order to prosper, that Ben's ambition places him, somehow, outside of his own home. All of these distortions can be attributed to the author's decision to exclude from her pictures even a hint of touching, talking, or sharing, between Ben and his family in order to heighten artificially the poignance of Ben's life. Black life is poignant enough without this type of artistic license.

Of course the trumpet player from the Zig Zag Club appears to redeem this abject portrait and all should be well. In my view, all is not well. The Jazz Man, as I will call him because he has no name within the story, is an outsider—not in real life, but within the simple dynamic established by the author. In Ben's reality, there are two worlds: home and outside of home (and this is probably an accurate reflection of a child's world view). But Isadora creates an unbridgeable dichotomy here which only further emphasizes the image of Ben divorcing himself from his home. In other words, *I* know that the Jazz Man exists within the Black family of community, a symbol of the power of art to transform reality, a symbol of history and continuity. However, the structure of *Ben's Trumpet* neither acknowledges nor attempts to convey the idea of community, and the Jazz Man remains a nameless stranger who appears out of the dim shadows of the Zig Zag

Club (an outpost) to rescue Ben from his plight. Therefore, even though Ben's friendship with the Jazz Man effects a "happy ending" and elicits a welcome sigh of relief, it is a double-edged sword that effectively removes Ben from any meaningful association with his family. He falls helplessly into the presumptive stereotype of the exceptional Black having to disavow and throw off the drag-down atmosphere of Black family and community in order to succeed. Ben's ultimate success is implied at the end of the story but again, it is success occurring "in spite of" his familial associations rather than growing out of a generative or positive home/community experience. Even if he achieves his dream of musicianship, Ben has been effectively marooned and, through his friendship with the "stranger," succeeds only by disavowal, becoming an outsider himself.

What is the author's intention in portraying in her illustrations such an unredeeming picture of a Black family? Possibly it was the author's intent to tell a very familiar story, a story focusing upon the feelings of isolation a child can sometimes experience even when surrounded by family and friends, feelings which usually arise from such realities as a parent's preoccupation with other more immediate problems: the exigencies of work, (or the exigencies of no work), preoccupation with other siblings, a personal problem, etc. More specifically, the isolation a child can feel when he or she first experiences "passion"—in this instance Ben's desire to create music—and there seems to be no one to share it with, the inevitable times when parents appear remote and peers suddenly seem too immature to understand. However, none of these qualifiers appear in Rachel Isadora's story— neither in the text, nor the illustrations. On the contrary, members of Ben's family appear merely cruel and distant. Their tangible silence leaves a subtle imprint—home for Ben is a cold lifeless shoulder. (An argument might even be made that the author intended to portray Ben's sensibility, rather than his reality, but if this were the case, the author would be obliged to make this plain.) The text is spare, leaving gaps in the story which could have been filled in with a little dialogue, some character insight, some suggestion of context. But instead the burden of explanation rests with the illustrations.

It would have been so easy for *Ben's Trumpet* to be an elegant depiction of a child's struggle towards an aspiration. There are several positive aspects to the story: 1) Ben lives in a Black world; 2) there is use of the extended family structure of many Black homes; 3) it is implied in the story's conclusion that Ben, primarily through his own desire and secondarily through the help of another Black person, will achieve his dream; and 4) jazz, a historically Black musical idiom, has been used as an element in the narrative. Unfortunately, buried in the illustrations is the awful "reef" of the unexplored assumptions of a writer who has nothing at stake in perpetuating the inaccurate portrayal of the Black family as a non-nurturing entity. Pity.

In addition to the question of subliminal messages in illustration, there are issues relating to a very different kind of ethics in *Big Sixteen*. Mary Calhoun has taken a traditional Afro-American folktale from the collection *Mules and Men* (recorded by Zora Neale Hurston, anthropologist and folklorist of the 1930s) and made changes which violate the intent and spirit of the original tale. It is a question of whether a writer has any obligation to respect and preserve the integrity of a borrowed literary artifact. There is nothing subtle about the images to be found in *Big Sixteen* and, unlike *Ben's Trumpet*, it has no mitigating positive aspects.

In order to read any Black folktale and understand its meaning and style, one has to have access to certain "in-house" assumptions within the Black tradition regarding the nature of racism. There must be an ability to appreciate the biting sarcasm and irony which was frequently employed to protect the storyteller as he or she revealed the truth. *Big Sixteen* is not a story that can be fully comprehended unless one has some grasp of its historical and social context. The tale that Zora Neale collected told of "Big Sixteen," a powerful and capable Black man who followed his white master's instructions to a "T" without argument or excuse. The story operates on several levels. First, it asks and then proceeds to answer the question: What would happen if a white person's whims were to actually be fulfilled? In the original version, Old Massa loves to test the strength of his prime slave, so he routinely sets him to tasks that would be too difficult for the average slave. But "Big Sixteen" accomplishes each task with ease. Finally, the slavemaster, in awe of his slave's strength, exclaims ". . . you can do anything. You kin ketch the Devil." Naturally, "Big Sixteen" sets out to do just that. He digs a hole, descends to Hell, knocks the Devil over the head with a hammer, and finally places him at the feet of his astonished master. The story explores the nature of the master/slave relationship, hinting at the abuse of power by whites and suggesting a calculating savvy on the part of the slave. "Big Sixteen" is cunning enough to give his master what he asks for even when it's clearly to the master's detriment. The answer to the proposed question is that white men are capable, through their reckless toying with their own power, of throwing the entire cosmos—earth, heaven, and hell—into chaos.

On a second level, a different question is proposed: what happens to Black people who follow all the rules set up by white society, Black people who use their strength only to carry out the will of white people? What kind of reward can they expect? As the story goes, "Big Sixteen" attempts to enter heaven after his death and is refused admittance by St. Peter because he is too powerful: if he were to get out of hand, he could not be controlled. (An ironic touch that, even in heaven, Black people are to be controlled. And only a certain type of Black person will be allowed to enter.) Similarly, "Big Sixteen" is refused entrance to Hell because he has killed the Devil and is much feared. He is left to wander the earth with no final resting place. To take a step back, if we have our in-house assumptions in place, we know without being told that since whites run the world, they also are in control of heaven and hell. Therefore, "Big Sixteen"'s inability to gain entrance to either place is a biting, incisive, and still pertinent social commentary on the arrogance and ingratitude of whites and their gut-level fear of the people that they control. It is also a lesson for Blacks who suppress their personal strength, exhibit no anger at injustice, and do what they're told at all costs. It is clear that the only reward they can expect is a final cosmic kick in the pants and no place to go. This story was never intended as a simple children's fable. It is a subtle and stinging analysis of American social politics created by the folks who bore the brunt of its day-to-day implications.

I have taken the time to describe *Big Sixteen* in its original form and within its historical and social context—to discuss the intent and purpose behind the creation of the story—because it is precisely these elements that have been deliberately omitted, camouflaged, and distorted within Ms. Calhoun's retelling and Ms. Hyman's illustration of the story.

For the most part, the written text of Ms. Calhoun's version follows the original, but with some crucial omissions and changes. Immediately, the characters are removed from the context of slavery. This alteration is achieved through the omission of the first line in Zora Neale's version which prefaces the entire tale: "It was slavery time when Big Sixteen was a man." Zora's version also refers to the slave master as "Old Massa"; Ms. Calhoun chooses to refer to "Big Sixteen"'s master as "The Old Man," thereby camouflaging the nature of the relationship. By lifting the characters out of context, Calhoun paves the way for a series of illustrations which not only violate the story's vision and imagery, but are insulting and demeaning to any Black child who might happen across the book. From this point on, the original meaning and intent of the tale is systematically destroyed, not by any actual changing of the words, but through the misrepresentations of the illustrations.

Rather than being instructive or validating in the manner of the original tale, Ms. Calhoun's version of *Big Sixteen* is pure confusion, and the illustrations obscure the story, rather than illuminating it. In the images created by the illustrator, we are shown a Black cosmos where Black people are in control. There is no explanation as to why "Big Sixteen" performs these arduous feats of strength for "The Old Man." We are left to assume that he does these things because he either has nothing better to do, or because he just likes to show off. At any rate, the implications of the statement in Zora Neale's original version, that Old Massa "looked to [Big Sixteen] to do everything," is completely obscured.

Up in Heaven, St. Peter is a Black who is afraid of "Big Sixteen"'s strength for no apparent reason. And there can be no logical reason for his fear—weakness in Black men is only comforting from a white point of view. Black male strength is always *good* from a Black point of view. So who is this Black St. Peter who is afraid of an extension of himself? He is a lie concocted by a writer afraid of her borrowed material. In the original tale, St. Peter is presumed to be white; the reason for his fear of a Black man's overwhelming strength is perfectly clear within the political realities of a racist society.

Down in Hell, all the occupants are Black. And here, the illustrations take off into amazing grotesquery. The Black population of Hell is comprised of the Devil's widowed wife and orphaned kids, all neatly afro-ed and replete with the resurrected clawed feet, horns, and tails that it has taken decades to rid from the minds of bigoted whites. The Devil's wife is a sinister Black woman (also with horns, tail, and African-style, oversized jewelry) who tells "Big Sixteen" to get lost. Now really, if this version could be taken in its own context, as a Black woman, the Devil's wife would most likely be looking for a replacement for her dead husband and "Big Sixteen" would be a prime candidate. However, the Devil's wife turns him away for no apparent reason. The reason is not apparent because in the original tale, the Devil and his wife are presumed to be white. To eliminate this detail is to deny the possibility of logic. Only a white woman would be repelled by "Big Sixteen"'s strength (because even the Devil's wife adheres to the sexual strictures of society) and only she would have the power, bestowed by her whiteness, to be able to tell "Big Sixteen" where to get off.

The Black child reading this book will be left with a collection of images that portray a strong, noble Black man, who has committed no crime, as a universal pariah. A man who, despite his physical strength, is ultimately powerless to control his own destiny. Non-Black children are asked to envision a Hell peopled by Black folks, hideous in appearance. The irony of Hurston's tale, where the virtues of strength, nobility of character, obedience, and goodness are a Black man's downfall in a chaotic society, is deliberately altered through omission and through illustrations derived, not from the story, but from a twentieth-century white author's mind. These changes do not appear to result from a misunderstanding of the material, but from the author's efforts to confuse and misdirect. By destroying the integrity of the story of "Big Sixteen," Ms. Calhoun has clumsily attempted to absolve white people of the historic fact of their involvement in slavery, and their perpetuation of a racist system. It is unconscionable that a writer would maim and distort the vision of a classic Black folktale, transform it into a shambles of illogic, and for such a ludicrous, irresponsible and self-serving purpose.

Assessments of children's picture books are frequently incomplete in their analysis of the visual imagery. Such analyses, which ignore the presence and lasting impact of visual messages, tend to be superficial. In the two examples offered here, it is evident that the images have, consciously or unconsciously, served as vehicles for messages that would have been inarguably inappropriate had they been introduced in the written text. The fact that these ideas are only evident on the level of suggestion seems to have placed them outside the reviewer's critical arena.

A child's eye gives direct passage to his or her mind. Images have the power either to dispel or reinforce doubts and fears that are common to children. The ingrained assumptions of cultures can be edited out of textual narrative, but a picture can negate the good intentions of erased words.

19. THE BLACK EXPERIENCE THROUGH WHITE EYES—THE SAME OLD STORY ONCE AGAIN

Beryle Banfield and Geraldine L. Wilson

CHILDREN'S LITERATURE PROVIDES an almost unfailing gauge of the level of racism and sexism in a society. It must be recognized that the racism in children's materials is not a personal aberration on the part of an individual author but rather a reflection of societal attitudes and practices. In this connection, a look at children's literature during two critical periods of U.S. history proves instructive.

One hundred years ago, African Americans were at risk in every aspect of their lives—political, social and economic; the period 1877–1901 has been described by historian Rayford Logan as the Nadir of the Black Experience in the U.S. The period saw the betrayal of African American hopes for complete democracy and the destruction of the gains of Reconstruction.[1]

Following the end of Reconstruction, legal strategems forced Blacks to work for little or no wages. The Ku Klux Klan and similar terrorist organizations came into being to prevent African Americans from exercising their democratic rights. In 1883, the Supreme Court declared the Civil Rights Bill of 1875 unconstitutional; it also effectively blunted the Fourteenth Amendment by applying a specious and devious interpretation which held that the Amendment forbade states—not individuals—from discriminating. This interpretation paved the way for the enactment of a spate of Jim Crow laws which reinforced the separate and unequal status of African Americans. Influential academics proclaimed the virtues of the Anglo-Saxon race. Prominent professors flatly proclaimed Reconstruction to be a failure and asserted that Thomas Jefferson would have stated that he did not mean Negroes when he wrote "all men are created equal." A leading member of the clergy, much in demand as a lecturer, saw the Anglo-Saxon race "moving down upon Mexico, up Central and South America, out upon the islands of the sea, over upon Africa, and beyond." (The more things change the more they stay the same!) The leading literary magazines employed racially offensive terminology with impunity; words such as "darky" and "coon" appeared regularly, and African Americans were routinely portrayed as thieves, drunkards and immoral characters.

The children's literature of that period reflected societal racism, it extended the plantation tradition of literature which began in the early 1800s and depicted an idyllic plantation life with happy, "picturesque" slaves. This type of literature increased after the Post-Reconstruction period. Among its myths was the notion that African Americans in slavery had been happy, protected and well-cared for, and that they were ill-fitted for the responsibilities of freedom. Offensive racial stereotypes—the "comic Negro," the "contented slave," the "wretched freeman," among others identified in literature by Black poet Sterling Brown—were rounded out and solidified.

Two adept creators of juvenile literature that perpetuated these myths and stereotypes were Thomas Nelson Page and Joel Chandler Harris. In 1888, Page produced *Two Little Confederates*, complete with mangled Black "dialect," superstitious beliefs and contented, loyal, Yankee-hating slaves. Freedom is so abhorrent to Page's slaves that they eagerly cooperate in hiding their Confederate masters. Joel Chandler Harris contributed *Free Joe and the Rest of the World* (1888), which also perpetuates the myths and stereotypes of the wretched freeman and the contented slave. While contented slaves, secure in the knowledge that they would be adequately clothed and fed, sing happily at their work, Free Joe, with no benign master to guarantee his earthly comforts, looks on in wretched envy.

Uncle Remus, immortalized as the repository of the Br'er Rabbit Stories, is portrayed by his creator Joel Chandler Harris as the epitome of the Plantation Negro; Uncle Remus yearns for the security of the slave plantation and looks disdainfully on ex-slaves who prattle about freedom. The hugely successful *Bobbsey Twins* series made its first appearance in 1904, introducing Dinah, the buxom Black cook—a watermelon-eating, eye-rolling, superstitious, thieving Black.[2]

African Americans are now again at risk. There is a systematic and determined effort to wipe out the civil rights advances won in the 60s. Once again, the institutional arrangements that perpetuate racial inequities are being brought into play. Court decisions are severely hampering efforts to secure equal educational and employment opportunities. Agencies established to implement civil rights are being systematically weakened or their goals and purposes challenged. Fifty per cent of Black teenagers are unemployed. A report recently released by the Center for Social Policy reveals that on "measures of income, poverty and unemployment, wide disparities between Blacks and whites have not lessened or have even worsened since 1960." African Americans are keenly aware that in cities like Boston and New York there are places they may not go without fear of bodily harm. The Ku Klux Klan is increasingly and confidently active.

The appearance of books like *Jake and Honeybunch Go to Heaven* and *Shadow*—both highly acclaimed—serves to underscore the national mood. Their stereotypes and distortions are no longer subtle but blatant affronts to African American sensibilities, assaults on the cultural traditions and lifestyles of African Americans. The works reflect the increasing tolerance by society at large of the erosion of the civil rights so hard won during the 60s. [3]

Significantly, both books are based on aspects of the Black experience which the authors misunderstand and misrepresent. The damage is compounded by the fact that both authors are extremely gifted artists; the books therefore have a powerful impact and are extremely effective in reinforcing stereotypes of the African American.

It is worth looking more closely at some of the issues that these books raise, particularly given the acclaim that they have received.

In a society that practices colonialism, [4] the manipulation and control of symbols play an important role. Symbols relating to those groups excluded from power get particular attention. Although this practice affects all oppressed groups—women of all colors, disabled people among them—we will focus here only on those having to do with the Black experience.

Two sets of symbols specifically related to the African American community are at issue. One set consists of the distorted symbols (stereotypes, if you will) created by whites and intended to control, demean, and dehumanize African Americans; these symbols also serve to create or reinforce a sense of superiority in white people. These stereotypes often represent how whites *wish* "those people" would be; eventually, many whites come to believe that such "symbols" do, in fact, represent reality.

The second set of symbols are those actually based on the collective cultural experience of African Americans. They represent the important, valued characteristics and beliefs of the group. Many of these symbols have been passed down from generation to generation;

others, more recent, are no less valued. There is little opportunity for these symbols to appear in "public," meaning outside of the group itself; they are generally excluded from the media (books, TV, film, art, etc.) because African American behaviors and concepts are not generally acceptable unless controlled or exploited by whites. The African American world view can most freely be expressed within the Black community, but even there it may be monitored, repressed and/or punished by those in power—whites and sometimes Blacks who have internalized racism.

In practice, whites often assume, incorrectly, that everyone shares *their* set of European American symbols, or they deny the validity of the symbols of people of color by maintaining that they have no culture and therefore no valued symbols. Because African Americans—like other people of color—lack power, their cultural symbols are almost never reinforced in positive ways in the media (including children's literature) or by societal institutions. One result of cultural repression is that the very meanings of African American symbols become lost, unknown even to members of the Black community. This complicates the fact that people in many societies tend not to articulate certain aspects of their culture, though they respond to—and defend—those cultural practices and symbols they value.

There are at least two general responses by African Americans to the repression of valued symbols and the attempt to substitute distorted versions. First there are those who are knowledgeable about their culture, its values and symbols, and they move (and raise their children to move) to correct the distortions. Second, there are other members of the Black community who lack this level of awareness. This may be due to (a) a lack of information about their own cultural history, (b) the influence of white institutions, particularly the educational system and the media, and/or (c) an internalized poor self-image.

Recently one of the authors of this piece asked some Black parents if they told Br'er Rabbit stories to their children. "Oh, those stories by Walt Disney?" asked one mother. When the consultant replied, "They are not Walt Disney's stories," the woman answered, "Oh, yes, they are. Otherwise Disney wouldn't have put his name on the book. You can't put somebody else's name on a book. That's against the law, you know." The process of cultural repression had done its job. The questioner knew only the *appropriated* stories, stories in which the original symbols were transformed by European concepts, stories which do not give credit to the African and African American sources. She was *convinced* that falsehood was truth. (Her lack of information was, at least, not shared by the entire group. Another woman did say, "Girl, they ain't Walt Disney's stories; my grandmother knew them.")

Culture and how it is both expressed and repressed in a colonialist society has not received the kind of attention it needs. Nonetheless, much is known—and what we know gives added dimensions to the issues being addressed.

Consider the red head-wrap worn by African American women, a custom that crested in the late 19th and early 20th centuries. Although no accurate record has been kept of the extent to which women of African descent resisted the repression of their dress by whites and/or continue to express African elements of their dress, we do know several things about the red head-wrap: (a) women in certain African societies, especially those who were married and/or over certain ages, wrapped their heads in a variety of kinds and colors of cloth, (b) the method and style of wrapping varied from society to society, (c) the wrapping of the head was a mark of status and a woman with her head wrapped commanded respect, (d) during the height of the slave trade, women of African descent in the Caribbean, South and Central America continued to wrap (and still do wrap) their heads in ways similar to that of African women (women in Martinique tie their head-wraps in almost the same fashion as do women in Senegal), (e) enslaved African American women in the U.S. wrapped their heads, (f) women of African descent in the U.S. and elsewhere still wrap and cover their heads.

Some interesting facts emerge. One is that Black women in the U.S. bought enough red head cloths to support a factory in Texas at the end of the 19th century (at the same time, cowboys began to use that red cloth around their necks). Africans consider red to be positive and associated with life, blood, women; these connections are also expressed in African American literature and music. (European Americans value white as the color of virginity, purity and femininity—virginal brides wear white; "loose" women wear red.)

An interesting thing happened to the red head-wrap. In the late 19th century, during the intense campaign against Black people,[5] African American women were a major target. The red head-wrap became a symbol of derided Black womanhood, a mark of low status, a mark of servitude. In addition, in some areas of the South, Black women were not permitted to wear hats; hats were for "ladies," who, by definition, could only be white. Black women hated the restriction and grew to hate the head-wrap, the symbol of the personal and collective stylistic freedom denied them. As a result, many though not all Black women stopped wearing an important cultural symbol, a symbol that expressed the spiritual beliefs, the world view and the decorative, stylistic dress that continues to distinguish African people. (It is interesting to note that large numbers of Black American women still wear hats even when they are not in vogue, and these hats have been distinguished by their style and decoration.)

The anti-Black campaign did not only derogate women's use of red and head-wraps. The big gold earrings, the practice of piercing the ear, the word "mammy"—all these and other cultural behaviors and practices were caricatured, misrepresented, ridiculed. Piercing ears were considered "pagan," "savage," "un-Christian"—even though Ethiopians, Egyptians and other Africans who were among the first Christians pierced their ears. The word mammy was ridiculed as a mispronunciation of the English words "mommy" or "nanny," although mammy has long been a respected word in West Africa. (In Ghana and other countries, the economically and politically powerful market women are called mammies.) Mammy became a hated word and symbol in Black communities throughout the U.S. So did the caricatured face of Aunt Jemima, a symbol that derogated Black women, their dress (jewelry and head-wrap), their names (Jemima was a traditional African American name), and one of their titles of respect (Aunt or Auntie were—and still are—titles of endearment or respect for older Black women). African cultural aspects of femininity were labeled "unacceptable" by whites.

This brings us back to the two books under consideration. Both *Jake and Honeybunch* and *Shadow* contribute to the cultural repression of Black people by appropriating and misrepresenting important cultural symbols. Both convey misinformation about Black people, how they live, what they believe, what they consider sacred, what *they* consider appropriate to laugh at. (Whites ridicule Blacks in literature and other media and then accuse Black people of not having a sense of humor.)

The jacket of *Jake and Honeybunch* states that the story has been taken from African and African American sources. It was. The implication is that it is culturally authentic. It is not. The symbols that would have made it culturally authentic have been misrepresented or distorted (see chart at end of article).

Significantly, the book misrepresents the unique, culturally distinctive view of spiritual life held by people of African descent. We have, for instance, a wonderful, joyous vision of heaven. The scholars who have analyzed spirituals, other traditional songs and the literature of Black people (not to mention the show of Black folk art that the Brooklyn Museum organized last year) document quite clearly what heaven "looks like." Lucille Clifton refers to our view of heaven in *Good, Says Jerome,* the only children's book that mentions heaven in a distinctively African American fashion. (When Jerome asks his sister about death, she replies, life "ends when they meet old cousins and brothers and others at the meeting place. They'll wait for us, too. Me and you.")

Zemach has not used one culturally authentic clue about heaven as understood by generations of Black people. Those symbols that she has appropriated have been distorted. A real concern is that Black children will believe the portrayal of heaven in *Jake and Honeybunch* to be culturally authentic just as the young mother believed Walt Disney created Br'er Rabbit. Much of the furor about *Jake and Honeybunch* has to do with its violation of some highly valued symbols.[6]

Shadow, like *Jake and Honeybunch,* also misrepresents important cultural symbols but because it has to do with African life rather than African American culture, its flaws may not be so immediately apparent. *Shadow* lacks the cultural clues that would give an authentic picture of African life. Instead, the book violates some primary African spiritual/religious symbols (see chart at end of article).

Another dimension to the question of cultural repression must be noted here: the refusal of so many whites to even consider it as an issue. When some librarians, reviewers and individuals suggested that the treatment of African American culture in *Jake and Honeybunch* was racist, the classic forms of defense occurred:

Denial: Apparently, the easiest way to deal with racism is to deny its existence (see Dorothy Sterling, *English Journal,* September 1969). When interviewed on National Public Radio's "All Things Considered," a Farrar, Straus editor said that the charges of racism were "bizarre." In a separate incident, the editor-in-chief of that same house (who also serves as Zemach's editor) said that librarians who found the book racist evidenced a "misguided point of view."

Suppression of dialog: One can, in theory, raise almost any issue about a book and dialog will ensue—not necessarily dignified dialog if the issues are controversial enough, but dialog nonetheless. When racism is involved, however, the *possibility* of dialog is almost inevitably ruled out by those in power. (The reaction of the Farrar, Straus editors cited above is one way that dialog is suppressed.) The suppression of discussions of racism in children's books is a reflection of the general national suppression of such dialog. It is critical that this type of dialog take place; a suppressed criticism means a repressive literature.

Naïveté: Toni Morrison has referred to "the incredible innocence" that leads whites to profess great surprise when people of color object to manifestations of racism. Consider, for instance, the Farrar, Straus editors who asked why San Francisco librarians weren't buying the book.

Appeal to research: Jake's creator defended herself by saying that she did research and used African American sources. That is not the point. One would hope that such research was done. However, the sources selected, the researcher's understanding of those sources, her sensitivity to the tradition, her ability to identify and comprehend the important cultural symbols and their meaning within that tradition are critical issues that must be addressed.

Appeal to a group member: A white reviewer who praised *Jake* indicated that an unidentified African American artist-folklorist "considers" the book "rooted in traditional spirituals." An unidentified Black minister has been cited as liking the book very much. Such appeals to a Black authority (usually nameless) generate wry amusement in the Black community. Obviously, there will be some Black people who like such books. That is hardly the point. Producing a "witness for the defense" to justify a work's authenticity avoids what ought to be a collective responsibility to examine practices that result in the production of culturally inauthentic books. Such discussions ought to be welcomed, but unfortunately, sensitivity to issues of race and culture is considered outside the purview of craft.

Appeal to the concept of the writer's right: After years of denying that Blacks had a literary tradition, whites are "discovering" the reservoir of African American stories, epics, poetry, etc., and appropriating them for children's books. Whites frequently state that they have the "right" to use materials from other cultures more or less as they see fit. Sometimes citing the First Amendment, sometimes the sacredness of a writer's imagination, they refuse to acknowledge issues of cultural appropriation or misrepresentation. Surely these are issues all of us should want to discuss. (An increasing number of books on African American themes are being written by whites, even as works by Black authors are going out of print.)

Cries of censorship: Citing the First Amendment, some people all too often consider criticism of racism (or sexism) as tantamount to a call for book burning. In the course of their duties, librarians and/or reviewers may "not recommend" a book because of its poor artistic or literary quality; they may even suggest that a library not purchase a book for the same reason. No problem. Let someone say the same because of racist content, and all hell breaks loose. This tactic effectively shifts attention from racism to censorship, an irrelevant connection.

Denial of responsibility: Members of the it's-not-our-responsibility brigade—usually publishers and their apologists—are willing to acknowledge their obligation for selection issues such as those related to "literary quality" and finances, but unwilling to consider social justice issues or the effects of racist books on children. States the *Newsletter on Intellectual Freedom* published by the American Library Association's Office for Intellectual Freedom:

Whether or not *Jake and Honeybunch* is guilty of racial stereotyping, according to ALA policy as enunciated in the Library Bill of Rights and elaborated in the policy on *Diversity in Collection Development,* this is not for librarians to judge. (March, 1983)[7]

Some 100 years ago, Henry McNeal Turner made a telling—and still relevant—comment. Born enslaved, he fought in the Civil War, became the first chaplain permitted to serve with Black troops and was elected to Georgia's first Reconstruction legislature. He soon saw the gains of Reconstruction being taken away. When Blacks were illegally expelled from the Georgia legislature, he said:

We are told that if Black people want to speak they must speak through white trumpets. . . . if Black people want their sentiments expressed they must be adulterated and sent through white messengers.[8]

The crucial issue of cultural repression must still be addressed, particularly as it affects children's books. Until there is a forum for open, respectful discussion of the issue, it will be impossible to move toward an authentic, representative children's literature.

Notes

1. "Reconstruction lasted ten years. During that time, a coalition of Blacks, poor whites and some Northern Republicans who had moved South enacted far-reaching political and social reforms in the constitutional conventions and newly elected legislatures of

the South. The new state constitutions provided universal male suffrage (a few state constitutions disfranchised some former public officials who supported secession, but the disqualifications were minor and temporary). This gave the vote for the first time to newly freed Black men, as well as to thousands of poor whites, who before the Civil War had been deprived of the vote because of property-ownership qualifications. For the first time, Southern states provided free public schools for all children, a gain not only for Black children but for tens of thousands of poor white children who previously had been denied education. The property rights of women were protected, divorce laws written and imprisonment for debt abolished. Orphanages, asylums for the insane and schools for blind and deaf people were established." From *Violence, the Ku Klux Klan and the Struggle for Equality* (The Connecticut Education Association, the Council on Interracial Books for Children, The National Education Association, 1981). For additional information on the reforms of the Reconstruction era, see: Lerone Bennett, Jr., *Black Power USA: The Human Side of Reconstruction* (Johnson Publishing Co., 1967); The Council on Interracial Books for Children, *Reconstruction: The Promise and Betrayal of Democracy* (The Council on Interracial Books for Children, 1983); W. E. B. Du Bois, *Black Reconstruction in America, 1860–1880* (Atheneum, 1962); John Hope Franklin, *Reconstruction After the Civil War* (University of Chicago Press, 1961); and Kenneth M. Stampp, *The Era of Reconstruction, 1865–1877* (Knopf, 1965).

2. For a review of the treatment of Blacks in children's fiction of this period, see Dorothy Broderick, *Image of the Black in Children's Fiction* (R. R. Bowker, 1973).

3. This is not to suggest that the 60s were a period of bias-free literature. The stereotypes simply appeared in a more subtle form. For instance, the widely-acclaimed *The Cay* by Theodore Taylor (1969) carried the stereotype of the contented slave to its "logical" conclusion: Timothy, who establishes his servile relationship to a young white boy with his very first words, eventually sacrifices his own life to save his master. (The grotesque Negro stereotype also plays a part in this tale.)

4. Colonialism is a political system of relationships in which one group controls and oppresses another. Fanon, Memni and others have written about classic colonialism, in which the colony is located far from the metropole (*i.e.*, the colonial center). Lerone Bennett, Jr. discusses "internal colonialism," in which the colonized people live within the same geographic borders as the colonial center; he applies this definition to the situation of people of color in the U.S. Both classic and internal colonialism have five components: racism, cultural repression, political domination, economic exploitation and force. For further information, see Bennett's *The Shaping of Black America* (Johnson Publishing Co., 1975).

5. See Ida B. Wells-Barnett, *A Red Record* (Donahue & Henneberry, 1894).

6. It must be noted that the serious issues of appropriation and distortion are not the only problems with *Jake and Honeybunch*. There is, for instance, the lack of variety in the skin color of the Black characters (everyone is the same color, which is unrealistic), almost all of the Black inhabitants of heaven look miserable (hardly appropriate), Jake can't even be counted on to tend to his job of moon regulator (another incompetent shiftless Black worker). The list goes on.

7. Lillian Gerhardt of *School Library Journal* takes another position which clarifies the librarians' responsibilities and options regarding book selection:

> Farrar, Straus & Giroux has been behaving as if librarians are obligated to buy *Jake and Honeybunch* . . . for their children's book collections whether or not they wish to use it with children. No such obligation exists. Nor is any apology due to the publisher for a decision taken against the purchase of the book in accordance with established library book selection policies and procedures. That's book selection. (*School Library Journal*, March, 1983)

8. "Participation of Negroes in the Government 1867–1870" by Ethel Christler, unpublished Master's Thesis, Atlanta University, 1932.

Jake and Honeybunch: An Analysis of Its Cultural Symbols

SYMBOL	JAKE AND HONEYBUNCH	AFRICAN AMERICAN PERSPECTIVE
The Train	A train kills Jake and his mule, Honeybunch.	It is not at all likely that a traditional African American author would use a train to *kill* a character. A train is a symbol of transport to glory, to "heaven," to "home" (meaning heaven, the place where family is, the place where God is, Africa). The train was also a symbol of transport to the North and Canada and therefore freedom. Still in use as a major symbol. God drives trains, or the train, in a symbolic way, is driven by the energies of Black people.
	A billboard that reads "travel while you sleep" shows a Black man who seems to be in a railroad sleeping car.	Black people were not permitted to use sleeping cars when the story takes place.
	A Black man is shown driving the train that kills Jake and Honeybunch.	Black men were not allowed to drive locomotives, although they were permitted to be engineers, the most dangerous job.
Green Pastures	A sign at the Pearly Gates reads "Heavenly Green Pastures," and when Honeybunch looks through the gates, she sees "the	"Green Pastures" is *not* an African American symbol; Blacks consider it a disrespectful portrait of heaven. Green Pastures is a

(*continued*)

SYMBOL	JAKE AND HONEYBUNCH	AFRICAN AMERICAN PERSPECTIVE
	Great Green Pastures of Heaven."	Euro-American symbol that caricatures and ridicules African American spiritual life. It was popularized by the 1930's play "The Green Pastures," which white playwright Marc Connelly based on an earlier work that was also written by a white author—"Old Man Adam and His Chillun" by Roark Bradford.
Heavenly Clothing	The inhabitants of heaven are shown wearing everyday clothing—chefs' uniforms, overalls and the like—of various colors.	Clothing has a variety of spiritual meanings based on an African world view that goes back centuries. For example, the type of cloth used, its color, its patterns, the occasion on which it's worn, all have meanings that can be "read." *Standard for heavenly wear is the color white* (see below), with silver or gold shoes, gold wings and gold crown.
Heavenly/Spiritual Colors	Heaven is depicted in a variety of colors—some pastel, some bright, some dark.	White is associated with heaven, ancestors and the spirit world in both African and African American life. Bright colors are not appropriate for heaven. Neither are dark colors (note the black sky).
Heavenly Food	Barbecued ribs, chicken, pies and other foods are shown floating around as the inhabitants of heaven prepare a meal.	Milk and honey are the only foods mentioned in spirituals. Eating is not a heavenly concern. The foods shown are appropriate

(*continued*)

SYMBOL	JAKE AND HONEYBUNCH	AFRICAN AMERICAN PERSPECTIVE
		for earthly celebrations, not in heaven—and any heavenly food would not float chaotically around. (A survey of picture books about Judeo-Christian heavens revealed that none showed cooking as an activity!)
Heavenly Movement	It takes Jake ten minutes to "flip-flop his way along the glory road" to the Heavenly Gates.	Traditionally, those who have been transported to heaven dance, "shout" or "stomp" (both "shouting" and 'stomping," forms of African American holy dancing, have been suppressed by Euro-Protestant faiths). Jake's behavior conveys laziness or sloppiness—it is entirely inappropriate for approaching heaven.
Music	The musicians look like a jazz or blues band playing in a nightclub.	Heavenly music is supplied by choirs.
"Flying Fool"	Jake says, "I'm *just* a flying fool" (emphasis added).	In traditional African American stories, a Black man goes to heaven and is expelled by a white God and angels because he flies extraordinarily well and/or fast and thus upsets heaven. He calls himself a "flying fool" because he did well! (If someone says "Tyrone was a dancing fool," it does not mean Tyrone is a fool. It means he dances well!)

(continued)

SYMBOL	JAKE AND HONEYBUNCH	AFRICAN AMERICAN PERSPECTIVE
		The original stories convey the African American practice of doing "extra-well" in white settings. The statement "I was a flying fool" also has a "self-praising" aspect: even though a white God puts the Black man out of heaven, he knows he did well. Learning how to gauge one's own performance is important for Black people because whites rarely recognize or validate what Blacks do. Jake's statement makes him seem foolish instead of accomplished.

Shadow: An Analysis of Its Cultural Symbols

Note: The chart below does not convey the feeling that the book evokes: that Africa is an unpleasant, frightening place. In *Shadow,* Africa is a place only of extremes; of heat-seared deserts and of jungles with snake-draped trees, a place of crawly things—snakes, scorpions and worms—with eagles and vultures hovering overhead.

SYMBOL	SHADOW	TRADITION
Masks	A large brightly colored mask appears on a double-spread captioned, "Here it [*i.e.,* Shadow] is in a mask." The same spread shows several white disembodied mask-like faces; similar mask-like faces also appear on the frontispiece and title page.	The large mask in *Shadow* is grotesque, frightening and inaccurately colored with large dots and stripes. African masks, made by artists trained in traditional values, are used in religious and ceremonial services; they are not considered grotesque or frightening. As George Tabman, a member of the Dan society in Liberia, has noted, "Beautiful masks keep

(*continued*)

SYMBOL	SHADOW	TRADITION
		children from fright, because it is through the masks that they will learn the tradition." The use of ghostly white "masks" is also inappropriate; see below.
White	Some streaky white disembodied faces that seem to be based on African masks appear in several illustrations (see above).	The white mask-like faces in *Shadow* seem spectral and frightening. White signifies ancestors and other positive spirits, a major element in African spiritual life. It is a color having spiritual, not ghostly or frightening, connotations. The African religious practice of applying white to the face (not to masks) has been caricatured as well as misinterpreted.
African People	The black cut-out figures have few or no features except for large, slanted white eyes.	The features of African people vary greatly. Many have almond-shaped eyes, dramatic against their dark skin, a characteristic that has been stereotyped and caricatured. African people are a variety of beiges, browns and blacks, a reality obscured by the illustrations in *Shadow*.
Clothing	The silhouetted figures (almost all appear to be men) seem to be wearing grass (or feather) "skirts."	Grass "skirts," which are actually worn in very few tropical societies, are not the standard dress for African men or women. The clothing of the hundreds of different African societies varies greatly. A unifying principle, expressed by each society, is the concept of

(*continued*)

SYMBOL	SHADOW	TRADITION
		personal adornment, which requires decorating the body or wearing decorative clothing. Clothing styles distinguish Africa's people and identifies them as belonging to a particular society. A note on sex roles: African women—who are barely visible in *Shadow*— play important roles in African society as mothers, warriors, rulers, etc., and their importance is reflected in the extent to which they appear in the art of the continent.
Architecture	A number of round, thatched "huts" are shown.	The caricatured "huts" depicted have become a shorthand symbol conveying "primitive" people. African architecture is rich and varied; it ranges from the great North African Islamic temples, Egyptian palaces and tombs to Dogon terraced stone homes and Ethiopian stone cathedrals to round buildings covered with woven grass or palm-frond roofs (local materials).
Spears, Shields	Various figures with "spears" (called lances when used by Europeans) and shields are shown. One spread with such figures is captioned, "It [*i.e.,* Shadow] follows man everywhere, even to war."	The depiction of individuals with "spears" and shields reinforces the stereotype that Africans are war-like. It also reinforces the notion that Africans are "primitive," with weaponry that is inferior to that of the Europeans; this obscures the fact that various African peoples routed European invaders for many decades, until the repeater gun was perfected.

20. JAKE AND HONEYBUNCH GO TO HEAVEN
Book Review

Nancy L. Arnez

THIS BOOK STEREOTYPES black people as a group as well as black home life and religious practices. It appears to be a take-off on the movie "Green Pastures," a white portrayal of pseudo-black religious practices. None of the characters in the book are depicted in a full and/or real manner. They are depicted in stereotypic roles, such as the following: playing music, singing, dancing, clowning, eating, cooking, trying to get into Heaven.

The author shows black environments which are unrealistically negative with no redeeming features. The buildings are depicted exclusively as cluttered, ugly and dilapidated. There is confusion in the yard and street as there is in Ms. Zemach's image of Heaven.

The subject matter is poorly treated and gives an unrealistic portrayal of black relgious life. Actually, the author is making fun of one of black people's most serious values.

This book is replete with more of the demeaning, derogatory, negative references and illustrations of black life than any children's story that I have ever read. Here, we note witches, devils, circus clowns and buffoons, shoe shines, unrealistically drawn black features, obese women, mainly tattered or mismatched clothing, exaggerated emotional expressions on the faces (overly sad, astonished or angry), and the unrealistic and stereotyped goal of the main character (to get into Heaven rather than live on earth).

The circumstances depicted provide other negative images of blacks as lazy, clumsy, sleeping, slouching, slow-moving, superstitious, good-timing, always eating, ignorant, foolish, crazy-acting, never getting things right, comic and confused. It is a caricature, indeed a comic or grotesque imitation of black life.

Jake and Honeybunch Go to Heaven is entirely demeaning to black people and is not recommended for purchase by any public school system, any public library or for any home. The book reinforces the white child's negative view of black people and destroys the black child's positive self-concept.

Part V

RACISM AND PUBLISHING

21. BLACKS IN THE WORLD OF CHILDREN'S BOOKS*

Jeanne S. Chall, Eugene Radwin, Valarie W. French, and Cynthia R. Hall

THIS ARTICLE REPORTS a study of representation of Blacks in children's trade books published from 1973–75. It attempts to replicate Larrick's study (1965) of the quantity and quality of children's books containing Black characters published from 1962–64.

From a survey of children's trade books published during 1962–64, Larrick concluded that "non-white children are learning to read and to understand the American way of life in books which either omit them entirely or scarcely mention them." We sought to determine whether the situation had changed over the eleven year period, and if so, in what ways.

The years between the two surveys brought many changes. Minorities made gains in their fight for equality, and more and more children were learning to read and write in schools that were mixed racially and ethnically. It therefore seemed appropriate to determine whether children's trade books reflected these changes.

As Larrick had done for her study, we surveyed publishers who were members of The Children's Book Council. Specifically, we sought answers to the following questions.

To what extent are Black characters found in children's books and how does this compare to Larrick's findings for the 1960s? Also,

---

*Editors' Note: The optimism expressed in this article about small presses is, unfortunately, not justified. Among the few that published children's books, Afro Am Publishers and Broadside Press went out of business, and Johnson publications have been severely cut back. It should also be noted that a more comprehensive study of the cultural content in books about Blacks is necessary, if one is to understand the meaning of the statistics. This would mean a study that extends beyond the limited goals of the Larrick report (1965)—as useful as that report and its sequel by the Harvard group are in indicating some of the superficial shifts in the publishing industry. Another industry shift is indicated by the fact that the 1984 edition of the New York Public Library's bibliography, "The Black Experience in Children's Books," is only about half the size of the 1979 edition. (See *American Libraries*, September 1984, p. 601.)

how prominent are the Black characters? Are they found in major or minor roles? In what settings, locales, and situations are Blacks presented? Do particular types of children's books tend to have a greater or lesser number of books with Black characters?

The study aimed to deal with both the quantitative and qualitative aspects of children's books containing Black characters. It was hoped that the results would be of some assistance to those responsible for writing, producing, and selecting books for children.

Assumptions and Related Literature

Underlying this study was the assumption that books influence the way children view themselves and others. By providing depictions of various cultures and life-styles, books can help children gain a more realistic picture of the world in which they live. By the same token, if the books to which children are exposed fail to represent the diversity of our multiethnic and multiracial society, they will not be serving our children and society at large.

A number of studies of the 1960s and 1970s concluded that children's books were important for the development of self-concept, world view, and language and reading. Cohen (1969) and Miel and Kiesten (1967) concluded that the images to which children are exposed can affect the ways they view themselves and the ways they view members of other groups. Somewhat later, Gast (1970) and Dieterich (1972) reported that books transmitted social values and attitudes about minority groups, and Glancy (1970) held that a healthier psychological growth can be achieved through books by increasing the child's awareness of people of different backgrounds. According to Davis (1972), when Black children who have a strong sense of radical identity are exposed only to literature containing poorly depicted or stereotyped Black characters, they may develop a negative outlook on books and reading.

Carol Chomsky's (1972) study of linguistic maturity and book exposure and the analysis of reading development by Chall indicated that the quantity of books read by children is positively related with their language and reading development. Thus, the quantity and kinds of books available to minority children may affect not only their developing self-esteem and attitudes but their language and reading development.

Studies were also conducted during the 1960s and early 1970s on the depiction of minorities in children's books. Shepard (1962) found from a content analysis of 16 popular children's books that only 4% of the "favorable characters" were nonwhite while 38% of the "unfavorable characters" were nonwhite. Heroes and heroines tended to be "clean, white, healthy, handsome, Protestant Christian, middle-class people."

In probably the most comprehensive study to date, Larrick (1965) sought to find through an industrywide survey the amount of representation of Blacks in children's trade books. Of the 5,200 books published in 1962, 1963, and 1964 by 63 publishers, only 6.7% had even a single Black character in either text or illustration. Of the books including Blacks, nearly 60% were set either outside the U.S. or before World War II. Only eight-tenths of 1% of all children's books had Black characters depicted in contemporary American settings. Of equal importance was Larrick's conclusion from a qualitative evaluation that the portrayals of Black characters were often biased and stereotypic.

A later survey by Sterling (1968) concluded that only 1% of the books written for children were germane to the Black experience. Baronberg's (1971) study of selected preschool picture books found that in one-half the books designated as integrated, the illustrations were of children of unspecified color.

Studies conducted in the early 1970s tended to express optimism that more children's books appropriate for Blacks and other minority groups would be published (Gast 1970, Cornelius 1971, Muse 1975). Wunderlich (1974) claimed, on the basis of studying 25 books, that there had been a substantial increase "in books which include today's Black America." Davis (1972), however, lamented a dearth of children's books depicting the life of Blacks in America.

In summary, the studies of the 1960s and early 1970s found few Black characters included in children's books. When included, they were often in derogatory roles. During the early 1970s, some investigators reported an improvement. Others reported no change.

Collection of Data

The basic data for the current study were collected in two stages.
1. A questionnaire based on the one used by Larrick in 1965 was

sent to the 58 publishing firms that are members of The Children's Book Council. The questionnaire asked them to supply the following information: the number of children's trade books published during 1973, 1974, and 1975; the number of these books which included one or more Black characters in the text or illustrations; and the titles of this latter group of books.

    2. A random sample of approximately one-sixth of the books with Black characters from those listed by the publishers on the questionnaires was closely analyzed to determine how Black characters were depicted.

Limitations of the Study

One of our limitations was that we surveyed only The Children's Book Council members, since we sought to compare our findings with those of Nancy Larrick. Since Larrick's 1965 study, there have been many new publishing firms founded to publish books for and about Blacks and other minorities. These new publishing houses are not members of The Children's Book Council, whose members publish from 80 to 90% of all children's trade books (books not intended as school textbooks) in the U.S.

    Thus, the extent of representation of Blacks found in our survey may be an understatement. The minority presses may in fact increase the number of books on minority topics or themes, but because they are small companies, it is difficult to know how much total impact they have. Overall though, many believe that these small publishing houses have enriched the store of children's books about Black folk literature and other ethnic topics.

    Another limitation is our focus on Black characters only. This should not be interpreted as a lack of concern for other minority groups. Rather, there were realistic reasons for limiting the scope of the study. First, a major goal of the survey was to allow meaningful comparison with the findings from Larrick's study. Second, time did not permit our conducting a detailed and thorough analysis of the representations of more than one minority group in children's literature.

Results of Questionnaire Analysis

Of the 58 publishers belonging to The Children's Book Council, 51 returned usable reports. (Several publishers either did not provide the titles of books with Black characters or did not provide a year-by-year breakdown.) These 51 reported publishing a total of 4,775 children's trade books during 1973–75. Of this number, 689 or 14.4% included one or more Black characters in the text or illustrations.

This number was more than double the 6.7% found in 1965 by Larrick for children's books published during 1962–64. In the period of her study, 87.3% of the publishers produced books with at least one Black character (Nancy Larrick 1975: personal communication), while we found 94% for the period 1973–1975. (Tables on which these findings are based may be obtained from Professor Jeanne Chall, Graduate School of Education, Harvard University, Cambridge, Massachusetts 02138.)

Most of the books with Black characters were designated by the publishers for use by children in grades four through eight; the next largest group of books were for preschool to grade three.

Content Analysis

A random sample of 115 books (one-sixth the total which included Black characters for 1973–1975) was analyzed for genre and for various other emphases.

The most common genres were contemporary fiction, biography, books on social and historical issues, and general nonfiction. These accounted for almost 80% of the sample. Of the remaining genres, not one composed even 5% of the sample.

Almost 85% of the 115 books sampled contained both text and illustrations. The predominance of illustrated books was evident within all genres except historical fiction.

Seventy percent of these 115 books were set exclusively in the United States and another 11% were set in both the United States and in another country. Few books were set exclusively outside this country.

Overall, most books were set in a variety of locales or in no specific locale. Neither urban nor suburban settings predominated.

For the books with characters—the fictional genres and biographies—the race (Black, White or other) of main, secondary and tertiary characters, and of illustrations was determined. (Books were classified as follows: "all Black"—only Black characters; "chiefly Black"—White, or other non-Black characters appeared at no higher than a tertiary level; "emphasis Black"—White or other characters appeared at no higher than a secondary level; "integrated"—Black and White main characters; "emphasis White"—Blacks at no higher than a secondary level; "chiefly White"—Blacks at no higher than a tertiary level; and "other"—a character neither Black nor White appeared in one of the remaining role designations. "All White" did not exist as a category since, by definition, the analyzed books contained at least one Black.)

In general, Blacks had significant roles in the majority of the books analyzed. (Roles were classified as "main," "secondary," "tertiary," or "illustration only," and were considered to represent a hierarchy from "main" to "illustration." Books were designated at the level of the most significant Black characters.) Over 75% of these books had Blacks in main roles and another 16% had Blacks in secondary roles. This was particularly evident in the biographies and contemporary fiction.

Overall, about half of the books were either "all" or "chiefly" Black, that is, containing only Black characters or having non-Black characters in tertiary roles. Within genres, this was particularly noted for folktales and biographies, and to a lesser degree in books of contemporary fiction. Historical fiction and fantasy tended to have a more varied racial composition. In general, the difference between the number of books which might be classified as relatively unintegrated and those classified as relatively integrated was small.

Book jackets and illustrations were also analyzed to estimate the relative prominence of Blacks. Of the 61 nonfiction books which had people on their jackets, Blacks appeared alone on 57%, and 31% of these depicted Blacks together with another racial group.

Most of the biographies had only Blacks on their jackets. The books on social and historical issues and general nonfiction books tended to depict only Whites on their jackets, although many depicted both Black and White characters.

Generally, Black characters were not as well represented in text illustrations as on the book jackets. Almost half, 46.6%, of the 115 books analyzed had Blacks in no more than 20% of their illustrations which contained human beings. Only the biographies contained a substantial percentage of illustrations of Blacks.

In summary, the content analysis revealed that when Blacks were shown in children's books published in the period 1973–75, they were represented in a variety of settings and locales; they were well represented in numbers in contemporary fiction, nonfiction, and books on social and historical issues; and they were generally given important roles in these books.

Other Findings from 1976 Survey

Besides the previously noted increase in the percentage of books with Black characters over what Larrick had found, our study found several other advances since Larrick's work: a greater proportion of books of contemporary fiction; a greater representation in nonfiction of Blacks functioning in a variety of situations; and a substantial number of biographies of Blacks. It should be noted, however, that the majority of these biographies were about sports figures and popular entertainers. Of the nearly 700 books with Blacks, 79 were biographies, and of these, 50 dealt with sports figures or entertainers. On the whole, biographies of Blacks published during 1973 to 1975 did not present many quiet heroes. There was one of Langston Hughes, one of Sojourner Truth, and one of Arthur Mitchell. But there were two of Muhammad Ali and five of Henry (Hank) Aaron.

Historical fiction, fantasy, folktales, humor and poetry comprised a small percent of the books with Black characters. While it appears that more folktales and poetry are being published currently than in earlier periods (Nancy Larrick 1977: personal communication), our estimates for the years 1973–75 indicate that the numbers are low for such books with Black characters. This is unfortunate, for books relating folktales of the Black experience in this country and in Africa could aid Black youngsters in developing a positive sense of themselves as members of a group with a rich and long tradition. And non-Black youngsters would gain from learning that the traditions of Blacks are as vital and legitimate as those of other groups.

Qualitative Impressions

We report here on matters that cannot be easily presented in statistical form but rely on judgments about the quality of the books.

Some of the books are a pleasure to read. Such titles as *The Third Gift* (Carew 1974) and *The Hundred Penny Box* (Mathis 1975) provide beautifully illustrated, sensitively executed descriptions of the experiences of Black people. *That New Baby* (Stein 1974) and *Do A Zoom Do* (Bernice 1975), both nonfiction, depict Black people in a realistic and natural manner. Among the biographies, *Sojourner Truth* (Ortiz 1974) is exemplary in its depiction of a strong, warm, courageous and real person.

Not all of the books are of such high quality, however. Some are still characterized by the stereotypes that have long been decried. For example, in one of the history books, the Black slaves are depicted as ever high-spirited, smiling, and fun loving. The biographies of Black athletes also tend to emphasize their exuberance and joyfulness without also including their serious competitiveness.

Another type of stereotype is conveyed by a book designed to teach children the fundamentals of basketball. While it includes many photographs of Black collegiate basketball players, the photographs which were specifically staged to demonstrate basketball skills include no Blacks. In several of the social studies books, the role of Blacks in American history seems generally underplayed. A book designed to dispel the myths of American history seemed to perpetuate some itself in its neglect of Black participation in the American Revolutionary War and in the winning of the West.

Changes from 1965 to 1976

Some changes did occur with regard to Black representation in children's books. In a year and a decade, as we have noted, the percentage of children's books which depict Black characters more than doubled—from 6.7% found by Larrick in 1965 to 14.4% found by our 1976 survey. There has also been an increase in the percentage of publishers producing books with Black characters, from 87.3% in 1965 (Nancy Larrick 1976: personal communication) to 94% in the present study. (It should be noted, however, that in the Larrick study, 63 publishers responded and reported publishing a total of 5,260 books in 1962–64; in the present study 51 publishers responded and reported publishing 4,775 books in 1973–75.) Both of these changes may, in fact, reflect at least in part the impact of Larrick's study and report.

Other changes were also discernible, Larrick had found that over 60% of the books with one or more Black characters were set outside the United States or before World War II. In the 1976 survey, we found that fewer than 20% of the books with Black characters were set entirely outside the United States, and less than 16% were set in the years before World War II.

Larrick had found that 14% of the books with Black characters had contemporary settings while we found 28%. By adding to the contemporary fiction all other books having a contemporary setting, 75% of the 1976 sample of books were set in a contemporary world. By extrapolating from these data, it was possible to estimate that nearly 11% of all children's books published depicted at least one Black character in contemporary settings. These figures represent a substantial increase over Larrick's eight-tenths of 1%.

Conclusions

Overall, compared to 1965, definite improvements can be seen in children's books containing Black characters. The percent of books with one or more Black characters in text or illustrations doubled. The 1976 survey also found that the Black characters in children's books were placed in more contemporary settings and had more prominent roles.

However, much still remains to be done with regard to both quantity and quality. A 100% increase still leaves 86% of children's trade books in an "all White world," to borrow Larrick's phrase of 1965. Perhaps the best way to improve the situation further is to encourage and recognize talented writers from various minority groups who will create the literature from their own experiences. There are many recent and encouraging developments in this respect. We agree with Ethel Heins of *Horn Book* magazine that children's literature must always be judged as literature, regardless of theme, content, or author.

To conclude, we raise some of the many questions that occurred as we sought answers to the questions raised in the present study. How are minority groups other than Blacks depicted in children's books? Is this depiction similar to that of Blacks? Do children like to read about ethnic groups? About people of their own ethnic background? About people of other ethnic backgrounds?

References

Baronberg, Joan. "Black Representations in Children's Books." *ERIC–IRCD* Urban Disadvantaged Series, No. 21, May 1971. ERIC ED 050 188. Arlington, Va.: ERIC Document Reproduction Service.

Bernice, Chester, Ed. *Do A Zoom Do*. Boston, Mass.: Little, Brown & Co., 1975.

Carew, Jan. *The Third Gift*. Boston, Mass.: Little, Brown & Co., 1975.

Chall, Jeanne S. "The Great Debate: Ten Years Later, with a Modest Proposal for Reading Stages" *Theory and Practice of Early Reading*, vol. 1, L. R. Resnick and P. A. Weaver, Eds. Hillsdale, N.J.: Lawrence Erlbaum Associates, 1980.

Chomsky, Carol. "Stages in Language Development and Reading Exposure." *Harvard Educational Review*, vol. 42, no. 1 (February 1972). pp. 1–33.

Cohen, Sol. "Minority Stereotypes in Children's Literature: The Bobbsey Twins, 1904–1968." *The Educational Forum*, vol. 34 (1969), pp. 119–25.

Cornelius, Paul. "Interacial Children's Books: Problems and Progress." *Library Quarterly*, vol. 41 (1971), pp. 106–27.

Davis, Mavis Wormely. "Black Images in Children's Literature: Revised Editions Needed." *Library Journal*, vol. 97, Part 1 (1972), pp. 261–63.

Dieterich, Daniel J. "Books That Lie and Lullabye." ERIC/RCS Report. *Elementary English*, vol. 49, no. 7 (November 1972), pp. 1000–09.

Gast, David K. "The Dawning of the Age of Aquarius for Multi-Ethnic Children's Literature." *Elementary English*, vol. 47 (1970), pp. 661–65.

Glancy, Barbara. "The Beautiful People in Children's Literature." *Childhood Education*, vol. 46 (1970), pp. 365–70.

Larrick, Nancy. "The All-White World of Children's Books." *Saturday Review*, (September 11, 1965), pp. 63–65, 84–85.

Mathis, Sahron Bell, *The Hundred Penny Box*. New York, N.Y.: Viking Press, 1975.

Miel, Alice and Edwin Kiesten, Jr. *The Shortchanged Children of Suburbia: What Schools Don't Teach about Human Differences and What Can Be Done About It*. New York, N.Y.: Institute of Human Relations Press, American Jewish Committee, 1967.

Muse, Daphne. "Black Children's Literature: Rebirth of a Neglected Genre." *The Black Scholar*, vol. 7, no. 4 (December 1975), pp. 11–15.

Ortiz, Victoria. *Sojourner Truth: A Self-Made Woman*. Philadelphia, Pa.: Lippincott, 1974.

Shepard, John P. "The Treatment of Characters in Popular Children's Fiction." *Elementary English*, vol. 39 (1962), pp. 672–77.

Stein, Sara, B. *That New Baby*. New York, N.Y.: Walker & Co., 1974.

Sterling, Dorothy. "The Soul of Learning." *English Journal*, vol. 57, no. 2 (Febraury 1968), pp. 166–80.

Wunderlich, Elaine. "Black Americans in Children's Books." *The Reading Teacher*, vol. 28, no. 3 (December 1974), pp. 282–85.

22. THE BLACK EXPERIENCE IN CHILDREN'S BOOKS: ONE STEP FORWARD, TWO STEPS BACK

Walter Dean Myers

I WAS AT A CONFERENCE at a small school in Michigan. The focus of the conference was on literature for children. My talk had gone reasonably well, touching upon my own publications and my seven-year career as an editor. The question and answer period was divided into two sections, interrupted by a more than welcome coffee break. At the beginning of the second session a young man in the front of the auditorium raised his hand. He hadn't participated in the earlier session although I had noticed him taking careful notes.

"Mr. Myers, apart from your personal interest in multi-ethnic literature," he asked, "don't you think we've been harping on the issue of racism in children's books for some time now?"

The inference, of course, was that the "some time" had been too long a time. I asked him to elaborate on his question and, rather uncomfortably it seemed, he expressed the view that the push against racism in children's books, while commendable in itself, had become anachronistic in these enlightened times. What's more, the issue was being greatly overplayed by some people and some groups.

The response from the rest of the assembly was immediate. What buzzing there had been ceased. This was clearly a question that had been on more than one mind—and indeed I had heard similar questions from librarians and educators in Michigan, Kansas, New Jersey, New York and Texas, mostly within the last two years.

This essay is an attempt to answer, from my own viewpoint, this question: Is it time to say "enough" about racism in children's literature? I think I can express my viewpoint best by sharing my experiences as a Black writer.

I first became involved in writing for children some ten years ago by entering the CIBC's first contest for unpublished Third World writers. Before that I had been writing short fiction primarily, with only a dim awareness of the crying need for children's books reflecting the Third World experience. It became clear upon examination of the materials then available that books did not do for Black or other Third World children what they did for white children—they did not deliver images upon which Black children could build and expand their own worlds. But this was in 1969 and publishers and librarians alike were voicing similar concerns about the lack of suitable materials for Blacks and other Third World children. It was just, I felt, a matter of time before the situation would be rectified.

But I soon discovered that there was a lot of resistance, even resentment, to this idea. I visited my daughter's grade school in Brooklyn at the request of the school librarian. After speaking to a bright group of seven-year-olds I was introduced to the principal. I showed him my first book—*Where Does the Day Go?* (Parents, 1969)—and he thumbed through it quickly, looking at the pictures. I fully expected him to say something tactfully complimentary. Instead, he said that he didn't feel that the book belonged in his school's library. There were no white children in the book! There were several Black children, a Japanese girl and a Puerto Rican boy, but no white child. I began to wonder if my work would be ignored—or remain unpublished—if I did not include white children. Would I be unable to write about all-Black neighborhoods?

My next book, *The Dancers* (Parents, 1972), was published some two years later. I need not have been worried about not having white children in this book. The publisher introduced a white character for me. He's not in the story, but he appears in as many pictures as possible and seems to be in the story. This being a Black writer was not going to be an easy task.

The Dancers and *The Dragon Takes a Wife* (Bobbs-Merrill, 1972) inspired some of the most virulent hate mail imaginable. I've received hate mail in response to my magazine articles—an article about interracial adoption drew a lot of angry letters from whites, for instance—but the mail about these children's books represented a different beast altogether. The letters were primarily from parents, people who could keep my work from school shelves and from local libraries. Many correspondents were furious that I—a Black author—had "invaded" the white world of fairy tales; "obscene" was one of their milder labels for *The Dragon Takes a Wife*.

But, despite these minor annoyances, I still felt that the time was soon coming when literature for Black children would really blossom and that all children's literature would be truly humanistic. The accusations that Black writers wouldn't or couldn't write well was being mocked by the CIBC contest, which had attracted a host of good Third World writers, excited by the opportunity to chronicle their own experiences. Such writers as Sharon Bell Mathis, Ray Shepard, Virginia Driving Hawk Sneve, Margaret Musgrove and Mildred Taylor were demonstrating that not only were they excellent writers but that their work did have viable markets.

By the mid-seventies, however, the promise of the late sixties and early seventies seemed suddenly hollow. The number of Black writers being published decreased as Black political activity decreased. The reasons for this were clear. Publishing companies had never tried to develop markets for Third World literature. Instead, they had relied upon purchases made through Great Society government funds, and when these were phased out the publishers began to phase out Third World books. Books were spaced so that their publication would not coincide with other Black books because sales representatives complained that they couldn't represent too many at one time. A look at the most recent catalogs shows that there are fewer books being published for Black children now than a decade ago.

Publishing Follows Market

The publishing industry has always followed the market, and the supposed commitment to multicultural literature of the sixties was sincere only to the extent that *some* editors did and still do feel a commitment to publish books for all children. Today, as major conglomerates take over publishing, and marketing people answering to these conglomerates have an increasing say over what does and does not get published, even concerned editors don't feel that they can encourage Third World writers since, given present realities, very few Third World writers will be published.

But if the publishing industry is primarily concerned with sales, how about the institutions that serve the public? If editors are unable or unwilling to publish books for which there is a need, why don't librarians and school officials take the initiative and press for more books to meet the needs of their communities? Why is it that a generally accepted concept of the sixties—i.e., that we have to reflect the experiences of all Americans in children's literature—has been forgotten or ignored? I don't have Black children in my school, so I don't need Black books in my school, a librarian told me last week. (But when I asked him if they taught European history in his school, he said that of course they did.) It seems to me that more and more librarians feel that their role is to bring *some* good literature to *some* good students. They are willing to accept public positions but not public responsibilities. "Enough!" they cry; "let us go back to the heart of what we are all about—good literature for children."

What Is "Good" Literature?

Good literature for my children is literature that includes them and the way they live. It does not exclude them by omitting people of their color, thereby giving them the impression that they are less valued. It does not exclude them by relegating them to a life style made meaningless by stereotype. Good literature for my children celebrates their life and their person. It upholds and gives special place to their humanity.

I am sorry if some librarians and some teachers find the constant vigilance for racism in children's literature anachronistic, or the organizations concerned with it bothersome. I don't feel sorry for the librarians or the teachers, however, but for the children, who have to suffer their insensitivity.

I am sorry if some librarians and some teachers feel they are being subjected to censorship by efforts to expose and label some books as racist. I've had my books taken out of schools, I've had my books "integrated," I've had people tell me what I should and should not write,* so I know what censorship means. (I have learned what all other Black artists learn—that our survival as Black artists will depend at times on tolerance of racism and at all times on keeping a low profile.) But I personally would rather have my children exposed to explicit and prurient sex, which librarians do not mind censoring, than racist books. I believe that the human values I give my children

---

*Editors have insisted that I justify a white character's presence in a Black neighborhood, told me that a Black character's speech was "unbelievable" because it was not stereotypical slang, and said that I should only write about Black themes because "there are already enough white writers around."

will help them deal with filth. It is a far more difficult task to help them deal with the concept of being less worthy because they are Black, especially when that concept is being reinforced in the school. If you choose to deal with my children then you must deal with them as whole people, and that means dealing with their blackness as well as their intellect.

I have had good experiences in my writing career as well as bad. But while I am hopeful for my own efforts I am not hopeful for the body of literature that still needs to be produced. I am not hopeful for the writers who are being turned away because "Black books aren't selling." I am not hopeful for the librarian who claims to love children and children's literature and yet can tell me that American children who are white do not need to learn of the Black experience, or that the Black experience need no longer be chronicled with truth and compassion. But most of all I am not hopeful for the millions of Third World children who will be forced to grow up under the same handicaps that I thought, a decade ago, that we were beginning to overcome. I'm afraid that the time has not yet come to say "enough" about racism in children's books.

23. THE SOUL OF LEARNING
(Excerpt)

Dorothy Sterling

I HAVE HAD A GENERAL IMPRESSION, which perhaps you share, that there has been an outpouring of books about Negroes for young people. The impression has certainly been bolstered by an outpouring of book lists. In Erwin Salk's handy *Layman's Guide to Negro History* (Mc-Graw-Hill), he notes more than a dozen bibliographies prepared by public libraries in New York, Chicago, Philadelphia, Milwaukee, by American Friends Service Committee, the American Jewish Commit-tee, etc. While doing my homework for this confrontation, I dis-covered several others, including two that I think you'll find particu-larly useful: "Books by and about the American Negro," selected by Young Adult Librarians at the Countee Cullen Branch of the New York Public Library, and "Bibliography of Materials by and about Negro Americans for Young Readers," prepared by Atlanta Univer-sity, for the U.S. Office of Education.

But aside from the lists, what about the books themselves? Are there enough books—and enough good books—that present honestly the Negro experience in the United States?

Thirty years ago—and indeed for a long time before that—books about Negroes were, to borrow a phrase from Hollywood, box-office poison. There were exceptions, of course. *Uncle Tom's Cabin* sold well. A century after its publication, Ralph Ellison won a National Book Award for *Invisible Man* (Random House). In between a handful of Negro writers managed to break into print.

In an article titled, "Uncle Remus, Farewell," Arna Bontemps tells of haunting the public library in Los Angeles when he was a youngster, seeking a recognizable reflection of himself and his world. "What I found was of cold comfort, to say the least," he writes. "Nothing more inspiring than *Our Little Ethiopian Cousin* was on the shelves, and I read almost every book in the room to make sure. Moreover, *Our Little Ethiopian Cousin* was not me and his world was not mine."

Two decades later, when his children were growing up, all he could locate for them was *The Pickaninny Twins*. Trying to provide them with something less damaging, he began to write children's books with Negro characters and themes. In the thirties he had the field almost to himself. His first book, *You Can't Pet a Possum*, published in 1934, was marred by stereotyped illustrations, but he continued with *Sad-Faced Boy, Lonesome Boy, The Fast Sooner Hound* (all Houghton Mifflin) and others. In addition to fiction, he edited *Golden Slippers* (Harper), an anthology of Negro poetry for young people, wrote *We Have Tomorrow* (Houghton), a book of biographies, and *The Story of the Negro* (Knopf).

Langston Hughes collaborated with Bontemps on *Popo and Fifina*, a story with a Haitian setting, and prepared a collection of his own poetry for young people, *The Dream Keeper* (Knopf). Then Jesse Jackson came along with some boys' stories: *Call Me Charley* (Harper) and *Anchor Man* (Harper), Ellen Tarry wrote *My Dog Rinty* (Viking), about a boy and his dog in Harlem, and Ernest Crichlow and Jerrold Beim collaborated on *Two Is a Team* (Harcourt), the first "integrated" picture book, and for a long time the only one.

In 1947, Shirley Graham won an award for the "best book combatting intolerance in America" with *There Was Once a Slave* (Messner), and thousands of people encountered Frederick Douglass for the first time. I know, because I was one of those people. With my children, I continued to read her groundbreaking string of biographies—of Phillis Wheatley, Benjamin Banneker, Jean Baptiste du Sable, George Washington Carver, Booker T. Washington. I remember listening to a radio adaptation of her *Story of Phillis Wheatley* (Messner) with a Negro friend. My friend burst into tears during the program. "Why didn't somebody tell me about this?" she sobbed.

In addition to these Negro authors, a small number of white writers—people like Marguerite de Angeli, Adele DeLeeuw, Florence Means, Hope Newell (I think they're all white)—began to tackle the problems of prejudice and explore Negro history. In 1951 Elizabeth Yates won the Newbery Medal for *Amos Fortune, Free Man* (Dutton), a biography of a slave in eighteenth-century New England who earned his freedom. It's a well-written carefully researched book, but I was a bit suspicious about the thinking behind the award. Almost until the end, Amos Fortune kept saying "No, I'm not ready for freedom—don't give it to me yet." I couldn't help wondering if his humility wasn't a part of the book's appeal. However, it is described enthusiastically in the Atlanta University bibliography, so perhaps I'm wrong. Still, if I were a teacher in a ghetto school, I wouldn't put it on my reading list.

Around the time of the Supreme Court decision on school integration there was a flurry of interest in books about Negroes. Gwendolyn Brooks published her *Bronzeville Boys and Girls* (Harper), Langston Hughes wrote *Famous American Negroes* (Dodd) and *Famous Negro Music Makers* (Dodd). Emma Gelders Sterne revived the Amistad case in *The Long Black Schooner* and followed this with a biography of Mary McCleod Bethune. I wrote *Freedom Train, The Story of Harriet Tubman* (Doubleday) and a year later came Ann Petry's excellent biography, *Harriet Tubman: Conductor on the Underground Railroad.*

The flurry didn't last long. The white South, you will remember, soon reacted to the Supreme Court with a loud "Never!" This was the period when White Citizens Councils mushroomed, when the Klan was revived, and southern librarians were attacked if they displayed a copy of Garth Williams' *The Rabbits' Wedding* (Harper), a picture book describing the marriage of a black rabbit and a white rabbit.

I can speak at first hand about these years. In 1955 I went to South Carolina to work on a biography of Robert Smalls, a slave who became a Civil War hero and, later, a Congressman from South Carolina. The reconstruction period, as it emerged from my research, was totally at variance with the then cherished notion of "the tragic era." When my editor read the manuscript of *Captain of the Planter* (Doubleday), she was frankly reluctant to publish it. It was one thing to write about Harriet Tubman who fought against slavery. By 1955 even White Citizens Council members admitted that slavery was wrong. But to tell the often brutal, truly tragic story of Negro disfranchisement and the birth of Jim Crow was something else again. All southern markets would be closed to the book, and she wasn't at all sure about northern ones. Fortunately for me, she sent the manuscript to Arna Bontemps for his opinion, and he was so enthusiastic that it was finally published. Although it has never been a best seller, it is still in print. In fact, it is now on the list of books approved for schools by the South Carolina State Department of Education!

After I finished *Captain of the Planter*, I traveled through the mid-South to talk with the Negro and white children who were entering integrated schools for the first time. Myron Ehrenberg, a photographer, accompanied me and together we turned out *Tender War-*

riors, a picture and text report of the unbelievably brave young people who were walking through screaming mobs to go to school. The text consisted largely of the students' own words, along with interviews with their parents. It was really a moving little book and the first thing of its kind. Few people were interested, however, and it soon went out of print.

I mention it now only to tell you of a curious incident connected with it. *Tender Warriors* was published by Hill & Wang in 1958. Months before its publication, the publishers were informed by the U.S. Information Agency that the book was disapproved for export under the informational media guaranty program. This is the program that guarantees dollars instead of francs, marks, etc. to U.S. publishers who export books. Without the guarantee, of course, it's scarcely worthwhile to attempt to sell a book overseas. The Hill & Wang people were sufficiently piqued about the rejection of a book before it had been read that they pursued the matter further. In reply to a series of letters, the U.S. Information Agency informed them that the disapproval was on the description of the book in their catalogue. Therefore, when the book finally appeared a copy was sent to the clearance officer at the Information Agency for re-review. His answer came promptly: "We regret to inform you that this publication is not eligible for export under the informational media guaranty program." No reason was ever forthcoming. Was the book disapproved because of its subject matter? Your guess is as good as mine. However, I think the incident sheds some light on the national mood in the late '50s.

Tender Warriors was intended for adults and young adults, but I was so emotionally involved with the children I had met in the South that I went on to write *Mary Jane* (Doubleday), a fictional account of a Negro girl's first year in an integrated school. My editor at Doubleday winced when I told her about it. "Couldn't you set it in the North?" she asked.

I couldn't. I wrote it as I saw it and, after some backing and forthing, Doubleday published it in 1959. At a cocktail party that fall—sometimes you learn more at a party than at an editorial conference—a salesman told me that although he liked some of my books he wouldn't dare enter a bookstore in Chicago with a book that had a picture of a Negro on its jacket. But this story has a happy ending, for *Mary Jane* won a few awards, sold well in 1959, and is selling better now, even in Chicago. And, as a footnote for the U.S. Information Agency, it has been published in seven European countries.

I was lucky. My publishers were willing to gamble. Other writers were not as fortunate. The same year that *Mary Jane* appeared, an acquaintance wrote a far less controversial book about a Negro child visiting a white family for a Fresh Air Fund vacation. Her book was already in galleys when the sales department heard about it. They were so dead set against it that she was obliged to revise it, transforming the Negro youngster into a white one. At still another publishing house, an editor reports that during the '50s she brought out three books in which Negroes appeared. "The books won favorable comment," she said, "but the effect on sales was negative. Customers returned not only these titles but all stock from our company. This meant an appreciable loss and tempered attitudes toward further use of Negro children in illustrations and text."

Of course, there wasn't a total white-out of books about Negroes during these years. Arna Bontemps wrote *Frederick Douglass: Slave, Fighter, Freeman* (Knopf); Henrietta Buckmaster, *Flight to Freedom* (Crowell); Jean Gould, *That Dunbar Boy* (Dodd); Mimi Levy, *Corrie and the Yankee* (Viking); etc. But no one was holding out a carrot or swinging a stick to induce authors and editors to enter the field.

Then came the student sit-ins and freedom rides, the Birmingham bombing, the Civil Rights Acts, the struggle against *de facto* segregation in the North. In every section of the country there has been a growing awareness of civil rights and a growing demand for picture books, stories, biographies, history about Negroes. We have seen a number of severely critical studies of the history textbooks used in schools, as well as blistering attacks on the Dick-and-Jane type readers that show only middle-class white suburban families.

I won't pretend to be an expert on primers but, from newspaper stories and an NAACP study on "Integrated School Books," I gather that Dick and Jane have been making new friends—and some of them are black. The Bank Street Readers series, the Skyline series, and others show children in urban as well as suburban settings and dark faces appear increasingly in spellers, science, and math books. Some of these changes are a bit mechanical. At the Education and Labor Committee hearings I learned of one textbook publisher who instructed his artist to make very tenth person a Negro in his illustrations. Another temporarily solved his marketing problems with three editions of a primer. In one, all the children portrayed are white. In the second, some are brown. In the third, the children are white, but the teachers pictured wear nuns' garb. One edition for the South, one for urban schools in the North, one for parochial schools!

The picture is far less bright in the field of history texts. Adult readers can find new interpretations of the slavery period, the anti-slavery movement, reconstruction, and so on. A little of this "new history" which should be more correctly called "true history," has begun to trickle down to school texts. A study made by Irving Sloan for the American Federation of Teachers shows that generally the history texts of 1966 are an improvement over 1956. But not much. Some now have inserts describing the death of Crispus Attucks at the Boston Massacre. Harriet Tubman and Frederick Douglass are mentioned. Readers are told that 200,000 Negro soldiers fought in the Civil War. There is a slightly more balanced but still woefully inadequate treatment of Reconstruction, and a few books have a supplement covering the civil rights movement and the Negro today. Among the thirteen books Sloan analyzed, only one, *Land of the Free* (Crowell) by John Hope Franklin, John W. Caughey, and Ernest R. May, comes close to presenting the "true history." And the picture is even darker than Sloan paints it because schools don't buy new textbooks every year. Many are continuing to use the same old distorted ones. I went through the textbook assigned to the seniors in the high school in my community—it's called *History of a Free People* by the way—and found it disappointingly full of misstatements, omissions, and bias.

As you undoubtedly know, textbook publishing is a multi-billion dollar industry. Each text represents a large capital investment so that asking a text publisher to rewrite a history book is a little like asking General Motors to design a new car. Trade books, however, are issued in much smaller editions. Because there is less money riding on an individual book, trade publishers are able to respond more rapidly to new ideas, new programs, new audiences. . . .

Let's play a numbers game for a minute. There were roughly twelve thousand children's trade books issued in the seven-year period from 1960 through 1966. If we say that eighty, perhaps one hundred and twenty, dealt with the Negro past and present in the United States, that means that at best 1 per cent of the total output of books for young people are devoted to the Negro.

Is this possible? Have I made a mistake in arithmetic? I don't think so. Two years ago Nancy Larrick, former president of the International Reading Association, jolted the publishing world with an article in *Saturday Review* titled "The All-White World of Children's

Books." She sent a questionnaire to the seventy members of the Children's Book Council. From sixty-three replies she found that out of 5,206 children's books issued between 1962 and 1964 only 6.7 per cent included a Negro in text or illustrations. Her figure is higher than mine because the questionnaire replies included books that showed Negroes only in illustrations, as well as books about Africa, the Caribbean, etc. When she subtracted these and the histories and biographies she reported that only four-fifths of 1 per cent of the books told a story about American Negroes today.

Since it takes a year or two to write a book, and another year before publication, perhaps the situation has changed since her article appeared. Twice a year *Publisher's Weekly* puts out a special Children's Book Number reporting on forthcoming books. Their issue of July 10, 1967, describes the children's books that will be published this fall. I always go through these special numbers with a sinking feeling, afraid that the books I would like to do have already been done by others. I needn't have worried. From the ads and thumbnail descriptions of more than five hundred books I found just fourteen about Negro Americans. And that *really* gave me a sinking feeling.

Four are biographies, two collective biographies, one an anthology of poetry. The fiction includes two sports stories about boys who want to become boxers, one about integrating a school, one about two girls who go from a city slum to a summer camp, and one about a boy living in a mixed neighborhood in Brooklyn. Good enough as far as it goes, but it doesn't go very far, does it?

Only 2.8 per cent of the current output of books for young people are concerned with the most burning issue of our time. When Arna Bontemps' grandchildren go to the library they won't have to read every book on the shelves and find only *Our Little Ethiopian Cousin.* But they will have to read ninety-seven books before they discover three that speak to them.

And it is not only Negro youngsters who are being deprived. As Nancy Larrick says, "The impact of all-white books upon 39,600,000 white children is probably even worse." How can they understand the news on television and in the newspapers? Increasingly isolated from their darker contemporaries, how well are these white children being prepared for the larger adult world in which they are globally a minority?

I'd like to carry this discussion a step further by asking "Why?" Are editors and authors less liberal, more prejudiced than the rest of

American society? Certainly not. Those I know, at least, are probably more concerned, more open to new ideas than the average citizen. Are they then only interested in money? The dollar is a factor, of course. Both writers and publishers must be paid for their efforts. But the economic picture has changed radically since the 1950s—and most radically since the passage of the Elementary and Secondary Education Act of 1965, which released millions of dollars to libraries and schools for the purchase of books for the educationally deprived. There's gold in them thar hills now. I doubt if any trade publishers or book salesmen would turn down a reasonably well-written book because it portrayed a Negro.

Then why? President Johnson has said "You do not wipe away the scars of centuries by saying 'Now you are free to go where you want.' You do not take a man who, for years, has been hobbled by chains, liberate him, and then say, 'you're free to compete with all the others.' It is not enough just to open the gates of opportunity."

He was speaking of Negroes, but his words could also be applied to editors and writers. You do not take minds that have been hobbled by centuries of racism and say, "Now you're free to write the truth." What is the truth? Most white people and many Negroes don't know. And there's more than that, of course. When you begin to write the truth, you bump into all sorts of obstacles. Consider the rule of the happy or at least upbeat ending. Should we tell the children that in real life people do not always live happily ever after?

I faced this problem when I was writing *Mary Jane* and didn't really solve it properly. I compromised by letting her make one friend in school and ending with the hope that she would make more next year. When the book was published the bright, warmhearted little girl who lives next door asked, "Is it really that bad?" "Much worse," I answered. "Why, today's paper tells about the bombing of the home of an eight-year-old boy because he went to a 'white' school." "Oh, don't tell me about it!" she said and ran home.

Should she be told? I think so.

Even more ticklish are the rules of American society. A policeman is a boy's best friend. Is he? Does a black boy in Philadelphia, Mississippi, think that about Sheriff Rainey, accused of conspiring to kill Chaney, Schwerner, and Goodman in 1964? Does a boy in Newark or Detroit think so? Not according to what I see in the newspapers.

Recently I've read two books that every high school student should read. One is *Mississippi Black Paper* (Random), published in

1965, with a foreword by Reinhold Niebuhr and an introduction by Hodding Carter III. It consists of the testimony of fifty-seven Negro and white civil rights workers on the breakdown of law and order, the corruption of justice, and brutality of the police in Mississippi. The other is *The Torture of Mothers* by Truman Nelson. Nelson tells, largely through tape-recorded interviews, of the arrest of six Harlem boys for a murder they did not commit, of beatings administered by the police, and of slanted stories in the press. There is plenty of raw material for books for young people here—really raw.

Books that tell it like it is—and nothing less will be acceptable today—must challenge all sorts of hitherto cherished beliefs. You were probably as shocked as I was, a couple of years ago, by the plot to blow up the Statue of Liberty. I'm still not sure there really was such a plot, but think how the Goddess of Liberty welcoming the world's poor and oppressed must look to a Negro teen-ager. When I was growing up, I recited the pledge of allegiance, "with liberty and justice for all," with real emotion. I was not aware—I had no way of learning—that the Goddess of Liberty was saying "But not for you" to large numbers of my fellow citizens. We have to tell young people about this, particularly white youngsters.

History must be completely rewritten, not just revised with supplements tacked on to the end. Seven biographies of George Washington Carver, three of Harriet Tubman, two of Frederick Douglass, one of Benjamin Banneker—it's like a giant jigsaw puzzle with most of the pieces missing. There's a scrap of blue sky, the top of a tree, but you can't even guess what the whole picture looks like.

Where is Paul Cuffee who built up his own fleet of ships in the eighteenth century and carried Negroes back to Africa when he couldn't find justice in his home state of Massachusetts? And James Forten, sailmaker for the U.S. Navy and Revolutionary War veteran, who was penning antislavery pamphlets as far back as 1812? And Forten's son-in-law, Robert Purvis, handsome, well-educated, wealthy, who sheltered thousands of escaping slaves? And William Still who kept the records for the Pennsylvania branch of the underground railroad? And black abolitionists like the Remonds and Henry Highland Garnet, William Wells Brown, Alexander Crummell, whom you read about in *Souls of Black Folk?*

I'm out of breath and I'm barely up to the Civil War. Why has so little been written about the twenty-two Negroes who served in Congress during Reconstruction and after? The black Populists? The men

and women of the early twentieth century who spoke, wrote, fought
for Negro freedom? It's time for young people's biographies of
W. E. B. DuBois, A. Philip Randolph, Marcus Garvey.

I can think of a dozen episodes from history that should be
written about, not only because they demonstrate Negro courage or
the Negro's contribution to American society, but also because they
would make darn good stories. And there are hundreds more.

Who will write these books? And who will write about today's
young people in urban ghettoes and the rural South?

I believe that publishers are ready to bring out the books. However, they are somewhat in the position of a manufacturer who puts a
sticker—a small one—in his window announcing that he is an Equal
Opportunity Employer and then says, "But no Negroes have applied."
Not many Negroes are likely to apply. The welcome mat has been out
for such a short time that they have not had a chance to see it.

Whitney Young of the Urban League has proposed a "more-
than-equal" program in which employers seek out qualified Negroes
for jobs and train those who lack qualifications. "For more than three
hundred years the white American has received preferential treatment
over the Negro," he says. "What we ask now is that there be a
deliberate and massive attempt to include the Negro citizen in the
mainstream of American life." I'm asking editors to make a deliberate
and massive effort to seek out Negro writers and manuscripts with
Negro themes. By this I don't mean that only Negro writers can do the
job. I happen to be hooked on Negro history, and I don't plan to give up
my addiction. But from my comfortable suburban home, I cannot
write a story about a girl in Harlem or a boy in Lowndes County,
Alabama—and doubtless other white authors feel the same way.

I can almost hear rumbles from editorial offices. . . . You can't
write books to order. . . . You can't commission books. . . . You'll
only get formula books with pat solutions. . . . Nonsense! Books are
written to order all the time. Three of my books—not about
Negroes—were written because Doubleday salesmen said there was a
need for them. I've just completed a book suggested by my editor—and
the suggestion, I'm glad to say, was that I write about the civil rights
revolution. I am definitely *not* asking for formula books with pat solutions. That's why I believe Negro writers should be sought out and
convinced to try their hand at books for young people.

An organization that feels as I do about this is the Council on
Interracial Books for Children, which was founded by a group of

children's book writers and children's librarians, along with such concerned citizens as Harry Golden, Benjamin Spock, and Harold Taylor. They are currently sponsoring a contest for the best children's books by Negroes, with $500 prizes for the best manuscript for ages three to six, seven to eleven, and twelve to sixteen.

There are also two Negro organizations turning out reference books. The Negro Heritage Library is planning a twenty volume encyclopedia and has already issued seven volumes, one a *Negro Heritage Reader for Young People* which reprints folk tales, songs, poetry, and prose by Negro authors. The other books in the series—none too difficult for high school readers—include *Profiles of Negro Womanhood*, *A Martin Luther King Treasury*, *The Winding Road to Freedom*, *Negroes in Public Affairs and Government*, etc. The Association for the Study of Negro Life and History which, for too long a time, was the only group that knew there was such a thing as Negro history, is preparing an International Library of Negro Life and History (Books, Inc.). Their first five volumes cover *Negro Americans in the Civil War*, *The History of the Negro in Medicine*, *Anthology of the American Negro in the Theatre*, *Historical Negro Biographies*, and *The Negro in Music and Art*.

Aside from these, Doubleday is, I believe, the only trade book house that has begun to make the sort of deliberate effort I am suggesting, with its Zenith series which, incidentally, was initiated by a Negro editor. Ordinarily I dislike series books. They tend to be pedestrian and, over the years, to run downhill. The Zenith series is uneven. Some of the books are very good and some only fair. But in this long, hot summer of 1967 wouldn't you rather give a youngster a fair book that tells the truth, instead of a pretty good one about, say, a talking mouse? Let's face it. Not all of the books published each season contain deathless prose—and these books that were written to order stand up very well. . . .

The fantastically difficult and yet hopeful job that confronts us as teachers and writers is to provide the young with the vision of conciliation, and the frame of mind and intellectual materials which will make conciliation possible. And perhaps I have hit quite by accident, on the significant word of the immediate future—*conciliation*. The concept of "soul," no matter how many ways you define it, expresses the growing Negro reaction against oppression and rejection on one hand, and against assimilation or absorption on the other.

Integration, in the light of Negro experience since 1954, has lost considerable credibility among Negroes, as a goal which is either attainable or desirable. But conciliation remains applicable, not merely as a semantic convenience but as a social process; because it means the coming together of antagonistic equals to resolve their antagonisms on a footing of mutual respect. If this happens, and only when it happens, will America stand a chance of becoming "the dream the dreamers dreamed"—

> The land that never has been yet—
> And yet must be—
> The land where every man is free.

We are among those who have to help it happen.

24. AN INTERVIEW WITH HAKI MADHUBUTI (DON L. LEE): POET, PUBLISHER, CRITIC, EDUCATOR*

Publishing is not intended as an activity that will obstruct the progress of children, yet it has done just that for some groups of young people. How do you assess the dimensions of this problem?

WELL, I WOULD DISAGREE with the premise of your question. Publishing has a very political bent to it. Certain books are published because they are politically correct; other books are published because they are compatible with the political attitudes of the day. There have always been—well, at least in the nineteenth and twentieth century—Black writers writing books. The problem has been in getting them published. Publishing is not neutral; people publish in the United States for economic, political, and cultural reasons. Publishers pay money to publish books and they receive money in return for selling the books, and so publishing cannot be removed from the realm of economic reality, human error, human prejudice, racism, and so forth. I think that needs to be very clear. Doubleday and Random House, Bobbs-Merrill, Harper and Row, the major publishers are really not concerned about trying to portray an accurate, culturally unbiased America or world. Very few people want to deal with this, but essentially you've got nine percent of the world's population, people of European extraction, running the world. Take publishing, for instance. Last year in this country, forty-five thousand books were published. A very small percentage for children and even less directed to a Black reading public. In a place like Nigeria, they publish fewer than two hundred books in a year. And one of the sad things about

* *Editors' note:* Donnarae MacCann taped this conversation with Haki Madhubuti when he was Visiting Professor of Afro-American Studies at the University of Iowa in 1984. Children's books published by Professor Madhubuti's company, Third World Press, include *I Look at Me* by Mari Evans, *The Tiger Who Wore White Gloves* by Gwendolyn Brooks, *I Want to Be* by Dexter and Patricia Oliver, *The Day They Stole the Letter J* by Jahari Mahiri, and *The Story of Kwanzaa* by Safisha Madhubuti.

those two hundred is the fact that the great majority were in English. Therefore the indigenous languages of Nigeria are not represented. So the concept referred to as cultural imperialism (and I use the term with some thought) is accurate. In some African countries, English has become most certainly the second language and sometimes the first language in many Third World countries. The books from this country and from other Western nations are coming to these countries at a much faster pace. What this does, essentially, is paint a biased picture not only of Black people, but of the world. My answer to the question is that publishing—although it may not always be intended—is certainly biased. And I think that is where the danger is and that's all part of the problem. Therefore we need men and women in publishing who go into publishing with a mission to accurately deal with the world. Essentially in the West and other parts of the world, the accent is on making a profit. And for the most part when people try to do things that are right, there's very little profit. You're lucky if you can really take care of yourself. And that's why there's the mission attached to it. At some point profit must take a back seat to education and enlightenment.

How did you experience literature in your own childhood and young adult years?

My childhood was not unlike that of many Black children in the country, as well as Indian children and Asian children to a certain extent. Within the context of my family there was very little reading going on. And there was so much happening that distracted us from reading—like trying to make a living. However reading, for me, became an outlet and became a way of understanding the world. Of course, I did come up with television; we had one, but it never worked. And school, at least to me, was like an escape because at school I was at least able to question the unknown and eat at least one balanced meal a day. I worked for it, but the point is, we were very poor, excruciatingly poor. It was a debilitating poverty. So you did not have those luxuries, and books, of course, were luxuries. Even magazines and sometimes even newspapers. We didn't have a telephone. It was just very difficult. The major thing I remember about my early life is working all the time; I just worked all the time.

The place where I came across books was in Detroit; there was a children's library. And they used to have a children's hour, and my sister and I occasionally went to these children's hours. We didn't stay often because in many cases the books that were being read just didn't have any attachment to our reality. We would leave. But we did become, at least I became, a regular visitor and I would take books out. The books I took were more culturally neutral. I would take books about trains and buses, books about airplanes, books about how to build things, rather than books that would lie within the context of the humanities or social sciences. One day when I was about thirteen years old, my mother asked me to go to the library to get a book entitled *Black Boy* by Richard Wright. And I kind of rebelled because I didn't want to go anyplace and ask for anything Black. (This was back in the Fifties and "Negro" was the "correct" designation at that time.) I did get the book and she read it and I read it. I didn't understand everything, but Richard Wright hit a core. I read *Black Boy* several times. The next book she asked me to go get was *Cast the First Stone* by Chester Himes, which was really an adult book. I read that. But I used Richard Wright as a pivotal point. When I left home at sixteen years of age and began to try to map out a future for myself, I started with Black literature, and Richard Wright was the starting point. So I went back to *Black Boy, Native Son, Uncle Tom's Children, The Outsider,* and just went through his entire works: *White Man Listen, Pagan Spain, 12 Million Black Voices*—the whole range of Richard Wright from essays to fiction and even his poetry. So it was a good starting point for me, and of course from Richard Wright I went to Chester Himes' very serious novels, then to the detective novels and things like that. So I was hooked on books early. but not as early as a typical white child. "Early" in terms of the opportunity afforded a Black young person who is not brought up on books. So books became not necessarily an escape, but an education.

In the kind of educational system I came through, there was never any encouragement for Black young people to go to college. It was never even spoken of in the high school I was in. I lost my mother early, at sixteen years of age, so I was on my own. And coming up in a working, poverty-ridden family, what I was expected to do essentially was go and work at the Ford Motor Company (this was Detroit, Michigan) or for General Motors—to work in a factory. Basically that was the only aspiration; or else hit the street, become a pimp, work the streets. Or to do other things to make money, but one did not seek a higher education. After losing my mother, I ended up in Chicago, and joined a magazine selling group. We traveled across the lower southern part of Illinois, going from door to door selling magazines and lying about wanting to go to college. And the important thing about this is that this is the first time that college or university education had even entered my mind. At least the idea had now entered my mind, and it just stayed there.

I ended up in St. Louis, got sick, pawned everything I had, and finally joined the U.S. Army like most destitute young Black men. I ended up in the army at the age of eighteen. That's when I began to really question the world. It was the first time in my life I had been around so many white men. Just three Black men in the company—an entire company of white men, and the three Black men were the youngest because most of the white men were draftees. They had got drafted, you see; we joined. As a result of that I went on an entirely different educational program and re-educated myself. I learned how to read. That was during the Kennedy years—they were talking about the Evelyn Wood reading course, so I took one. And learned how to read with a high level of comprehension. And I began to systematically devour libraries. Most importantly, I was looking for myself, looking for that which was Black.

It was a real problem for me coming up because nothing in my world was "Black," absolutely nothing. The only Black literature that I found during my early years was some of the poetry. I remember reading Sterling Brown's poetry, Langston Hughes' poems, Gwendolyn Brooks to a certain extent. But more importantly, Sterling Brown, because Brown's poetry was more like folk poetry, it had more rhyme to it, it had a different kind of rhythm to it. These poems had always made an impression on me, but the type of impression they made, too, was that he was talking about what was happening in the country. I began to feel that more and more as a young man.

This experience for me meant two things. One, that there may be a place for writers, but most certainly there would be a place for publishers. But not having the money, I had to go the writing route first. So I started writing in the army. What I was reading did not accurately portray all of Black life, at least from my vantage point, and so I began to basically deal with that.

Tell me how you made the transition from army life to the world of book publishing.

I came out of the service in '63. I had been involved in a lot of civil
rights activity in the service, and had been in a lot of trouble. When I
got out, I went basically to the streets—to SNCC, CORE, SCLS, and so
forth—and I continued to write. I worked for the Du Sable Museum
of African American History in Chicago, and the director of the museum, Dr. Margaret Burroughs, had written children's books. I had
not been aware of them because they were basically published by a
small company in Chicago; they had not been distributed widely. Of
course, when I came upon them, I was mainly into adult literature,
but I began to see the possibilities of publishing. Working with her
and her husband, Charles Burroughs, was a great education; I de-
voured their library. They had a massive library, especially strong in
Black literature and Russian literature. They were the first people to
introduce me to Russian literature—Tolstoy, Dostoevsky, Pushkin
(who was Black), and other major Russian writers. The Burroughs
began to open up another world and I began to understand the power
of world literature. The problems we have in the U.S., other people—
especially if they are a minority within the context of a larger society—have as well. And so I began to become aware of that.

I continued to write, and in 1966 I decided to publish my own
book. As a writer, I was a critic of the society, the critic of white
people. And as one who was essentially trying to come to the core, to
understand, to bring some change, it did not even enter my mind to
take my book to a white publisher. If you're talking bad about somebody, you don't take it to that person and say, "Will you please publish
me and then pay me for talking bad about you?" It was street logic;
that's what I used. So I'm saying that I did not come into writing as a
writer, I didn't come out of the Village; I didn't come out of the Bay
area; I came out of the Lower East Side of Detroit. So I came basically
from the streets. As a result of that, you have a different type of logic.
I wasn't concerned about reviews; I was not concerned about interviews. What I was concerned about was reaching Black people. And so
my first book was *Think Black*. I took a selection of poems to a printer,
had them printed, paid the bill myself.

So, in effect, I became a publisher. At that time (this was the
tumultuous Sixties), because I was not coming through the regular
literary route, I did not have on me the stigma of self-publishing, you
see. Very few writers who consider themselves writers would ever
self-publish. You see, they feel that's beneath them. If you publish
yourself, you're not a writer. So coming in the back door, trying to

move at a different level, I published it and sold it on street corners. I sold *Think Black* for a dollar. A year later, I met a man by the name of Dudley Randall who had just started a publishing company in Detroit (Broadside Press). He had come to Chicago to talk to Margaret Burroughs because they were going to edit a collection of poetry on Malcolm X. I was very shy, so I didn't get into that discussion, but I knew what they were doing. I didn't even contribute a poem. I finally submitted one for the revised edition. But I did have enough nerve to ask Dudley Randall if he would consider publishing my next book: *Black Pride*. He published it and he wrote an introduction for it. My publishing activity stopped at that point—in about 1966.

Next I began to work with Gwendolyn Brooks in her workshop. I met Hoyt Fuller, who, as far as I am concerned, is probably the major editor we've produced, other than W. E. B. Dubois (who was editor of *Crisis,* the NAACP magazine for so long). Fuller was an editor extraordinary. He was a very committed Black man, committed to Black people, committed to a new way of life, committed to excellence, committed to developing a magazine that truly portrayed the multifacets of Black culture. Even though you might describe him as a nationalist, a Black nationalist, if you look through all the issues of *Negro Digest* (later re-named *Black World*) you will see that his point of view was not the only one represented. I think that was the quality and the beauty of the man; he was able to see that there were ideas just as substantial as the ones he had, and he gave them a voice in a magazine. *Negro Digest,* which was a Johnson publication, was the first publication to give me a national voice and the first to pay me. Hoyt Fuller and I became very close friends. He, along with others and myself, started the Organization of Black American Culture, a writer's workshop which still exists today. It produced many of the major young Black writers that came out of Chicago in the Sixties.

But I decided shortly after that (with encouragement from Hoyt Fuller, Gwendolyn Brooks, and Dudley Randall) to return to publishing. I and Jahari Amini and Carolyn Rodgers started the Third World Press. I felt kind of, not guilty, but uneasy about receiving money for my work, as well as for readings and things like that, so whatever money I received I put back into the publishing company. We published poets, mainly, but we got to a point where I felt that we needed to branch off and become a much more substantial press. Not necessarily a large press but a press that began to meet other needs than just the needs of poets. We went into children's books and we went into

political and historical books. A children's book was one of the first
books we published, a book called *Jackie* by Luevester Lewis; and one of
the major children's books that we published, *The Tiger Who Wore
White Gloves* by Gwendolyn Brooks, is still in print. Moving into
children's books was a logical step in terms of finding a larger market.
Every place we go the children's books just go well. So there's a great
need, and then there's a whole new crop of young Black writers dealing with children's books now, too. So that's how, you know, we got to
where we are now.

*Racist books that are viewed as good (even classic) in "mainstream" Ameri-
can culture are often read aloud in classrooms where Black children are
taught, as well as white children. What does it take to enable white librarians and teachers to break with their own culture, so to speak, to
withdraw support from "prestigious" books that misrepresent a culture?*

That's very difficult to do. But it will have to be done if there's going to
be any substantial change. All we ask for, what any people should ask
for, is an honest depiction. But the great majority of the material is
culturally biased, insensitive, racist, often very naive. It is often
downright treacherous in its depiction of, not only Black people, but
other people of color—especially Blacks and Indians.

How do you change this? Number one, you have to begin to have
some influence on the major schools of library science. Librarians are
not being educated to deal with the multifacets of culture; they do not
understand the psychological makeup of people, how they perceive the
world and so forth. I really feel it's dangerous that the schools of
library science do not have strong anthropological and social science
courses that future librarians are required to take and do well in.
Undergraduate and graduate. What I mean by that is, I think we have
to have a cultural view of the world. Racism really did not come into
existence until Europeans discovered that they were in a minority, an
acute minority, and began to push their supremacy. And in the process
they began to define the world from a European-white perspective.
And in doing that they began to push their interpretations; yet the
European interpretation is not universal, it's European. And the danger with that (why I call for a culturally unbiased, anthropological
approach) is that in order to understand any people, you've got to go to
the core of why people act or react a certain way to a given stimulus.

You cannot stand on the outside and just observe and think that you're going to get the truth or the answer. You have to become a part of it. You have to become culturally immersed in that people, in their mores, their science, religion, music, technology, art, their language. If you do not become a part of that people in such a manner, then your depiction of them is going to be faulty.

That's essentially what has happened to the majority of white men and women who have written books about Black people. They've taken European/American eyes and focused them on another culture, and they think what they're getting at is the truth. Of course that is not what has happened. So it's important that librarians are trained adequately, are educated culturally to understand the very important and very human differences that exist among cultures. It has nothing to do with whether one culture is superior or not. Cultures are not measured that way, you see. The key thing is to understand a particular culture's way of doing something. Now of course there are universals, but you cannot culturally color them. How can you culturally color fire? Or water? Or land? For Europeans, the land was to put barbed wire around. Nobody else ever did that. But that had come out of their culture, you see. I'm saying that in schools of library science we need another approach to the understanding of people. To understand the world, one has to go beyond one's own world.

Librarians must be the carriers—that's a good word—they must be enthusiastic about what can be gotten from books. Because only with your enthusiasm will other people pick that up and say, "This is worthwhile." In my role as a poet, publisher, and book critic, I see my job as one who pushes the literature. Very few things develop the mental faculties as well as language. When you get people who deal with language, generally they can think. And what I'm trying to push people toward is the ability to think critically. You've got millions of people who just believe everything you tell them. If you get people to think critically and constructively, you can change the world. I'm convinced that change is possible with an informed public.

I'd like you to comment on something that has turned up in research about children's book publishing. Various mainstream book editors have said that Blacks are included in books if they "fall naturally" into a narrative. Those of us who review books often come across a narrative about a family having an adventure, and we wonder why this isn't a Black, or perhaps a Hispanic or Asian family, rather than almost invariably Anglo-European. How could one group "fall" into this narrative more "naturally" than another? And yet, at the other extreme, it is a mistake to think that faces can just be shaded in.

I'll tell you what happens when you paint the face white. Again it gets back to who was doing the publishing. It gets back to the problem of not really understanding that people of color are the majority in the world. But the great majority in the U.S. is not concerned about this. The members of the majority are essentially concerned about writing books to themselves. There is nothing wrong with that, per se, but it creates a problem when you have a multicultural society, when you've got 35 million Black people and in the neighborhood of 15–16 million Hispanics, plus many Asians and Native Americans. You cannot just live as an island anymore. You have to begin to understand that there is something greater out there than the white, Anglo-Saxon, Protestant middle class.

I don't think that this Black family (if what you are envisioning in the question is an integrated setting for a narrative) is going to fit neatly within this white crust. If it does, then it's not going to be a Black family, because given the politics of this country, it's very difficult for families who are racially different to live together without being antagonistic. When there is harmony among families, that means that essentially these families grew up in close proximity. I'm not saying that this is impossible. But in most cases, when we read stories like that, we are really being asked to stretch the imagination. I think we can look back and remember, perhaps, one white person we kind of grew up with. And at a certain point, at a certain age, that growing together just stopped. We were going two separate ways. Generally when young people become close to adulthood (16 or 17 years old) it's just another world out there.

But thinking about what you said about books that come to reviewers (especially those for very young children), books must at some point talk about possibilities, not only about what exists. The average child grows up knowing what is, especially in the context of his or her life. Many of us come up in single-parent homes, going through the welfare system. What's the value of reading about that? We know about it. I think that literature— if it's working—talks about the possibilities, about what you can become, what is beautiful in the world. The rest of that stuff you can leave for adults. I'm thinking about Lucille Clifton's books, which basically deal with very poor children, but they're always talking about the possibilities, talking about the beauty. I think this is why she's so successful. We have to think about what is best for the child, and we can do that in ways that do not compromise the intelligence or development of the child. I'm pretty sure that can be done.

When you're talking about possibilities, it makes you think on another level. One of the things I like about some of the books that are coming out, especially the African folktales, is that these folktales for the most part are dealing with moral and ethical questions. These questions are being put to children, which is very good. And even the Ezra Jack Keats books, although there are minor problems with some of them, are for the most part culturally straight. I think he does a good job. I think that we need more books like this, stories that get the children excited.

The possibilities are great. We just have to have imagination, and stop trying to force circumstances when it's just not going to work. The great majority of this society is separated. So I'm saying that in order to improve reality we can start by talking about the possibilities—about what is possible if changes occur, rather than saying "this happened." Try to begin to depict a world where people are not judged by the color of their skin and so forth. It just seems to me that writers, creative writers, have got to be bold, have got to be innovative. It might even require them to publish their own books, which is fine. The small presses tend to be overextended. It's very seldom we can take anything, unless it's so unusual and magnificent that it just shines through.

What kinds of institutional changes are needed in order to expand the circulation of existing non-racist books about Third World groups? How can they be discovered when they do not receive the publicity that other books receive?

Well, I think you have to give credit to people at the Council on Interracial Books for Children for doing what they have been doing for the last 17 years or so. I've never met them personally, or the man who's most responsible for *Interracial Books for Children Bulletin*, Brad Chambers, but I'm aware of the literature and aware of what they're trying to do. So they have to be commended for trying to do what they've been able to do on limited resources.

But what I would suggest is that the American Library Association develop a search committee. That committee's responsibility would be to do a systematic study of books that are now in print, and begin to categorize them. Now that's different from saying ban them or saying they can't be printed. I'm just saying that if this book is a racist book, then just say that. All right? You see, you're not trying to stop it from being published or to take it off the shelf. The point is that people would begin to understand intentions and what you're trying to do.

At the same time, I think that librarians need to write. I think it's a real problem that those who know the most about the problems are not dealing with it even in their own creative environment. I think that those persons who are aware of the problem need to write, they need to organize, and they need to be involved in whatever change they can bring about in their space. And often that's very dangerous. I mean, you may lose your job. But those persons who generally take stands are those persons who are going to leave a legacy. Otherwise you may as well just be a sheep, you see. It's best to leave your mark doing something worthwhile, rather than just sitting back and saying, "Well, I knew about that, but didn't do anything about it."

Can you tell me something about how you seek out writers and illustrators—people who perhaps haven't thought about children's books as a medium of expression? Until 1980, the Council on Interracial Books for Children had prizes that were effective in bringing new Black writers into the field. There doesn't seem to be any specific channel now.

We're going to initiate some prizes, not only for children's books but for fiction and poetry at Third World Press. I'm not sure—possibly the Council on Interracial Books stopped the prizes because they didn't have the money. As far as I know, they're pretty independent also. It's just very difficult to keep anything going without resources— it's extremely difficult.

When we first started out, I had to literally beg writers to come; but now since we've been in existence 17 years, we get all kinds of manuscripts. It looks like we'll be publishing a new children's book by Nora Blakely and one by Sharon Opuku this year. So for us there is not a problem of finding Black writers. The problem is in starting out, in gaining exposure (not only for children's writers, but for all writers). The white publishers are not usually interested unless someone is a truly tried writer. Eloise Greenfield, Sharon Bell Mathis, Lucille Clifton, Virginia Hamilton—most of what they write is published. Those are some of the major writers of children's literature. Then of course, the Fieldings: they've got several books out which are very popular. And you've got this Black/white husband and wife team, the Dillons. Everything they touch just turns to gold. And their depiction is very beautiful. And John Steptoe—his books are very good. But it's just hard to get a start.

Now we still need children's books that cover the lower age categories (preschool up to the fourth or fifth grade) and some books for that age range are coming out. But the virgin soil is in writing for teenagers, young adult Blacks. You have a lot of books about white people, but for Black teenagers and preteens almost nothing. My daughter is eight and she's reading at the teenage level. It's hard to find material that will challenge her. So we need writers for those areas. We just published a book in that area by Sonia Sanchez: *A Sound Investment.*

Having contests that are nationally sponsored is one way to seek out writers. Another way is to go to the institutions like the Writers' Workshop in Iowa City and urge them to give some emphasis to children's books. In a workshop atmosphere, you generally find very few who are dealing with children's books. This is one of the shortcomings of many of the writing schools.

Now I feel that the education of children is the most revolutionary thing anybody could do. When you leave your children to be taught by those who do not love them, or do not care about them, then what may be the results of that act are children who are not loving, who are not considerate, who are not in tune with what's the best in the world, and we then end up repairing broken adults. And so you have to place special attention on education of the young.

So I will look where writers are and encourage young artists to go into children's books. At the same time I will try to develop an interest in writing in other people—people such as librarians. Or people in the humanities or social sciences. Even if you cannot write yourself, if you have a concept, you could find a writer to work with. I'm saying that you've got to have good concepts and good values and move on from there.

Librarians, I think, do not deal with small presses very well. Is it necessary then, for a small press to try to become a big press?

I'd like us to become an influential press. Bigness is not the direction in which we're going. We're trying to become influential within the context of the publishing world and have an influence on the population that we impact upon. Our special role is to be what we call a cultural house. We publish books by and about Black people, and that's where the void is. When we started out, there were about seventeen Black publishers and now we're really about the only ones who publish children's books. We're going to continue to make it a major part of our whole publishing apparatus.

Most small presses start out (whether they're Black or Hispanic or even white) with a special mission. They see that there's a certain void that's not being taken care of within the traditional houses, so they try to fill the void. One reason why my goal is to publish whatever is best for Black people is that if a text is not best for Black people, then it's probably not best for anybody. Because essentially we're at the bottom of the totem pole all around the world. That is not the only criteria, however; what I'm looking for is the best in the world, and the best in terms of *truth*. We have to present those things which are essentially uplifting for everybody.

The Western way, which has been described as universal, is not universal. Now you find that this kind of bias exists in every culture. However in the West, racism and white supremacy is pervasive in everything—law, textbooks, the arts, government, education, the entertainment world, sports—everything. The type of multicultural world view that we were bringing can just never get in there. It's controlled by a very small group of white men for the most part. They don't even let too many white women in.

In other publications, you've written about the ideology of Third World Press in terms of social values—especially in relation to unity, cooperation, and communality. Would you, in closing, say a word about accommodating both artistic form and social content?

That's where creativity comes in—when you are presenting values within the context of literature. What I've seen children do with books is often very creative. The key thing always is how the material that they're reading relates to reality. I'm not saying that children are geared toward only one set of realities. What they're looking for, I feel, is challenge.

People who are serious about change have to begin to make

regular, substantial visits to the real world, especially this world right here, and just find out what is going on. Then life-giving and life-saving values can be incorporated into the literature in a way that enriches and entertains at the same time.

As the 20th century closes, we are already living in a service-oriented and an information-gathering economy. In order to deal with information, you've got to be comfortable with language, have the research tools; you have to deal with reading. And reading must start young. You just can't start with a child who is nine or ten or eleven years old. You've got to start young in developing literary appreciation.

However, the best teacher is still the day to day example set by those persons closest to the child. If the parents read, the odds are that the children will read. Our homes have got to become mini-learning institutions. In-home libraries should not be exceptions but common realities. One can tell where a family is culturally by viewing the children's rooms. Are there books and book cases? What type of music are the children listening to? What's on the walls? The education and cultural development of the child is the *first* responsibility of the parents. *Children are more important than careers and cars.* Reading (study), unlike eating, is not natural; however, if we read as much as we ate, we'd all be in better condition intellectually and physically. Most people who are serious about contributing something positive to the world must understand the world, and the best way to do that is to explore the literature.

Part VI

INTERNATIONAL AND LEGAL
PERSPECTIVES

25. ETHNOCENTRIC IMAGES IN HISTORY BOOKS AND THEIR EFFECT ON RACISM

Roy Preiswerk

MANY OF THOSE who have gathered ample evidence of the distorted images, stereotypes and prejudices held by Europeans about people in other parts of the world, say that racism is rampant. This may be true, but the author's contention is that a study of racism which does not take ethnocentric distortions into account may well overlook some of the worst obstacles in the way of intergroup relations through official images transmitted by our knowledge-producing institutions. In written materials, racism in its crudest forms has greatly diminished since the 1940's, except in specific countries where it is a severe domestic problem or, worse, official government policy.

True, this change may not be a result of less racism on the part of writers and textbook authors. Crude racists who write for a wide public, and particularly for children and adolescents, probably realize that it is no longer so easy to get away with a generalized glorification of whites and a simplistic denigration of others. An example is Hergé's 1929 edition of *Tintin in the Congo* as compared to the author's more recent work. His first "magnum opus" is a revolting piece of racism. Today, the approach is more subtle through a negative presentation of cultural differences which, because of the generalized confusion about race and culture, may actually produce racist attitudes in the reader's mind.

The Ethnocentric "Input" into Racism

The subjects of racism and ethnocentrism can be theoretically approached in a variety of ways (theories of learning, socialization, communication, etc.). Without in the least minimizing the importance of these approaches, we would like to suggest a few concepts which can quite easily be used for experimentation and empirical research. One of these is *individual centration* which is of major importance in Jean

Piaget's work on the development of intelligence in children (genetic psychology). In its first years of life, the child is a "primary narcissist," as Anna Freud put it, unable to decenter itself. In a spatial perspective, for instance, the child does not recognize the relativity of its observation point. It does not comprehend that an object placed to its right is located on the left for a person standing opposite. Similarly, a child who understands that it is of Swiss nationality will consider itself Swiss when at home and Swiss when abroad, but will see a Frenchman as a foreigner when in France and as a foreigner when in Switzerland. Generally, around the age of six or seven, a child becomes capable of what Piaget calls "decentration" or recognition of reciprocity. It will then accept the status of being a foreigner when going abroad.[1]

Corresponding to centration on the individual level is *collective centrism*, when group behavior is studied. Sociocentrism is a characteristic of any group, whether it defines itself in terms of a class (class sociocentrism), a nation (nationalism), a culture (ethnocentrism) or a race (racism). The political, economic and human functions of these various forms of sociocentrism are quite different: class struggle may be a necessary way for an exploited segment of a population to defend its legitimate demands; nationalism is an instrument of resistance of small countries as much as an ideology to justify aggression against others; racism is mostly used to deprive members of the out-group from political rights, economic benefits, social justice and so on.

Of all possible forms of sociocentrism, it is really racism and ethnocentrism which need some terminological clarification. To put it briefly: race is based on biological characteristics and ethnicity on cultural identity. But who really knows what a race is or how cultural boundaries are determined? In the history of science, geneticists and physical anthropologists, joined by philosophers and a good number of self-styled "experts," have listed anything from two to sixty-five "races."[2] Such differences probably arise because a race is usually a subjectively determined group, which is identified as being different in one society but not necessarily in another.

Yet biological features, such as skin color, are more visible than cultural traits. When conflict situations arise, values, behavior patterns or religions are not as quickly identifiable as physical appearance. The racist is one who attributes cultural differences to biological factors: he believes, for instance, that certain forms of behavior (attitude towards "modernization," family structure, dance, and so on) are in-born rather than learned. He also generalizes, taking the characteristics of one member of a physically identifiable group and applying them to all those which he subjectively associates with that group (stereotypes).

These forms of *racist* attitudes are already well known, and we should therefore concentrate on substantiating the view that such an approach is also the result of *ethnocentric* resistance to the behavior of groups subjectively considered to be outside of where one "feels at home" and among the "likeminded." Ethnocentrism was first defined in 1906 by William G. Sumner as a "view of things in which one's own group is the centre of everything, and all others are scaled and rated with reference to it. . . . Each group nourishes its own pride and vanity, boasts itself superior, exalts it own divinities and looks with contempt on outsiders."[3] This may well look to some like a definition of racism, but there is an essential difference. The ethnocentric says: our religion is the only true one, our language is more refined, our material objects are more sophisticated, our artefacts are more beautiful, we have better clothes, food, literature and theater. The racist says: this is only possible because we are hereditarily superior. He thereby goes an enormous step further in attempting to give a biological foundation to feelings of cultural superiority.

A famous example is provided by Kenneth Clarke, well known for his television series on civilization in the US and Great Britain (and not to be confused with the American psychologist of the same name), who comments on an African mask and an Apollo statue in the following way: ". . . the Apollo embodies a higher state of civilization than the mask. They both represent spirits, messengers from another world. . . . To the Negro imagination it is a world of fear and darkness, ready to inflict horrible punishment for the smallest infringement of a taboo. To the hellenistic imagination it is a world of light and confidence, in which the gods are like ourselves, only more beautiful, and descend to earth in order to teach men reason and the laws of harmony."[4] Few authors have succeeded in expressing so many prejudices in so few words. First of all, there is an association of ideas, contrasting the color black (fear, horror, taboo) with the color white (confidence, beauty, reason, harmony). Then a few assumptions: on the states of civilization or that all blacks participate in a culture that is associated with the mask. Finally, the author compares what for him is the best of one culture with what is worst in another. Surely African art contains masks that are not terrifying, and all the symbols of Greek mythology are not Apollos.

Mr. Clarke stands out as a supreme case of cultural arrogance.

But it would be futile to launch an extravagant research program to find out whether *he* is a racist. He obviously is the product of a culture which produces the type of ethnocentric images he so profusely projects around him. The more important question is whether *the reader* transforms cultural centration (or, collectively speaking, ethnocentrism) into a racist attitude. If he does, he believes that the difference between the mask and the Apollo comes from behavioral differences between blacks and whites (which may be historically true) and that these differences are "explained" genetically (which is scientifically false). This is where we find the subtle and dangerous input of ethnocentrism into racism.

Forms of Ethnocentric Distortion

Any research on ethnocentric or racist texts presupposes an analytical framework. Far too often, individual researchers launch into content analyses without a prior intercultural exchange of views, and the results are superficial and irrelevant. The most obvious cases of inadequate results due to such methodological deficiencies are the Unesco studies on the mutual appreciation of eastern and western cultural values and the publications of the International Institute of School Textbooks in Braunschweig (Federal Republic of Germany).

The following categories have proved particularly useful in the study of history textbooks.[5] However, they can also be applied to a wide variety of other source materials, ranging from cartoons to Tarzan and James Bond movies, tourist information booklets, novels, newspaper reports, books on philosophy and United Nations resolutions on development. Similar patterns of ethnocentric distortion emerge in all these cases, although the analytical grid needs to be adapted to each particular type of source.

1. The Ambiguity of the Concepts of Culture, Civilization and Race

As is very often the case with widely used terms, they are not defined or are given meaning only through indirect references to situations where their use is assumed to be appropriate. In history textbooks, all of the following assertions, and more, are made or implied:

• some people are "still" part of nature (*Naturvölker*), others have evolved to the "stage" of culture (*Kulturvölker*);

- civilization is a higher stage of culture;
- civilization is the unique achievement of only one people (usually the Greeks, from whom Europeans have inherited it);
- there can be a variety of civilizations but certain minimal conditions must be fulfilled to "deserve" the qualification;
- "signs" of civilization can be anything from human rights to industry or hair style, jewelry to democracy;
- the "purity of blood" of a people of "superior stock" is sometimes a condition for the preservation of civilization; and so on.

Fortunately for the school child, not all these confusing affirmations are found in one single textbook. What is typical of almost all books, however, is the absence of any explanation of the following three facts:

- That every human group (family, class, tribe, nation, etc.) identifies with a set of values, institutions and patterns of behavior. This is what we call culture. By definition, there can be no human beings without culture, as there are no human beings without values, institutions and patterns of behavior.
- That the meaning of the term "civilization" is never clear in any reading material children ever come across. A nation may be called civilized due to its wealth and refined technology. It is often assumed "natural" that such a nation may (sometimes "must"!) conquer others, destroy them, exploit them, subjugate them. Attila the Hun and Adolf Hitler are the only true villains in history books. Other aggressors, leading their countries into expansionist adventures, are more often than not heroes.
- That race does not determine culture, in other words that culture is socially and not hereditarily transmitted. Note, in this context, how innocent-sounding terms such as "blood" and "stock" are creeping in to replace the word "race."

2. Linear Evolutionism

Although the *term* "evolutionism" is entirely absent from all school books, the *idea* is omnipresent. As such, it has more profound implications than any outright racist statement, for while the latter can be easily detected and denounced, the former infiltrates the realm of what we would like to call nonconscious knowledge. In other words, some cognitive mechanisms, in addition to affective or emotional factors, influence our thinking and behavior although we are not aware of it.

According to evolutionist theories, all of humanity must pass through the same stages of development to reach a level defined as the ultimate form of social organization and economic well-being. To the evolutionist, the final stage is already known: Marx called it communism and Rostow thought it would be mass-consumerism with self-sustained growth. Others have found more fanciful earthly paradises, but essentially all evolutionists have postulated their own preferred version of the world as the indispensable "happy end" for everyone. Evolutionism thus means: "they" will all end up being like "us," it is just a matter of time for them to catch up. Anyone interested in the Third World can well imagine what devastating effects such implicit theories of the development of humanity can exert on the behavior of experts, advisers, volunteers and various brands of self-appointed "developers."

In the textbooks examined, two main versions of social evolutionism appear. One is rather direct and presents a sequence of stages: this group is primitive, that one is feudal; here we find capitalism (the final stage of neo-liberals and the last but final one for neo-Marxists). The other is more subtle and is part of second-degree ethnocentrism: these people "still" use mules, those are "already" urbanized; these here do "not yet" use computers, those "are building" the post-industrial society. The whole process of social change is presented in terms of the necessity of change in a certain direction, of the inevitability of predetermined stages. Simple words such as "still," "not yet" or "already" weigh heavily in favor of a deterministic and linear concept of history. There is no room for reversals, cycles or unexpected evolutions of which history holds the secrets. Thus it becomes quite apparent that very often a departure from the ethnocentric/evolutionist scheme devised by a particular author is used—by conscious or nonconscious consumers of the theory—as a basis of racist attitudes. If *they* have "not yet" reached a particular stage in a sequence devised by Europeans or North-Americans, they must be backward. In the same simple-minded mental process, the next step consists of saying: it is because they are of a different race that they have not yet done so.

3. Contacts with Us Are the Foundation of Their Historicity

In history books (at least, in those written for schools), the "others" do not exist unless they have been in touch with "us." The worst situation we can imagine for them is that they have not recorded their history in writing. In that case, they do not exist at all (a-historicity). But presuming they have an official history, decipherable by Europeans, they are mentioned only insofar as they have been "discovered" or "awakened" by the explorers. Even the distinguished historian E. H. Carr is capable of an ethnocentric statement such as the following: "Modern history begins when more and more people emerge into social and political consciousness, become aware of their respective groups as historical entities having a past and a future, *and enter fully into history.*"[6] Isn't the question here: whose history are we talking about?

Every human species has concepts of time, of the past and of the future. It has been the privilege of Europeans to postulate that their definition of these concepts is the only acceptable one and that other cultures are non-existent or a-historic if they fail to conform to this pattern.

The phenomenon of contacts is introduced in a rather arrogant fashion through the so-called "discoveries" of continents inhabited for up to hundreds of thousands of years by non-Europeans. Thus, the Chinese are "awakened" to civilization(!) and the "dormant" Africans are brought within the realm of history. The travels of a Vasco da Gama, a Marco Polo or a Savorgnan de Brazza are all it takes to needle these giants into making them aware of a destiny they were unable to discover on their own.

4. Glorified Self-Presentation: The Value-System

The final stage of evolution, which Europe is said to have almost reached, can be idealized in a variety of ways. One very common form consists in stressing a set of values which supposedly characterize the European way of life and are intrinsically superior to the values of others. These values, we are told, are not culture-bound, specific to Europe but, potentially at least, of universal validity. Any culture which does not accept them is "still" caught in a lower stage of evolution.

The values which appear most frequently in history books are: the unity of the group (from the family to the nation), order (implying the existence of a strong state capable of guaranteeing Law and Order), a religion based on the worship of a single God (monotheism), democracy (in the sense of a pluralistic, parliamentary political system), a sedentary way of life, the industrial mode of production and writing as the highest stage of communication. The antithesis to this value-system would be represented by an illiterate splinter-group living in relative isolation, disregarding the law foreign powers wish to impose on it, believing in several gods but ruled by one autocratic leader, leading a nomadic life and living from the products of the earth. This would apply, for instance, to nomadic groups in the Sahara region which are usually dealt with in extremely violent terms. If aggression and expansion were added to the negative list, Attila the Hun would again come out as the chief villain. But aggression and expansion are not there, because their opposites are not on the positive list of the European value-system. How could they be, when we are dealing with a continent whose past is described by its own historians as a sequence of wars and expansionist movements? All these expressions of violent behavior are, as we shall see, either legitimized or camouflaged in some form. Psychoanalysts with a patient on the couch would call this respectively rationalization and scotomization. Thus, for instance, an African historian thoroughly indoctrinated at Oxford University calls the beginning of the European colonization of his continent the "coming of Law and Order." The violence of the oppressor is turned into a positive value (rationalization) and its negative effects are omitted (scotomization).

Quite a few values which are certainly prevalent in European societies are not on the official lists drawn up by textbook authors. Except where Soviet authors denounce capitalism and private property, not a word is ever said about the worship of money and material goods in western societies. Nor are such values as individualism as a principle of person-person relations, or anthropocentrism in the realm of person-nature relations, ever touched upon.

Thus, self-glorification through the presentation of a value-system not only occurs when some values of the in-group (Europe) are introduced as though they "naturally" had universal validity, but also when the selection of these values is arbitrary.

5. The Unilateral Legitimation of European Action

Legitimation consists in presenting a particular form of behavior in such a way that it looks acceptable to others. This may become necessary when a certain action is criticized by its victims or when the actors themselves begin to realize the true significance of their past behavior.

The main sources of guilt feelings giving rise to legitimizing formulations are colonization and slavery. Lengthy explanations are given to justify European expansion. They usually include the benefits gained by "primitive" peoples from their conversion to the Christian faith, the technological superiority of Europe which made it "inevitable" to navigate round the globe and conquer other people's territory, the sufferings of the conquerors in the face of mosquitoes, swamps and "inhospitable natives" (in that order) and, finally, the right to occupy land containing unexplored natural resources.

In the case of slavery, rationalization is a little more difficult in view of the monstrosity of the crime. Attempts to cover up what happened usually result in a clumsy association of totally unrelated events. A Portuguese author speaks of slavery in the same breath as he exalts the attempt to fight malaria, and a British colleague comes to his rescue by stating: "The effect of the slave trade on Africa was undoubtedly harmful. Yet the balance was not altogether unfavorable. The Portuguese, for example, introduced a variety of new vegetables and fruits. . . . Later in her history, Africa . . . was to make good use of these new imports—as food for her people and as exports." Three cheers for the improvement of the balance of payments as a by-product of slavery! But the author persists: "The European conquest certainly brought more violence and attempted [sic] slavery, but it also brought towns, with parks, churches, schools, hospitals and an ordered way of life."[7]

6. The Intercultural and Intertemporal Transfers of Concepts

Concepts are strongly culture-bound and related to a particular epoch. They originate in a specific social context at a given time in history. Their applicability to other societies and to different historical periods cannot be assumed *a priori*. Yet it is very common for historians, other social scientists and "developers" to use the same vocabulary indiscriminately wherever they go in time and space. This may be done consciously and stem from feelings of cultural arrogance and elitism ("we" know better anyway) or it may happen unintentionally. The non-conscious transfer is probably more frequent. It is the result

of the very widespread unawareness of the circumstances under which
the words we use were given meaning and substance.

Transfers of concepts have done considerable harm to histo-
riography and are very frequent in development studies. This applies
to both normative and descriptive transfers. A normative transfer occurs when an attempt is made to influence the goal-setting process in
another society with heavily value-loaded ethnocentric concepts such
as progress, stages of growth, rationality, modernization or wester-
nization. A descriptive transfer consists of using words in different
societies without noticing, or wanting to notice, that they cannot
possibly embrace the same reality everywhere. The simplest notions
such as time, space, work or family have different meanings in different societies.

An intertemporal transfer may occur when contemporary European historians apply such concepts as the "state" or "nationalism" to
ancient Greece or Rome. An intercultural distortion is likely to be
added if the same is done with ancient civilizations in Africa, America
or Asia. One may be closer to an adequate description when examining
our present societies with the concepts of our time, particularly since
the vast majority of scientific concepts have been introduced or refined
over the last hundred years. Probably the most frequent distortion
occurs when concepts originating in our present societies are applied
to contemporary societies in other parts of the world.

Quite often, attempts are made to describe past phases of our
own history through the present situation of other societies. "They
still live in the Stone Age" is not only an arrogant ethnocentric pronouncement. It is also a misleading statement if, on the basis of the
survival of a particular trait, such as the way one uses natural resources, an entire social system is projected back in time. Similar
problems arise when the present social systems of other societies are
described with concepts from our past. The term "feudalism," for
instance, is still used when speaking about some twentieth century
societies in Africa or Asia. A closer look may show that certain social
inequalities and forms of exploitation resemble those prevalent in me-
dieval Europe, but may also reveal that the entire legal system and
particularly the law of land ownership have nothing in common with
it. In this latter category, linear evolutionism is again particularly
strong. The "temporal" distance between "them" and "us" (back-
wardness, gap, lag) becomes identical with the "cultural" distance
(underdevelopment).

Conclusion

We have seen that ethnocentrism can be a dangerous ingredient in the formation of racist attitudes and that it is rampant in children's books and school texts. But a word of caution is needed now: while racism has at long last come to be seen as the source of many evils, as a way of denying equality, of taking away job opportunities, of preventing inter-marriage—in short, as a technique for preserving privileges for some and making others miserable—ethnocentrism must be viewed in a much more differentiated manner. Indeed, ethnocentrism is not just cultural arrogance on behalf of expansionist countries (e.g. European) or of relatively isolationist powers (e.g. China, Empire of the Centre and Middle Kingdom). It is also a powerful weapon for many people, particularly cultural minorities all over the world, who are struggling for the recognition of their identity in the face of the uniformization, standardization and "cocacolization" of the world. To defend the values of one's own group is perfectly respectable. But everything de-pends on the attitude adopted towards others: Is it ethnocentric or respectful of cultural diversity? Is it racist, nonracist or anti-racist?

Notes

1. For more details and bibliographical references, see Roy Preiswerk & Dominique Perrot, *Ethnocentrism and History, Africa, Asia and Indian America in Western Text-books*, NOK Publishers, New York, 1978.
2. The inventory can be found in G. E. Simpson & J. M. Yinger, *Racial and Cultural Minorities: An Analysis of Prejudice and Discrimination*, Harper & Row, New York, 1953.
3. *Folkways: A Study of the Sociological Importance of Usages, Manners, Customs, Mores and Morals*, Ginn & Co., New York, 1906.
4. *Civilization: A Personal View*, Harper & Row, New York, 1969.
5. The study mentioned in note 1 covered 30 textbooks from France, French-speaking Africa, the Federal Republic of Germany, Great Britain, Nigeria, Portugal, Switzerland and the USSR. The same analytical grid was used in a study on US textbooks by Sandra Wagers, *Non-Western Cultures in a US World History Textbook, with Reference to Preliminary UNESCO Work*, Graduate Institute of International Studies, Geneva, 1973, unpublished diploma thesis.
6. *What Is History?*, Penguin, Harmondsworth, UK, 1964, p. 149 (italics added).
7. See the book quoted in note 1, example 157.

26. LIBRARIANS AND FREEDOM FROM RACISM AND SEXISM

Howard N. Meyer

WHEN INTRODUCED as the author of a book on the Fourteenth Amendment,[1] I have not infrequently been asked, "what is the Fourteenth Amendment?" This question, with the puzzled look that accompanies it, has come not merely from college-educated lay people, but from law school graduates and some practicing lawyers. Therefore, I do not think that a group of librarians should necessarily feel self-conscious about needing a little more information on the subject.

Merely to read the language of the Fourteenth Amendment might not be enough to introduce it although it is worth stressing three of the key phrases in its operative ninety-five words—"due process of law," "equal protection of the laws," and "privileges and immunities of citizens of the United States." It is worth saying, in addition, that although there were six major articles in the United States Constitution as originally ratified, and twenty-six amendments since, for more than half our history just those few words quoted from the Fourteenth have been the focus of almost as many constitutional law cases as the rest combined.

In the first part of the Fourteenth is found the authority for the protection won in the last two decades for the rights of the poor, of women, of aliens, of the young—in and out of school—and their teachers, for the strengthening of safeguards against lawless police and unfair judges. There is much more! The Fourteenth furnished the foundation for the process of restoring state and local democracy under the slogan "one person, one vote" and above all, it was the spur and the shield for the aspect of the Civil Rights Movement launched in 1955.

The story of the Fourteenth Amendment could go on for hours; but let me focus on the connection with the subject of awareness of racism and sexism. Let me quote in this connection Sheldon Ackley, Chairman of the Board of Directors of the New York Civil Liberties Union, who wrote some years ago: "We Americans have traditionally spoken well of equality . . . racial discrimination exists in this country today, not through ignorance or indifference, but through active opposition to racial equality . . . our commitment to equality is less firm than our commitment to freedom . . . if equality is indeed, like freedom, fundamental to a democratic society, then what obligation does the state have to insure its reality for all citizens?" And to these words I would add—what obligation does each and every American have to help the nation make up for past errors of omission and commission? Another question might be, what special obligation, if any, do librarians have?

I salute the professional librarians of America for their consistent courage and capacity to defend intellectual freedom as shown by the activities of various bodies of your association. But without diminishing the tribute that intellectual freedom activism is entitled to, I would like to suggest that there are dimensions of freedom other than intellectual freedom that have equal importance.

Intellectual freedom in a democracy is devalued when freedom to choose one's associates, one's place of residence, or one's career are impaired by racism or sexism or other invidious forms of discrimination.

Freedom is indivisible, and intellectual freedom in a society permeated with racism is counterfeit.

I can find no more to say on this subject than is stated by the American Civil Liberties Union itself in its own official policy guide, 1977 supplement, which declares:

The central concept of civil liberties is that all individuals have the fundamental right to be judged on the basis of their individual characteristics and capabilities, not the characteristics and capabilities that are supposedly shared by any group or class to which they might belong. This fundamental right is the premise of the Fourteenth Amendment to the United States Constitution which guarantees equal protection of the laws to all individuals.

The premise of the Fourteenth Amendment is still not much more than an ideal. We are reminded violently and tragically every once in awhile, most recently by news from Miami,[2] that racism survives in this country. We know from evidence that repeatedly surfaces that sexism persists. The connotations and effect of racism and sexism are flatly incompatible with the Fourteenth Amendment. With respect to each, there is massive evidence that they are reflected in

and perpetuated partly by books and materials offered and dissemi-
nated by schools and public libraries.

To the extent that library materials may be instrumentalities of
sexism or racism, what is the constitutional standard by which they
are measured?

It was not until 25 years ago, when *Brown v. Board of Education*
was decided, that the constitutional mandate of equal protection of the
laws began to approach the reality that had been designed by its framers. The accumulated effect of many decades of legitimization of racism had created a situation which could not be dissipated overnight.

The *Brown* decision is particularly relevant to the present problem. Its keystone finding was that the doctrine of "separate-but-equal"
could not stand because, as the Chief Justice said for the unanimous
Court, segregation [of Black children]

generates a feeling of inferiority as to their status in the community that may
affect their minds and hearts in a way unlikely ever to be undone.

It is my thesis that not only segregation has that effect: so do
books permeated by the consequences of the racism of the period in
which they were written. And the adverse impact is as detrimental to
those led to a false belief in their superiority as it is to the victims.

The applicability of the *Brown* decision to the content of educational and library materials is self-evident.[3]

I do not propose to make a full legal argument, but suggest that
there is no reasonable doubt about the proposition stated in an article
on sex discrimination in Volume 62 of California Law Review at page
1338 in an article by Carol Amyx:

Sex stereotyping denies both boys and girls basic personal liberty to develop as
individuals, not to be required to conform to standard personality types; the
denial is more destructive to girls since boys are encouraged to have a positive
self image and an expansive view of their own potential, while girls are taught
that they are inferior, are given a negative self image and a limited view of
their own potential.

That applies equally well to racist content in school and library
materials. In the light of *Brown*, there would be a difference in approach to juvenile and adult collections.

There is no doubt that libraries are subject to the Fourteenth's command that no state shall "deny to any person within its jurisdiction the equal protection of the laws." In plain English, what the State is forbidden to "deny" it is obliged to grant; that is, to provide by affirmative action.

As applied to the literary legacy of racism, the necessary corollary is that the state has the power and duty to act against the consequences of the presence of pernicious anti-group content in libraries.

Reserving comment as to what is specifically appropriate to be done, it should be understood that since the "State" means public authority at every level, librarians share the responsibilities of the states under the Fourteenth Amendment to the extent that libraries are sustained by public funds.

There is no freedom protected by the First Amendment that would be threatened by the application of the principles that follow from the Fourteenth Amendment.

The First Amendment is a protection of group and individual freedom of expression and thought and association. As such, it is the fountainhead of intellectual freedom. But when educators or librarians select books as texts or for inclusion in libraries, they are acting as officials, charged with making judgments as to how to spend public-state funds.

They are not acting as individuals engaged in their own self-expression. In acting as public officials, they have no protected First Amendment interest in being free from regulation of their activity by or under authority of the Fourteenth Amendment. The First Amendment does not establish rights for government officials or bodies acting as such. On this subject, Professor Thomas Emerson, who is as close as any good scholar can be to the so-called absolutist school of thought of the First Amendment, has written:

The government can restrict its own expression, or that of its agents (aside from their own private expression) without invading any First Amendment rights.

To be effective and to fulfill the constitutional requirements, a program addressed to the relation of libraries to patrons should be framed in the light of some specific guidelines which will indicate what the components and qualities of racism and sexism may be, and to suggest what can be done.

The basic responsibility for the development, interpretation and application of such guidelines is that of the library profession itself.

But it should invite and welcome contributions that may be made by individuals and groups of supporters of libraries. The effort to make up for the accumulation of the errors of the past and contribute to a future free from the varied violations of the Fourteenth Amendment is challenging enough to require aid from every possible source.

Ironically, however, I have found that citizens' groups that have prepared and advocated acceptance of pro-humanistic guidelines have not merely been unwelcome; they have been sniped at and condemned by some as advocates of "censorship." In the circles where the word "censorship" is carelessly tossed around, the basic definition seems to have been forgotten. That is, that censorship constitutes "the activities of government agencies," as the grand old man of civil liberties, Roger Baldwin, noted.

To spell this out, I quote from a classic work on censorship, written in the early 1960s by Morris L. Ernst, long General Counsel for the American Civil Liberties Union:

The First and Fourteenth Amendments to the Constitution prohibit invasions of free speech and press by the federal and state governments; they do not prohibit countervailing private pressure. In a society such as ours, where ideas are supposed to prove their value by free and open conflict with other ideas, it is the duty and function of individuals, whether in groups or alone, to project their points of view so long as they act responsibly and with due regard for the rights of others. (page 240)

The intermittent confusion and occasional criticism charging censorship, which have followed the advocacy of racism and sexism awareness guidelines, have involved a confusion of terminology. The effect of using "censorship" as an epithet is the stifling of debate and controversy. That looseness of characterization has been employed to retard or set obstacles in the path of constructive groups which have published much useful material in the effort to enhance awareness of racism and sexism in school and library materials and provide criteria for selection.

The validity or phraseology of particular guidelines may be fairly debated. But to use the repugnant epithet "censorship" against organizations advocating guidelines conceived in good faith is contrary to the public interest.

As a writer, I reject the notion that the literary imagination is cramped, or that free flights of fancy are grounded by raising one's own consciousness with the aid of guidelines as to what elements of style are pernicious products and vestiges of slavery and racism.

There are no easy answers to the problems we are discussing. The implementation of the ALA resolution on racism and sexism awareness challenges us with the hard facts that it recites, namely that for two centuries we have "failed to equalize the status of racial minorities and of women" and that the association has "failed to aggressively address the racism and sexism within its own professional province."[4] Of course, the ALA is not alone in this. It was not until the 1950s that the American Bar Association even admitted blacks to membership.

The candid and honorable avowals in the resolution present us with the plain truth that the racist and sexist heritage of the past is not only manifest in the library shelves; it is present among those staffing the institutions. This obviously calls for discussion of a program of "affirmative action" to remedy this, analogous to such programs in the areas of employment and educational opportunity.

All difficulties in dealing with this must be surmounted since whatever produces unequal treatment of women and minorities and to which the state contributes, violates the equal protection guarantee of the Fourteenth Amendment. A constitutional obligation has been created and the freedom from racism and sexism that it guards must be vigilantly furthered.

Some have said that efforts in this direction will result in librarians ceasing to be "neutral"—that librarians will become involved in "social causes." I respectfully submit, as a constitutional lawyer, that bringing about obedience to the precepts of our Constitution and remedying past violations is not a mere "social cause" but an affirmative professional obligation.

We cannot continue to bring up children whose self image and aspirations are limited by racist or sexist or otherwise discriminatory library and school materials. We should find ways of helping adults to overcome the elements of racism and sexism that may have come from books of their childhood.

It would be presumptuous of me as a non-professional in the librarianship field to suggest particular solutions or the components of affirmative action. But librarians must have a greater awareness of how to seek out sexism and racism and recognize it where it exists. With all the good will in the world, it must be conceded that many of us—including myself—were socialized and trained in a society which was racist and sexist.

One major effort might be some kind of retraining or supplemental post-graduate training. This training could be aided by guidelines, particularly guidelines prepared with the assistance of some who have been historically victimized. The best assistants are, in all likelihood, those who are astute at recognizing bias against their group.

I do not appear as the advocate of any particular set of guidelines. Ultimately what are adopted and used must be decided upon by librarians. But I would like to contribute by offering one example of guidelines, which I can personally endorse, which I read in an article by Jessie M. Birtha, book selection specialist at The Free Library of Philadelphia, and reprinted in MacCann and Woodard's *The Black American in Books for Children* [also in this second edition, chapter 5]:

There are two questions which a librarian might ask herself when selecting books. First, "How would I feel upon reading this book if I were a black child? Particularly an inner-city black child?" Second, "If I were to borrow this book from the library, would I return to get another book like it?" These two questions can help to answer whether this is a suitable book for either a white child or a black child. If it contains material inappropriate for a black child, it is also unsuitable for a white child. . . .

The First Amendment must be construed in the light of the command of the more recently enacted Fourteenth, according to a basic legal principle. But there is no tension or conflict between them on the subject under review. Supreme Court Justice Frank Murphy, one of the great defenders of freedom in the history of the Court, in the *Chaplinsky* case declared, "utterances" that "are no essential part of any exposition of ideas" have a dubious claim at best to protection under the First Amendment. Serious thought should be given to the proposition that racism and sexism are not ideas or concepts worthy of further debate, and that they are evils outlawed by the United States Constitution.

Notes

1. Howard N. Meyer. *The Amendment That Refused to Die.* (Beacon Press, 1978).
2. A white jury in Florida acquitted a group of white police officers who caused the death of a Black suspect by severely beating him at the time of his arrest.
3. There has been a kind of absolutism on the part of some on the question of whether there can constitutionally be differential treatment of reading materials for children based on the difference between personalities and level of sophistication of children and adults. In that connection, it is worth quoting a paper delivered by Charles Morgan, Director of the American Civil Liberties Union in Atlanta, by invitation of

the A.L.A. Intellectual Freedom Committee at the Intellectual Freedom Conference of 1965:

> There are differences of library purpose. Libraries do and should have personalities. Grammar school libraries should differ in content from those in high schools. And neither college and university nor public libraries should be substantially governed by the rules applicable to those of children. Even though children often do seem more rational than adults, it may be that they are not capable of absorbing a radical literary content.

This paragraph was omitted when a portion of Morgan's address was anthologized in *Literary Censorship: Principles, Cases, Problems* by Kingsley Widmer and Eleanor Widmer. The irony and lesson of this should not be lost.

4. The A.L.A. membership passed a four-point "Resolution on Racism and Sexism Awareness" in 1976.

CORETTA SCOTT KING AWARD WINNERS*

1970 Lillie Patterson. *Dr. Martin Luther King, Jr.: Man of Peace* (Garrard)

1971 Charlemae Rollins. *Black Troubador; Langston Hughes* (Rand McNally)

1972 Elton C. Fax. *17 Black Artists* (Dodd, Mead)

1973 Alfred Duckett. *I Never Had It Made: The Autobiography of Jackie Robinson* (Putnam)

1974 Sharon Bell Mathis & George Ford, Illustrator. *Ray Charles* (Crowell)

1975 Dorothy Robinson & Herbert Temple, Illustrator. *The Legend of Africania* (Johnson)

1976 Pearl Bailey. *Duey's Tale* (Harcourt, Brace & Jovanovich)

1977 James Haskins. *The Story of Stevie Wonder* (Lothrop, Lee & Shepard)

---

* *Selection Criteria*: The award is made to one Black author and one Black illustrator for outstandingly inspirational contributions. The author and illustrator need not necessarily be associated with the same book. Joint authors and joint illustrators are also eligible.

The books to which the award is given:
   a. Must be appealing to children and/or young adults.
   b. Must portray people, places, things, and events in a manner sensitive to the true worth and value of all beings.
   c. Must be published in the calendar year preceding the year of the award presentation.
   d. May be either fiction or non-fiction.

1978 Eloise Greenfield & Carole Byard, Illustrator. *African Dream* (A John Day Book by Crowell)

1979 Ossie Davis. *Escape to Freedom* (Viking)
Tom Feelings, Illustrator. *Something on My Mind*/words by Nikki Grimes (Dial)

1980 Walter Dean Myers. *Young Landlords* (Viking)
Carole Byard, Illustrator. *Cornrows* by Camille Yarbrough (Coward, McCann & Geoghegan)

1981 Sidney Poitier. *This Life* (Alfred A. Knopf)
Ashley Bryan, Illustrator. *Beat the Story Drum, Pum Pum* (Atheneum)

1982 Mildred Taylor. *Let The Circle Be Unbroken* (Dial)
John Steptoe, Illustrator. *Mother Crocodile* by Birago Diop; translated and adapted by Rosa Guy (Delacorte)

1983 Virginia Hamilton. *Sweet Whispers, Brother Rush* (Philomel)
Peter Magubane, Illustrator. *Black Child* (Alfred A. Knopf)

1984 Lucille Clifton. *Everett Anderson's Goodbye* (Holt, Rinehart and Winston)
Pat Cummings, Illustrator. *My Mama Needs Me* by Mildred Pitts Walter (Lothrop, Lee & Shepard)
Special Citation to Mrs. Coretta Scott King for *The Words of Martin Luther King, Jr.* (Newmarket)

1985 Walter Dean Myers. *Motown and Didi* (Viking)

(*continued*)

HONORABLE MENTION BOOKS

1970*

1971   Maya Angelou. *I Know Why the Caged Bird Sings* (Random House)
Shirley Chisholm. *Unbought and Unbossed* (Houghton Mifflin)
Mari Evans. *I Am a Black Woman* (Morrow)
Lorenz Graham. *Every Man Heart Lay Down* (Crowell)
June Jordan & Terri Bush. *The Voice of the Children* (Holt, Rinehart & Winston)
Grossman, Gloom, and Bible. *Black Means . . .* (Hill & Wang)
Janice M. Udry. *Mary Jo's Grandmother* (Whitman)
Margaret Peters. *The Ebony Book of Black Achievement* (Johnson)

1972*

1973*

1974   Louise Crane. *Ms. Africa: Profiles of Modern African Women* (Lippincott)
Alice Childress. *A Hero Ain't Nothin' but a Sandwich* (Coward, McCann & Geoghegan)
Lucille Clifton. *Don't You Remember?* illustrated by Evaline Ness (Dutton)
John Nagenda. *Mukasa* illustrated by Charles Lilly (Macmillan)
Kristin Hunter. *Guests in the Promised Land* (Scribner)

1975*

1976   Shirley Graham. *Julius Nyerere: Teacher of Africa* (Messner)
Walter Dean Myers. *Fast Sam, Cool Clyde and Stuff* (Viking)
Mildred D. Taylor. *Song of the Trees* (Dial)
Eloise Greenfield. *Paul Robeson* illustrated by George Ford (Crowell)

1977   Lucille Clifton. *Everett Anderson's Friend* illustrated by Ann Grifalconi (Holt, Rinehart & Winston)

---

*Books in the Honorable Mention category were not selected for these years.

Clarence Blake & Donald Martin. *Quiz Book on Black America* (Houghton Mifflin)

The Editors of Franklin Watts. *Encyclopedia of Africa* (Franklin Watts)

Mildred D. Taylor. *Roll of Thunder, Hear My Cry* (Dial)

1978 James Haskins. *Barbara Jordan* (Dial)

Lillie Patterson. *Coretta Scott King* (Garrard)

William J. Faulkner. *The Days When the Animals Talked: Black Folktales and How They Came to Be* (Follett)

Eloise Greenfield. *Mary McLeod Bethune* (Harper & Row)

Ruth A. Stewart. *Portia: The Life of Portia Washington Pittman, the Daughter of Booker T. Washington* (Doubleday)

Frankcina Glass. *Marvin and Tige* (St. Martins Press)

1979 Carol Fenner. *Skates of Uncle Remus* (Random House)

Nikki Grimes & Tom Feelings. *Something on My Mind* (Dial)

Virginia Hamilton. *Justice and Her Brothers* (Greenwillow)

Lillie Patterson. *Benjamin Banneker* (Abingdon)

Jeanne Patterson. *I Have a Sister, My Sister Is Deaf* (Harper & Row)

1980 Eloise Greenfield & Lessie J. Little. *Childtimes: A Three-Generation Memoir* (Harper & Row)

Berry Gordy. *Movin' Up* (Harper & Row)

James Haskins. *Andrew Young: Man with a Mission* (Lothrop, Lee & Shepard)

Ellease Southerland. *Let the Lion Eat Straw* (Scribner)

James Haskins. *James Van Der Zee: The Picture-Takin' Man* (Dodd, Mead)

1981 Alexis Deveaux. *Don't Explain: A Song of Billie Holiday* (Harper & Row)

Carole Byard, Illustrator. *Grandma's Joy* by Eloise Greenfield (Philomel)

Jerry Pinkney, Illustrator. *Count On Your Fingers African Style* by Claudia Zaslavsky (Crowell)

1982 Alice Childress. *Rainbow Jordon* (Coward, McCann & Geoghegan)

Kristin Hunter. *Lou in the Limelight* (Scribner)

Mary E. Mebane. *Mary* (Viking)

Tom Feelings, Illustrator. *Daydreamers* by Eloise Greenfield (Dial)

1983 Julius Lester. *This Strange New Feeling* (Dial)

Ashley Bryan. *I'm Going to Sing: Black American Spirituals, Vol. II* illustrated (Atheneum)

Pat Cummings, Illustrator. *Just Us Women* by Jeannette Caines (Harper & Row)

John Steptoe, Illustrator. *All the Colors of the Race* by Arnold Adoff (Morrow)

1984   Virginia Hamilton. *The Magical Adventure of Pretty Pearl* (Harper & Row)

James Haskins. *Lena Horne* (Coward, McCann)

Joyce Carol Thomas. *Bright Shadow* (Avon)

Mildred Pitts Walter. *Because We Are* (Lothrop, Lee & Shepard)

1985   Virginia Hamilton. *Little Love* (Philomel)

Candy Dawson Boyd. *The Circle of Gold* (Apple/Scholastic)

NOTES ON CONTRIBUTORS

RAE ALEXANDER was trained in the field of early childhood education at Teachers College, Columbia University. She is the compiler of the anthology *What It's Like to Be Young and Black in America*.

NANCY L. ARNEZ is Chairperson, Department of Educational Leadership and Community Services, Howard University.

BERYLE BANFIELD is the president of the Council on Interracial Books for Children, and is a professor in the Department of Education, Bank Street College of Education.

JESSIE M. BIRTHA has been the children's book selection specialist at The Free Library of Philadelphia, and is a professor of children's literature at Antioch College.

JEANNE S. CHALL is director of the Reading Laboratory at Harvard University and professor in the Graduate School of Education. She is the author of *Learning to Read: The Great Debate* (1967, 1983) and *Stages of Reading Development* (1983).

PAUL C. DEANE is a professor in the Department of English, Bentley College.

VALARIE W. FRENCH is a graduate of the Harvard Graduate School of Education, and is now associated with "Research for Better Schools" in Philadelphia.

DONALD B. GIBSON is a professor in the Department of English, Rutgers University, and editor of the anthologies, *Five Black Writers: Essays on Wright, Ellison, Baldwin, Hughes and Leroi Jones*, and *Modern Black Poets*.

ELOISE GREENFIELD is the author of more than a dozen works of fiction, poetry, and biography for children (including *Sister*,

Paul Robeson, and *Honey, I Love and Other Love Poems*). She has been the recipient of the Jane Addams Award, the Coretta Scott King Award, and the Woodson Award.

CYNTHIA R. HALL earned a doctorate at the Harvard Graduate School of Education, and is working at Children's Hospital, Boston.

JULIUS LESTER is an author, editor, folk singer, and professor of Afro-America Studies at the University of Massachusetts. His works for children include *To Be a Slave* (a runner-up for the Newbery Medal), *Long Journey Home: Stories from Black History,* and *This Strange New Feeling.*

DONNARAE MACCANN is a columnist for the *Wilson Library Bulletin,* and co-author of *The Child's First Books* and *Cultural Conformity in Books for Children.* She has taught children's literature at UCLA, the University of Kansas, Virginia Tech, and the University of Iowa.

HAKI MADHUBUTI (DON L. LEE) is a poet, publisher, essayist, and associate professor of English, Chicago State University. He has also been a professor of Afro-American Studies at the University of Iowa. *Don't Cry! Scream, Think Black,* and *Enemies—The Clash of Races* are among his many books. His company, Third World Press, has published the children's books *The Tiger Who Wore White Gloves; or, What You Are You Are* by Gwendolyn Brooks, *I Want to Be* by Dexter and Patricia Oliver, and others.

HOWARD N. MEYER is a New York arbitrator and civil rights historian, as well as the author of the Pulitzer-nominated *The Amendment That Refused to Die* (a history of the Fourteenth Amendment). His Introduction to T. W. Higginson's *Army Life in a Black Regiment* (1869) is a study of this minister/abolitionist/feminist (Norton Library edition, 1984).

DHARATHULA H. MILLENDER is an adjunct professor at Indiana University Northwest, member of the Gary City Council, chairperson of the City Council committee on art, culture, and history, and library trustee.

OPAL MOORE is a graphic artist and poet. She has been an instructor in the Department of English at the University of Iowa, and in the Afro-American Studies Department's Black Poetry Workshop. She is currently a doctoral student in the American Studies program.

WALTER DEAN MYERS is the author of picture books and novels for children. His novel, *The Young Landlords,* earned him the Coretta Scott King Award, and his books have been selected for the ALA Notable Book List.

ROY PREISWERK (deceased) was a professor at the Institute of Development Studies and at the Graduate Institute of International Studies, both in Geneva, Switzerland.

EUGENE RADWIN has a doctorate from the Harvard Graduate School of Education, and is now working as an educational consultant for the Massachusetts State Department of Education and for private educational firms.

ALBERT V. SCHWARTZ is a professor in the Department of Education, C.U.N.Y. College of Staten Island.

RUDINE SIMS is a professor of education at the University of Massachusetts, and author of *Shadow & Substance: Afro-American Experience in Contemporary Children's Fiction.*

DOROTHY STERLING is the author of *Tear Down the Wall! A History of the American Civil Rights Movement, Captain of the Planter,* and many other books for children and young people.

ISABELLE SUHL, before her retirement in 1983, worked as a librarian at the Elizabeth Irwin High School (NY), the Adelphi Academy, the New York State School of Industrial and Labor Relations of Cornell University in Manhattan, and The New Lincoln School.

JUDITH THOMPSON is a lecturer at the University of Kansas, and has published poetry and critical essays in journals and anthologies. She received her doctorate in English in 1982.

GERALDINE L. WILSON is a freelance education and early childhood specialist, and curriculum consultant with the Children's Television Workshop.

FREDRICK WOODARD is Associate Dean of Faculties, and a professor in the English and Afro-American Studies departments at the University of Iowa.

GLORIA WOODARD is an elementary school library media specialist, Prince George's County, Maryland, and the co-author of *Cultural Conformity in Books for Children*. She has also been a teacher in Texas and Kansas.

GEORGE A. WOODS is the children's book editor for the *New York Times*.

INDEX OF CHILDREN'S AND YOUNG ADULT BOOKS MENTIONED

TITLE INDEX

283

AUTHOR INDEX

Fenner, Carol. *Skates of Uncle Remus* (Random House, 1978) p. 277.

Flower, Jessie Graham. *Grace Harlowe's Overland Riders Among the Kentucky Mountaineers* (Altemus, 1921) p. 164, 166–167.

Fox, Paula. *The Slave Dancer* (Bradbury, 1973) p. 34, 123.

Franklin, John Hope, John W. Caughey, and Ernest R. May. *Land of the Free* (Benzier Bros., 1966; rev.) p. 232.

Friedman, Frieda. *A Sundae with Judy* (Morrow, 1949) p. 53.

Glass, Frankcina. *Marvin and Tige* (St. Martin's Press, 1977) p. 277.

Gordy, Berry. *Movin' Up* (Harper, 1979) p. 277.

Gould, Jean. *That Dunbar Boy;* illustrated by Charles Walker (Dodd, 1958) p. 231.

Graham, Lorenz. *Every Man Heart Lay Down* (Crowell, 1970) p. 276.

Graham, Shirley. *Julius Nyerere: Teacher of Africa* (Messner, 1975) p. 276.

Graham, Shirley. *The Story of Phillis Wheatley* (Messner, 1949) p. 228.

Graham, Shirley. *There Was Once a Slave: The Heroic Story of Frederick Douglass* (Messner, 1947) p. 228.

Greenfield, Eloise. *African Dream;* illustrated by Carole Byard (John Day/Crowell, 1977) p. 275.

Greenfield, Eloise and Lessie J. Little. *Childtimes: A Three-Generation Memoir* (Harper and Row, 1979) p. 277.

Greenfield, Eloise. *Daydreamers;* illustrated by Tom Feelings (Dial, 1981) p. 277.

Greenfield, Eloise. *Grandma's Joy;* illustrated by Carole Byard (Philomel, 1980) p. 277.

Greenfield, Eloise. *Mary McLeod Bethune* (Harper, 1977) p. 277.

Greenfield, Eloise. *Paul Robeson;* illustrated by George Ford (Crowell, 1975) p. 276.

Grimes, Nikki. *Something on My Mind;* illustrated by Tom Feelings (Dial, 1978) p. 275, 277.

Grossman, Barney (with Gladys Gloom). *Black Means. . . . ;* illustrated by Charles Bible (Hill and Wang, 1970) p. 276.

Hamilton, Virginia. *Justice and Her Brothers* (Greenwillow, 1978) p. 277.

Hamilton, Virginia. *A Little Love* (Philomel, 1984) p. 278.

Hamilton, Virginia. *The Magical Adventure of Pretty Pearl* (Harper, 1983) p. 278.

Hamilton, Virginia. *Sweet Whispers, Brother Rush* (Philomel, 1982) p. 275.

Hansberry, Lorraine. *Raisin in the Sun* (Random, 1959) p. 64.

Harris, Joel C. "Free Joe and the Rest of the World" in *Free Joe and Other Georgia Sketches* (P. F. Collins and Son, 1887) p. 29, 123.

Harris, Joel C. *Uncle Remus: His Songs and Sayings* (Appleton, 1881) p. 29.

Haskins, James. *Andrew Young: Man with a Mission* (Lothrop, 1979) p. 277.

Haskins, James. *Barbara Jordan* (Dial, 1976) p. 277.

Haskins, James. *James Van Der Zee: The Picture-Takin' Man* (Dodd, 1979) p. 277.

Haskins, James. *Lena Horne* (Coward, McCann, 1983) p. 278.

Haskins, James. *The Story of Stevie Wonder* (Lothrop, 1976) p. 274.

Hergé (see Remi, Georges)

Hill, Elizabeth Starr. *Evan's Corner;* illustrated by Nancy Grossman (Holt, 1967) p. 44.

Hogan, Inez. *Nicodemus books* (12 titles) (Dutton, 1932–1945) p. 115.

Hope, Laura L. *The Bobbsey Twins at the Seashore* (Grosset, 1950) p. 167.

Hope, Laura L. *The Bobbsey Twins in the Country* (Grosset, 1950; rev.) p. 29–30, 163, 164, 166.